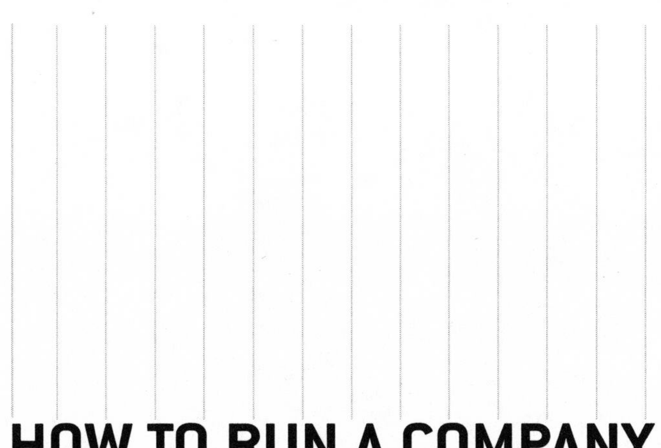

HOW TO RUN A COMPANY

Also by Dennis C. Carey

CEO Succession: A Window on How Boards Can Get It Right When Choosing a New Chief Executive (with Dayton Ogden)

The Human Side of M&A: How CEOs Leverage the Most Important Asset in Deal Making (with Dayton Ogden)

Dennis C. Carey and
Marie-Caroline von Weichs

HOW TO RUN A COMPANY

LESSONS FROM TOP LEADERS OF THE CEO ACADEMY

CROWN BUSINESS • NEW YORK

To my children, Maggie and Matt

—DCC

To all those who have participated in the CEO Academy

—MCvW

Published by Crown Business, New York, New York.
Member of the Crown Publishing Group,
a division of Random House, Inc.
www.randomhouse.com

CROWN BUSINESS is a trademark and the Rising Sun colophon is a registered trademark of Random House, Inc.

Printed in the United States of America

DESIGN BY ELINA D. NUDELMAN

Library of Congress Cataloging-in-Publication Data

Carey, Dennis C.
How to run a company : lessons from top leaders of the CEO Academy / Dennis C. Carey and Marie-Caroline von Weichs.
1. Chief executive officers. 2. Executive ability. 3. Leadership. 4. Industrial management. 5. Corporate governance. I. von Weichs, Marie-Caroline. II. CEO Academy. III. Title.
HD38.2.C374 2003
658.4'2—dc21 2003010402
ISBN: 1-4000-4927-X

10 9 8 7 6 5 4 3 2 1

First Edition

contents

PART IV

The CEO and the Outside World

foreword

Larry Bossidy, retired chairman and CEO of Honeywell and AlliedSignal

THE DAY A CEO takes on the job, he has to make it an immediate priority to address a question that his predecessors only had to keep in the back of their minds: What am I doing to ensure my survival?

Lest you think I am about to make a bid for sympathy, let me acknowledge the obvious: Being CEO of a major company is one of the greatest jobs in the world. That's not just because of the financial compensation. One of the best parts of the job is doing it; it's the chance to make decisions that make the world a different place than it would be if you weren't there. More than anything else, that is what ambitious people want to do—make a difference. If the company is prominent, the CEO is getting a chance to make history. He is given a gold-plated ticket to one of the most exciting games in the world. Holding on to that ticket has one cost: continually demonstrating that he deserves it.

The escalating challenge of CEO survival can be seen in the statistics. Between 1999 and 2001, 57 percent of the largest 367 companies in the United States removed their CEOs. I would challenge anyone to find another three-year period in which so many CEOs were replaced.

What has added this new dimension of job insecurity to the position of CEO? Changes in the nature of business, investment, and investors. Just consider three of the most obvious changes:

Constituent demands are greater. Like any decision-making position, the job of CEO has always come with stakeholders whose concerns needed to be addressed. There were always shareholders and analysts to be concerned about. There were always customers who needed to be pleased. There were always suppliers who required attention. That job alone has become tougher and in some cases more important—especially in light of dispersed stock ownership and increased investor activism. But now there are also active constituent groups that most CEOs of the past didn't even have to regard as constituents, including employees and communities. All of these groups have priorities. All of them feel entitled to attention. They may not all require the same amount of time, but a CEO who ignores any of them does so at his own peril.

Expectations are higher. The most obvious example of rising expectations is on Wall Street, where a difference of a penny or two in earnings can translate into a difference of a billion or two in market capitalization. But the Street isn't the only force driving up expectations. We are seeing a rising drumbeat for new governance standards, backed up by pressure to implement them from investor organizations, regulators, and governments. Many of these governance proposals are sensible and would not only help protect investors but improve corporate stewardship. But some governance proposals currently being discussed will not advance the interests of shareholders. Which governance processes to implement? Which not to—and how to communicate the reasons for the decision? These are judgments that a CEO must make, a new set of challenges and risks.

Competition is tougher. The growth of global competition is bound to change the nature of business in a number of ways. One of the first impacts we are already seeing is oversupply in almost every sector that is potentially vulnerable to the threat. Oversupply leads to commoditization, which leads to a decline in pricing power. Industries that depend on the investment of intellectual capital are finding themselves vulnerable as well. Pharmaceutical companies have always recognized the need to invest significantly in research and development. Despite the enormous costs entailed in developing a drug, once they brought a successful one to market, patent protection ensured a period of up to fifteen years to pay down the sunk costs and make a profit to justify the investment. Now, follow-on drugs that don't technically violate patent protection are cutting short the profitability period. In virtually every industry, CEOs can describe new competitive forces creating pressures on companies to find new ways to secure profitability. This is not necessarily a bad thing. In many instances, it is an example of the creative destruction that has allowed most of the world to raise its living standards and improve its quality of life so dramatically over the past three centuries. But in a competitive environment in which there are increasingly two kind of companies—the quick and the dead—CEOs find themselves under the spotlight, and under the gun.

Moreover, in the face of these growing challenges, CEOs cannot simply sit back in the confident expectation of improved profitability when the economy recovers. Different sectors will recover by different degrees; some will continue to stagnate. In the face of dramatic structural changes, a high tide does not lift all corporate boats. Some continue to run aground; others take to the high seas in their place.

Obviously, each of these challenges is greater than ever in light of the credibility gap that has grown between the corporate world and the public—especially between us and our investors. For most corporations and corporate leaders, the precipitous decline in public trust no doubt seems unfair. Never has it seemed more appropriate to raise the age-old question that has been asked since the dawn of trade during the agricultural age: Why should a few bad apples spoil the barrel? But who wouldn't be turned off by a barrel of apples with a few bad ones? There is no point bemoaning the problem. All we can do is address it. For CEOs, across America and beyond, the need to restore trust has suddenly shot to the top of an already-packed agenda.

As I said at the outset, the challenges facing a CEO are not something to complain about. They are something to act upon. The CEO Academy is a useful tool for proactive leadership; it is a unique opportunity to take a good look at the problems a CEO must address, and benefit from the thinking of people who have been there. No one can provide a blueprint for running a company, but a relatively few people can provide insight into the job from the position of having performed it. No academic text or seminar—no matter how insightful—can provide the sense of which approaches has worked and which have not from the point of view of people who have actually made them work, or had to turn things around after failure.

Getting the chance to hear from CEOs who have turned companies around or successfully shaped a new strategy strikes some as the business executive's equivalent of a baseball fantasy camp. It is a chance to learn from our equivalent of a Willie Mays or a Hank Aaron. But there is one big difference: The doctor or lawyer who attends a baseball fantasy camp does not get the chance to take what he has learned and put it into practice in real-life, major-league conditions. The CEO Academy—and this book—provide insights that can be thought through and tested in the real corporate world. It is more like a CEO reality camp.

More than anything else, in today's business world characterized by high expectations and demands for immediate results, CEOs must focus on the reality of the question that must be at the top of their minds: What can I do to ensure my survival, as opposed to just waiting for things to get better?

CEOs have to deal with immediate realities, in the strategies they pursue, the processes they put in place, and the methods by which they assess senior managers. They have to address questions like: "Am I showing enough discipline in how I use my own time, and enough judgment in how to lead a team?" They have to be able to look at the success of others and ask: "Why do they have better margins, better success in dealing with government, and better share price?" Of course, they also have to be able to understand what they cannot learn from other companies, and how to deal with the unique aspects of every sector and every company.

More than anything else, one of the first things CEOs should realize is how much they have to learn. And one of the next things they come to realize is how rare and valuable learning opportunities are. I have had the privilege of chairing the Academy on two occasions. One of the best things about it is that it does not purport to provide a how-to guide to avoiding problems and ensuring corporate success. Rather, it is a tool for dialogue. Corporate presenters will offer different perspectives and disagree with one another. It is a chance not just to learn *what* a successful CEO has done but *why*. This book is faithful to that concept.

INTRODUCTION

The Dilemma of the CEO: Uncertainty Amidst Insecurity

Dennis C. Carey and Marie-Caroline von Weichs

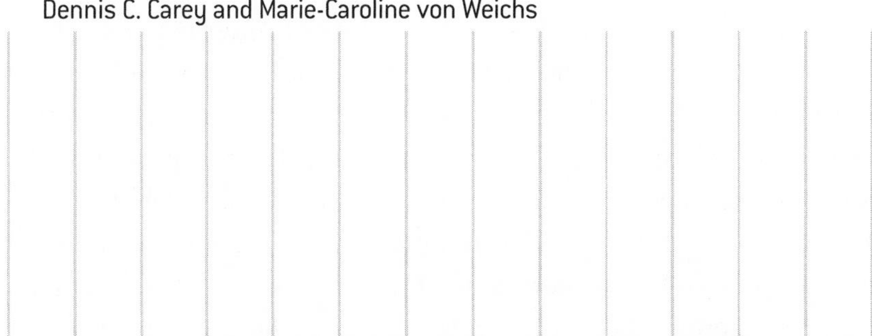

FOR MUCH OF THE PAST DECADE, the top executives at the world's largest corporations have enjoyed a level of prominence and public admiration that is unsurpassed in business history. A veritable library of business publications has chronicled the rise of influential business leaders and their companies, treating chief executives in a manner once reserved for movie stars and rock idols. Events such as the World Economic Forum in Davos and the rise of all-financial news cable channels have only heightened the near-celebrity status of the modern CEO.

It was that lofty and highly respected status of the top business executive that made the business scandals of 2000 and 2001 all the more shattering. Suddenly, many of the figures who had once appeared on magazine covers as rising stars or wily veterans worthy of emulation were at the center of scandal and criminal investigation. The esteem in which many corporations and their leaders were held dropped even more precipitously than the stock market. In the wake of these scandals, the integrity of corporate governance was questioned by shareholders, corporate financial statements were deemed untrustworthy, and corporate executives were treated with suspicion, seen by some as interested only in using their public company for their own personal enrichment. According to one poll taken conducted in August 2002, CEOs were ranked lower in popularity than politicians.

This new climate of distrust had an impact not only among investors—it sounded alarms among regulators and lawmakers. The result was the creation of new rules and new laws that surely will be seen as watershed events in the history of American corporate governance. The Sarbanes-Oxley Act, enacted with much fanfare during the summer of 2002, introduced new requirements on the composition of corporate boards and more demanding standards for financial reporting. Both the New York Stock Exchange and NASDAQ issued stricter requirements for the member companies on the roles and responsibilities of board members. What is clear from this activity is that the rules for all corporate executives at public companies have changed. It is safe to assume that any position of responsibility at a public company will invariably be subjected to higher standards of accountability. This greater scrutiny is likely to be a permanent feature of business life going forward.

Despite the apparent public hostility to corporate executives, their role in a public company—particularly the role of the chief executive officer—has remained poorly understood. Indeed, one of the paradoxes of business-press coverage of corporations is that while the personalities and wealth of CEOs have been exhaustively documented, there has been scant attention to what a CEO actually does. True, much has been written on the "leadership qualities" or "management style" of corporate executives. But this literature is very different from a description of the day-to-day demands of a CEO: how he develops strategy, how he motivates employees, how he works with board members, how he deals with the investor community.

The absence of attention to these "practical" features of a CEO's professional responsibilities is a conspicuous omission at a time when the business world is searching for a model of how a CEO ought to lead a public company. We believe the chapters that follow help fill that gap. The contributors to this book either have served as CEOs of some of America's most prominent companies or have been veteran advisors to and observers of executives who have a deep understanding of the dynamics of daily corporate life. In bringing their thoughts together, we believe they offer a fuller portrait of what kind of questions a CEO confronts when he or she first steps into the top job. Most of all, these chapters give a sense of what modern management feels like at the highest levels. The topics they tackle are familiar to anyone who has worked inside a corporation: how to manage a merger, how to incentivize employees, how to deal with concerns of corporate directors, and so on. In each case, the authors of the chapters try to put these issues in the larger context of juggling many problems at once, which is the reality that all senior managers must confront. Ideally, the portraits of "how to run a company" that they provide will be useful not only to chief executives but to any senior manager who has to think about everyday management problems in the broad context of how to move a company forward. While there are a number of chapters devoted to corporate governance and the relationship between the CEO and the board of directors, we believe these chapters give all current and aspiring executives a full picture of the kind of information and relationship that a board increasingly demands from management.

By their own admission, the CEOs and advisors who are represented here have not always succeeded. But the breadth and depth of their experience has given them the opportunity to reflect on what ultimately were the most important challenges they faced and how—often by trial and error—they tackled them. When we began this project, we suggested to each of the contributors that they address their topic as if it were the advice they wished they had received when they first started their job. Clearly, there is not an easy short list of "must-do" lessons. As virtually all the chapters note, leading a public company is a matter of dealing with constantly shifting circumstances. Fluctuating market conditions, new mergers, and unanticipated expansions demand that leaders develop certain management practices that they can rely on and that can help guide the company. These management habits, illustrated with personal anecdotes from the corporate front lines, are what we believe a wide variety of readers will find most helpful. Above all, the limitations of time demand that every executive at a significant company set priorities for others to follow. One cannot help but be struck in these chapters by the way in which even business strategies that did not fully succeed were led by executives who had a clear sense of where the business ought to be spending its time and resources.

Today, such advice about strategic priorities and management focus is much needed but hard to come by. CEOs—and anyone aspiring to a position of senior leadership inside a public company—understand that they are taking on a position that has become one of the most demanding and least secure jobs the private sector offers. The new CEO in particular takes on a post that is always demanding, closely scrutinized, highly criticized, and increasingly precarious.

What was once seen as a comfortable sinecure at the tail end of a successful career has become a job fraught with uncertainty and insecurity. According to a study by executive search firm Spencer Stuart, a decade ago the average tenure for a CEO was eight years. Today it is less than five. Some don't make it even that far: One study found that boards now expect the CEO to raise the company's stock price in the first nineteen months or be asked to step down. Just one in twenty CEOs hired this year will hold the job for the next twenty.

Not only is tenure far from guaranteed, but the demands of the job have escalated. Gone are the days when the CEO's role was a form of genteel stewardship: quarterly board meetings, international travel, and golf. Indeed, what clearly emerges from the chapters here is that much of what a CEO must do is often unglamorous, time-consuming, and professionally difficult. While the CEO is often portrayed in the business press as the captain of a ship, the better analogy may be with a state governor or mayor. Although the CEO of a large organization can do much to launch new initiatives, success depends entirely on how the organization's various constituencies behave. Despite many hyperbolic press accounts about the "power" of the modern CEO, we see in these chapters that corporate leaders face severe limitations on what they can accomplish by themselves. After all, customers, stockholders, and employees don't always cooperate. How these constituencies are managed is a leading preoccupation of all successful corporate leaders.

Today's chief executives also increasingly face highly independent and sometimes difficult board members. That situation has become even stronger since the reforms enacted in 2002. The New York Stock Exchange, for example, now requires board members of its listed companies to meet in a separate session, without the CEO present. For its part, the NASDAQ has raised its requirements for truly independent directors on its boards. These reforms no doubt strengthen the board and improve governance. Many CEOs welcomed the reforms, and many had instituted them long before they became required. But the practical implications of such changes in the boardroom are unmistakable: The CEO is more isolated than before. He cannot assume that his board is a rubber stamp or that a consensus on key strategic or management issues is a given. We have asked a number of contributors to offer their reflections on this central and intriguing relationship in the life of a public company, whether based on their own experience as chairman of the board or in light of the changes that have recently been introduced.

Of course, the duties of chief executives extend well beyond the boardroom. Readers will see in these chapters that contemporary CEOs necessarily become involved in every facet of a corporation's activities. They are intricately involved in investor relations, taking personal responsibility for the company stock price. They are responsible for recruitment of top executives and for making decisions about extensive job cuts. Top negotiating skills are required during delicate merger negotiations. They must develop professional public-relations skills to deal with the immense interest of the business press, especially during a crisis.

Above all, they are expected both to execute superbly and deliver long-term strategy—or face the wrath of shareholders and the scorn of Wall Street. What non-CEOs will gain from the descriptions of problem-solving in many of these chapters is the way essential functions—accounting, marketing, investor relations—are viewed at the top of the company. Very quickly, one sees how both successful strategy and execution are highly dependent on harnessing all the elements of a corporation, from financial metrics to internal newsletters.

Remarkably, most CEOs arrive to take on this towering professional challenge with little adequate preparation. Even those who have been carefully groomed for succession have not yet experienced the special job circumstances of the CEO. Senior executives may have been responsible for a business unit or a large division. But they have always been part of the chain of command, not at the top. Excellent managers are not necessarily excellent CEOs. Once they ascend to the top job, most of the training is on-the-job. Repeatedly, the new CEO—who may have worked in an industry for decades—will encounter problems and expectations never before confronted. CEOs with long tenure frequently remark that they wish they had known about a particular process or management skill ten years earlier, when they first took the job.

The Trials of an Emerging Corporate Leader

It is a problem that is etched in the nature of the top job. Chief executives are surrounded by advisors and lieutenants whose institutional bias is to please their boss—that is the way every organization works. But in most new and difficult situations, a CEO needs the counsel of an independent observer who understands the challenges that confront the person at the top. Often that type of corporate *consigliere* can be found among the board of directors—but not always. Especially during the first few years of his tenure, when setting a direction for the company, a CEO can be utterly alone in the final decision-making process. Trial-and-error is the only method he has available.

Perhaps the hardest problem a new CEO faces is taking control of a company that, until recently, was run and shaped by someone else. It is very common that a board of directors is leery of an incoming CEO, even one they fully support. Not all boards are unified to begin with, and it is more than likely that a CEO will face a hostile faction or troublesome members still loyal to the *ancien régime*. Two and a half years after he took the top spot at Coca-Cola, Douglas Ivester found himself at odds with the board members (including Warren Buffett) who had enthusiastically installed him. Richard Thoman was fired as CEO of Xerox after three years, during which time the board maintained a close alliance with Thoman's predecessor, who remained on as chairman. The board of directors at Gillette were less patient with CEO Michael Hawley and asked for his resignation after just eighteen months. These CEOs did not have a team of advisors or board members who were truly in their corner. Having reached the top position, they found themselves powerless to execute strategy in the face of a board they could not win over.

In the office, the CEO will find a team of direct reports who may have competed for and lost the top job. Down the hall, it is not unusual to find the recently retired CEO, as Thoman did, still serving as chairman of the board or perhaps staying on in some "emeritus" status. Regardless, the shadow of the former boss always looms large, making any change in management practice or strategy difficult to introduce without appearing to be an indictment of old ways. What we learn from our contributors is that transition in executive life is a process, not a one-time event. Change in personnel and succession planning is an ongoing activity—not only for the CEO but for the people who report to him. What we learn from our contributors is that a new leader is expected to make changes, and the company is best served if the changes are enacted quickly.

The CEO who arrives from outside the company faces even

higher hurdles. Not only must he learn the ropes of a new company, he has even fewer possible channels of trusted advice. He is unfamiliar with the culture of the company, its history, its top performers, and its underachievers. Yet he is responsible for not only crafting strategy but winning over the company, with all its idiosyncratic habits and practices.

On top of the general problem of harnessing the energies of a company comes the simple fact that a CEO may have very limited experience with some core responsibilities. Most new CEOs have never chaired a board meeting. Some may never even have attended one. Issues such as advertising, human resources, the press, Wall Street analysts, mergers, and board-member recruitment, which consume inordinate amounts of a CEO's time and attention, are activities that most senior executives below the top job deal with on an infrequent basis. In short, being the number-two person in a corporate organization doesn't provide enough practical experience or lessons on how to be a better-than-average CEO.

The Imperative of Distinct Leadership in the New Environment

Faced with these challenges, the new CEO—whether an insider or outsider—learns how to cope by muddling through. Once, if the economy was strong and the execution abilities of a company solid, a CEO who muddled through was good enough. That is clearly no longer the case.

Two recent developments have fundamentally changed the rules of the game for chief executives. The first, as mentioned above, is the series of high-profile cases of corporate malfeasance that came to public attention beginning in the fall of 2001. Corporate leaders such as Kenneth Lay of Enron, Dennis Kozlowski of Tyco, and Bernard Ebbers of WorldCom had been lionized by the business press as visionary leaders and exemplary managers. When it was stunningly revealed that they might have been directly implicated in wrongdoing, they became pariahs. But the impact of these scandals, along with the shakeup of the entire world of corporate accounting and governance, was felt not just by a few CEOs. Corporate integrity itself had been put on trial, and public distrust of CEOs was as high as it was in the robber-baron era.

The other development that has significantly changed the lives of CEOs is the noisy crash of the stock market and the accompanying bursting of the tech and telecom bubble. Here, too, CEOs who were once venerated by the business press saw both their reputations and business strategies evaporate.

Both these developments—escalating corporate scandal and cascading technology fortunes—will invariably shape the jobs and lives of executives and corporate managers for the foreseeable future. In the late 1990s, when major market indices seemed to hit new highs every month, the actual abilities of managers seemed irrelevant. If the stock was going up, it was taken for granted that management was doing everything right. Few analysts or journalists familiar with the financial details of some companies saw any reason for suspicion.

In today's environment, no senior manager has the luxury of operating without much examination or second-guessing. The market's tolerance for poorly defined business plans and extensive debt has shrunk. Today there is little enthusiasm for theoretical projections of future profits and more demand for proven management results.

We believe that the most vital element of corporate management is distinguished, confident leadership at the top. While there are plenty of models for organizational management and efficiency, nothing replaces the vitality and vision of a strong CEO who initiates strategy, demands the highest level of execution, and sets the tone and culture of a company. Leadership shapes companies. It sets new direction for a business in the midst of an industrywide change. It can create the work environment unique to an organization. But above all, corporate leadership ought to shape the future leadership ranks of a company. Good leaders invest in developing good leaders. Jack Welch and others have long argued that the particular products generated by their company were less important than the development of people. That approach is now widely embraced in corporate America, and, as these chapters make clear, human-resource issues occupy a significant amount of time for most corporate leaders.

Indeed, as the CEO-authors are quick to admit, their success has often depended on executing the insights of their senior or not-so-senior advisors. The conclusion we must draw is that corporate leadership is frequently the proper identification and deployment of human capital. Business reporters in the future eager to assess the performance of a CEO by something other than quarterly results would be well advised to look at the team of executives who have been put in place or promoted under his watch. So while the "cult of the CEO" may be fading, it would make great sense to replace it with a vision of a company—clearly shared by the contributors here—that is led by a dynamic individual who nurtures and promotes talent, builds a strong working partnership with the board, and is able to generate enthusiasm for an idea across the company by persuading employees to embrace a specific process or set of priorities.

The Education of a CEO

That returns us to the question at the heart of this book: Where can an executive turn when seeking training and advice on how to lead and manage a company? The answer, alas, is that there has been no fully satisfying way of introducing a CEO to the realities of life at the helm.

Our business schools have done an excellent job of providing mid-level and senior-executive training. They offer well-developed courses on management, finance, leadership, team-building, and negotiation. But the most critical part of a CEO's duties cannot be found in academic theory. While their contribution to the business literature has been significant, professors of business have not run companies. That experience gap is critical. The chief executive of today wants to know the dynamic of a boardroom. How to deal with an unproductive board member. How to negotiate with union employees. What kind of relationship to establish with skeptical Wall Street analysts. How to put together a senior team.

We believe there is an immense and largely untapped body of knowledge on these subjects. It resides among the fraternity of experienced, seasoned, and retired CEOs who have been working in the trenches for many years. They are a remarkable resource for current and future CEOs, yet their views on how to run a company get insufficient attention. When the business press interviews them, the focus is largely on their particular industry or the achievements of their company.

The most notable exception to this situation also proves the rule. For many years, Jack Welch, the former chairman and CEO of General Electric, has been promoted as the model of modern corporate management. *Fortune* declared him "manager of the century." Executives across the country have studied his methods in training, promotion, and measuring results. What is most interesting about the popularity of Welch among managers is that those who laud him speak little about the growth strategy of GE's plastics business or innovation at the company's aircraft-engine unit. What interests them the most is to hear frontline reports on how the manager of a successful company dealt with the everyday and often mundane duties of leading and motivating an organization.

At a time when there is great skepticism about managers' leadership skills and corporations' integrity, there is broad interest in any model for modern business leadership. The fascination with Welch's everyday habits of interacting with managers demonstrates that executives at every level are looking for a standard from which they can learn. That is what makes the chapters of this book so fascinating to us. Our authors provide a set of firsthand accounts of what worked and what didn't in their own companies. No one here suggests that the rules they used are universal maxims. Yet all our contributors demonstrate that they have thought seriously about the problems of running a company and uncovered lessons that can benefit anyone who confronts the same situations they have encountered. In doing so, they suggest how a successful leader approaches modern corporate management and governance.

We believe that models of thoughtful corporate leadership have existed for some time but that they are rarely studied. No one has approached veteran CEOs to get their collective thoughts on how they did their jobs. But it was clear by the end of the 1990s that an immense gap existed between the knowledge that senior and retired CEOs had accumulated and the widespread interest in finding a better standard of corporate management and governance.

As part of an effort to bridge that gap, we created the CEO Academy in 2001. Our purpose was to bring together a small group—fewer than thirty—of chief executives who had held the job for less than three years. Leading the conversation would be a group of some of the most seasoned CEOs and a few proven professionals who work with CEOs every day. The idea was to create a kind of education "boot camp"—a one-day session, closed to the press, in which CEOs with plenty of experience under their belt could share their thoughts with those who were still accumulating experience.

Sessions of the CEO Academy have been held twice a year in New York since our inaugural event. They have been consistently lively, engaging, and eye-opening. We have been very fortunate in being able to bring together some of the most dynamic and high-profile corporate leaders during a period in which corporate leadership has been on the front pages of newspapers throughout the world.

The parameters of these sessions are loose. Discussion and give-and-take are the rule. We deliberately select CEO "students" from a wide range of industries, whether it be mining or micro-processing. The premise is that, regardless of the specific characteristics of the business, chief executives share a number of burdens and responsibilities. Our faculty has also been diverse in both perspective and experience. It has included veteran CEOs like Larry Bossidy, who recently retired (for a second time) as CEO of AlliedSignal, and Ray Gilmartin, former CEO of Becton Dickinson and now CEO of Merck. It has included CEOs who have succeeded some of the most celebrated managers, such as Jeff Immelt of GE, as well as those who stepped in after a CEO resigned amidst scandal, as Edward Breen did in the case of Tyco. Given the high level of interest in corporate-governance issues, we have included a number of perspectives on how a CEO interacts with the board, especially given the new climate. John Smale, who stepped in as non-executive chairman of General Motors after the board dismissed the company's CEO in the early 1990s, remains a staunch advocate of separating the chairman and CEO functions; Kevin Sharer, Amgen's CEO, argues that for the sake of clarity and cohesion, the two roles must be filled by one person. On this subject and others, we also have some of the most astute observers of CEOs, including corporate counsel Ira Millstein; corporate watchdog Nell Minow; Mark Begor, who as head of investor relations at GE was Jack Welch's eyes and ears on Wall Street; and Robert Hurst, who as vice chairman of Goldman Sachs has seen up close how CEOs deal with the world of financial analysts. Each of them brings a wealth of experience—but not necessarily consensus.

When we considered the idea of taking some of this material and using it as the basis for a book, we knew that we could not do full justice to the give-and-take quality of the sessions. Yet we were also aware that our "faculty" had managed to dispense considerable amounts of fresh and insightful advice—advice that we believed deserved a much wider audience. What has been most rewarding about our CEO Academy sessions is seeing how many leaders, faced with the same problems, approach them in different ways.

The result, we believe, is exactly what we intended from the time we started the CEO Academy: frank, straightforward views on how to conduct the job of CEO from those who have actually led companies in good times and bad. There is very little management theory in these pages. Instead, these are firsthand accounts from those who have been "in the trenches," giving their views on how they succeeded or failed to meet the goals of a company.

Anyone reading just a few of these chapters will quickly realize that the value of their contents goes far beyond those already in the CEO chair or even those who aspire to it. This is a book about the preeminent corporate challenge in American business—the job of chief executive. But its lessons have obvious application to anyone who works in or studies the corporate environment.

For too long, the actual day-to-day challenges of a corporate CEO have been shrouded in mystery. People are accustomed to seeing CEOs speak at forums or discuss their companies' stock prices on CNBC. But we rarely get a glimpse of how the CEO views his own responsibilities—what guideposts he uses to stay on track. This subject, underreported, is inherently interesting.

But we have also discovered that our CEO contributors, while praised for their business accomplishments, are also first-rate teachers. Anyone interested in the life of business or anyone charged with management responsibilities at any level can't help but learn from the observations of those who have steered the ships of the world's largest and most complex organizations.

PART I

Management and Leadership in the Midst of Change

Over the past decade, the one experience common to all chief executives in corporate America has been the need to confront and manage change. That change has come in different forms. For example, the successful and predictable pace of a company can be suddenly disrupted when a merger or acquisition is suddenly announced. In short order, the culture, the business focus, the headquarters, and even the name of the company must undergo a change, affecting the lives of employees and executives alike. But change also comes without the upheaval triggered by a merger. A new strategy, new marketing plans or products, new markets, or simply the arrival of a new CEO forces a company to switch gears, to acquire new skills, or to reshape the way it has always done business.

For the most part, however, companies change because they must. The combination of technology, globalization, deregulation, and competition has made stability the rarest commodity in business life over the past decade. This environment, experienced by virtually all American companies and more recently by European and Asian firms, has shaped the life of the CEO and the senior leaders of every public company. The days when the leadership of a publicly traded firm could coast on reputation and hand over issues to operational leaders in the field have largely disappeared. With the rise of new, upstart competitors and Internet technology that made many old business models obsolete, CEOs at every type of company had the job of rethinking their firm's place in the market and how it needed to change, keep pace, or ward off threats.

In the chapters of this section, we get to see how change affected the thinking and role of five executives in dramatically different circumstances.

Michael Armstrong had spent more than three decades as a senior executive at the company that many once regarded as the exemplar of corporate stability: IBM. But in the 1990s, he made two critical career moves that put him at the very center of two industries undergoing top-to-bottom change: defense contracting and telecommunications. As he explains in his chapter, Armstrong watched from the perch of two different companies with storied histories as their traditional markets evaporated in a matter of months. In both cases, he chose to join rather than fight the change, leading both Hughes Electronics and AT&T into entirely new markets, unimaginable just a few years earlier. Today both companies have been radically reformed, due largely to the changes he instituted as CEO.

In Armstrong's case, change was thrust upon him. But in many situations, the CEO and the company's senior team are charged with making change—even when it is unclear what change is needed. When John Dasburg arrived at Northwest Airlines, he already knew that the company's strategy needed to be revamped. That was his mission, and he set about changing the way the company operated, introducing a new strategy and making the company adjust to it. Eleven years later, he was hired to do the same thing for Burger King. He is a "turnaround" CEO, and, as he reveals in his chapter, the critical tasks of a chief executive who is consciously trying to fix a company headed in the wrong direction is to establish a new strategy and, then, quickly develop the structure and people to carry it out.

Similarly, William Stavropoulos saw that changes were needed at Dow Chemical in the 1990s. He not only began turning around the company, he reintroduced focus to an organization that had taken on too many businesses in which it no longer excelled. He then helped the company pursue a series of divestitures and acquisitions that redefined the strategy for the business. Implicit in what both

Stavropoulos and Dasburg lay out in their respective chapters is that the very act of shaking a company up forces the CEO and the senior team to define a new set of goals from which a new strategy quickly emerges.

Of course, sometimes the biggest change a company confronts is the arrival of a new CEO. But here the circumstances matter greatly. Ray Gilmartin arrived as CEO of Merck after a successful tenure at another company. As he explains, Merck was doing well, even as the industry was undergoing significant change. He believed that his most important task was to listen to the senior employees and establish a flat organization that made acting on their ideas much easier. This dialogue with the existing staff made his transition very smooth, and he made few significant personnel changes at the senior level.

Edward Breen's situation at Tyco International could not be more different. Arriving at a deeply troubled company, with his predecessor facing criminal charges, Breen needed to introduce change quickly. Dennis Carey was a close advisor to Breen during this transition process. In his chapter, he argues that Breen had to move quickly during the first hundred days and create a completely new senior team. Only by introducing dramatic changes to the company's leadership and board of directors could Breen position himself to take full responsibility and ownership of Tyco's management challenges once his "second hundred days" arrived.

Together, these chapters form a picture of the wide variety of change with which the contemporary CEO must grapple as part of everyday management. In each instance, change was not a singular event but, rather, an ongoing feature of management that constantly required the attention of corporate leadership. Orchestrating that change, shifting the company's priorities, and keeping the business together while the company redefines itself have become, we discover from these authors, integral parts of modern corporate leadership.

CHAPTER ONE

Assessing a Company As an Outsider Coming In

Raymond V. Gilmartin, chairman and CEO of Merck & Co.

Raymond V. Gilmartin has worked in the healthcare industry for more than twenty-five years. He has been chief executive of both the medical device manufacturer Becton Dickinson and, since 1994, the drug giant Merck. During his tenure, the industry has faced dramatic changes and challenges, including the introduction of managed care, budget constraints, and remarkable innovation. These developments have presented several different strategic options for drug companies, and pharmaceutical executives have had to set clear direction for their companies.

Gilmartin has had the advantage of watching these industry changes from two key but very different leadership experiences. At Becton Dickinson, he was an insider who rose through the ranks to become CEO. At Merck, he was recruited from the outside and arrived at the job with a stellar record as an industry CEO. Unlike some corporate leaders who parachute into a position, Gilmartin did not launch wholesale changes among Merck's senior management team. Instead, he established a very flat and open organization structure and helped reassert the company's reputation as a leader in breakthrough research. In recent years, Merck has been included on *Fortune*'s list of the most admired global companies and the 100 best companies to work for.

WHEN A FORMER Harvard Business School professor learned that I was leaving the CEO job at Becton Dickinson to become CEO of Merck, he told me I now had a second chance to do it right. His forecast was accurate. I had an advantage my second time around—the advantage of being an outsider.

As it happened, I had a rewarding and successful career at Becton Dickinson. I had joined the company in 1976 as vice president of strategic planning. Over time, I moved up through various line positions until I became president and CEO thirteen years later. During my tenure the company grew, our stock price did well against the S&P 500, and, having groomed a successor, I felt comfortable moving to a new company.

But my experience at Becton had been strictly that of the insider. One of the most important things I learned at Merck is how valuable it is to approach corporate issues from an outside perspective. In fact, that makes sense even for a CEO who has been promoted from within the company. Becoming CEO is an opportunity to step back and take a good look at the company, even if you think you know it well.

Nineteen ninety-four, the year I arrived at Merck, turned out to be a pivotal year for the pharmaceutical industry. In many respects, the industry was in turmoil. President Clinton had proposed a far-reaching health-care plan that many observers believed would lead to government-imposed price controls on prescription drugs. Stock prices across the industry were depressed. Managed care had also emerged in the early nineties, and it was clear that, one way or another, it would have an impact on the drug business.

Merck, too, was going through a period of uncertainty. The company had developed only a few new drugs in the early 1990s, and some questioned the company's commitment to research. The year before I arrived, Merck had acquired Medco, the pharmacy benefit manager, which suggested a change in direction for the company. Many at Merck wondered what the future held.

A new CEO is expected to make changes, often dramatic changes. Given the industry environment, I suspect that's what many expected from me at Merck. But I believe that before any changes can be introduced, a new CEO has to take a close look at three constituencies within the first six months on the job: the management team, the board, and the previous CEO. Identifying your key constituencies and addressing them quickly is critical for anyone who takes on a new management responsibility.

The fact is that when you come in from the outside, the management team you inherit is someone else's management team. It was put in place by your predecessor. At the CEO level, it is very likely that one or two people on that team expected to get the top job and experiences lingering disappointment. Similarly, the board is not the new CEO's. Its members were appointed by the CEO's predecessor, perhaps even by prior CEOs. And more often than not, the former CEO is still involved, either as a director or possibly continuing as chairman; in some instances he may have an office down the hall.

CEOs who have not paid attention to these different constituencies whose companies are in the midst of some very dramatic change have gotten into a lot of trouble, and many have lost their positions.

Building Support in the Company

Dealing with your constituencies and carrying out corporate change is possible only with support throughout the company. Determining what changes need to be made requires tapping into the knowledge that is available throughout the corporate ranks. Ironically, that requires being able to look at a company from the outside. The knowledge you need—in terms of the kind of change that is required and where to enlist support for those changes—already exists in the organization.

I started my career as a consultant with Arthur D. Little. I worked on an assignment for an executive I respected very much. The company was about to embark on a major restructuring of its sales and marketing division. Although he was supportive of the plan, he was not directly involved with it. On his behalf, I gathered information from within the organization about employee attitudes toward the restructuring, which I then presented to him. What I shared with him was that there was considerable anxiety among employees about the restructuring. Many thought it was taking the company in exactly the wrong direction. Indeed, the restructuring seemed to have very little support below the senior levels of management. After I presented this situation to the CEO, he said to me: "What you found out is very important, it's very critical, but it's also very sensitive. I think one of the things we should talk about is how we're going to maintain the confidentiality of what you found out." And I said to him, "With all due respect, your organization knows all these things. What they are worried about is that *you* do not know them." To his credit, he reacted the right way and did not go through with the planned restructuring.

That's an important lesson for the CEO. People in the organization know its strengths and weaknesses. It is the CEO who has to get to know them and tap into the organization's institutional knowledge.

On the day my appointment was announced, I introduced myself to senior management. After a short hiatus between jobs, I started working right away. I brought considerable experience in how an organization works—how it operates across functions and locations. But I didn't want to impose anything. The first thing I wanted to do was get people's views as to where things stood. So in the first couple of weeks on the job, I undertook a series of interviews with about sixty people at all levels of the organization.

The interviewing process was easy. I was asking people to share their ideas and knowledge. As the incoming CEO, I was giving them an opportunity to talk about what was important to Merck. I asked only two questions:

- What do you think are the major issues that we face?
- If you had my job, where would you spend your time and attention?

These two questions formed the basis for candid conversations, because people care a lot about the future of their company and how to resolve some of the frustrations they must deal with. I gathered a great deal of candid information about what was wrong in terms of how the company worked, and what issues people were really concerned about. At the same time, I obtained considerable insight into the senior levels of management and middle management down through several layers. It was a valuable exercise—and would have been just as valuable if I had been moving up within the organization.

What I heard was not entirely surprising. People wanted to know what the future of the company would be. They were concerned about whether Merck was still committed to research. Some expressed concerns about the competitive environment within the company that led different functions to act as rivals. Marketing and research, for example, might have different views about how a drug should be developed or how clinical trials should be conducted. Their competitive approach to tackling issues affected the company environment. But beyond these issues, what was most important was that I was giving people a chance to speak their mind. I wasn't asking them to respond to my agenda.

It was clear from these conversations that I needed to focus on the future of drug research at Merck. With the senior leadership, I spent a few days together at an offsite meeting, specifically talking about where we were taking the company. From my point of view, it was critical that any commitment to the future needed to be a collective one. We concluded that breakthrough research remained crucial to Merck. In the age of managed care, it might prove even more important. As a result, we got out of a generic-drug business we had started in the early 1990s. At the time, it perhaps made sense. But now our goal was to re-commit to research and make sure the company was focused on that.

My thinking on these subjects was greatly influenced by the initial conversations I had with top people at Merck after I arrived.

Those conversations helped clarify what the leadership of the company needed to do, and it let the company leaders genuinely contribute to my transition process. I recognized how important clarity of purpose is to a company in the midst of a changing business environment. We needed to be clear about the future direction of the company and our commitment to research. We needed to establish firmly how work would get done—that meant more collaboration and less competition among functions. And above all, we needed to communicate heavily to the organization: Employees had to know about our priorities.

This process of listening to the top people in the company tell me what was on their minds was extremely helpful to me in understanding what Merck needed most. The experience was so positive that we have institutionalized it. To do this, we relied on Harvard Business School professor Michael Beer, who helped us establish a process he termed "organization fitness profiling." In fact, we have broadened the exercise to incorporate more people. We choose a task force of eight highly regarded managers with potential from across the company to conduct interviews with fellow managers about how the company is doing, what is working, and what needs to be changed. Once the data are organized, the task-force members take part in a roundtable session with a facilitator, with the management team listening to the discussion, in what's often called a "fishbowl exercise." What organization fitness profiling does for us, more than anything else, is give all of us in senior management a good look at how closely our operations are aligned with the company's goals. It gives us a chance to listen to others raise a problem and to how the task-force members talk about it. There's a big difference between hearing things from an outside consultant and hearing them from your own people. It lets you understand how problems are perceived and understood internally.

After these sessions, Merck executives discuss the problems they've heard and come up with proposals on how to address them. We then reassemble the group with the task force. Once again, we let the task force hear our proposals but then develop their own ideas about how to address the same issues they raised earlier.

The topics covered aren't necessarily lofty questions of vision and long-term planning. More often, they are nuts-and-bolts issues that weigh heavily on the minds of managers and employees. I recall one session in which we discussed whether our reward system was really aligned with the goals of the company. What came out of that meeting was a change in our incentive structure so that individuals were recognized for performance that was closely tied to achieving company goals.

Shaping a Management Team

I used the information I gained in my original one-on-one sessions not only to understand what issues the company was facing, but also to help me decide whom I was going to pick to help me deal with those issues, who was going to be on the management team.

I had a timetable in mind. I had started in June and spent the summer learning about the company. I had a sense that I wanted to announce a new management team on Labor Day.

The process of putting together the new team went smoothly. There were a couple of vacancies. One senior manager announced his retirement. Another had said that he would take retirement if he was not named chief operating officer. Merck did not have a COO when I joined the company, and I made it clear that I wasn't about to create the position. In fact, I flattened the organization and took on more direct reports, because I believe that a CEO must be able to ensure a close relationship between setting strategy and executing it.

That required using a team approach to discussing strategy and operations. Since I didn't have a COO, there was no layer of management between me and the people responsible for executing. That gave me a good sense of how things were going at any particular time. That closeness to the operations was particularly important at Merck, because we believed that shareholder value comes from organic growth. Other companies in the industry have decided that scale is everything. We looked at that option and came to a different conclusion. So my job as a leader was to be very aware of how the company was executing our strategy.

During my long series of interviews during the summer, I became confident that the talent I needed was to be found inside the company. I realized I didn't need to bring in anyone from the outside. All of the management team members came from inside the company. Some new members moved up from the ranks, others took on different jobs, and some stayed where they were. I had selected these leaders and given them specific responsibilities, but we quickly found ourselves working as a team.

I chose people not only because of their competence and their ability to perform the job. That is obviously necessary but not sufficient. I also drew on my conversations with people throughout the company and assessed potential management team members based on their ability to inspire confidence and trust within the organization. That is especially crucial at a time of change and uncertainty.

The criteria that I used were these: If I name these people, will the rest of the organization say that they are absolutely the right people for the job? Not only because of their competence but because of their values, their style, and the way they conduct themselves consistently with the values, traditions, and styles of the company. Do they treat employees with dignity and respect? Did I have a sense that I could really trust them in terms of ethical behavior in any situation? In other words, the people a CEO selects for the management team must inspire confidence and trust on the part of the entire organization as well as the CEO.

Developing a Working Relationship with the Board

The new CEO also inherits a board of directors, directors whom the CEO has not appointed and does not necessarily have that close a relationship with.

To get a sense of the Merck board, I used the same process that I had employed with management. I conducted the same kind of interviews with the board of directors: I asked what they thought of the major issues that the company faced, and where I should be spending my time. But I also asked a third question: How do you feel about the governance process, and the nature of the board meetings and the involvement and participation of directors?

Directors will probably want more time for discussion at the board meetings, and more time for discussion among themselves. Moreover, they will want a relationship with management that is open and candid.

I think this was the first time that many directors had really had an opportunity to express themselves in this way, because most board meetings are not structured to allow such views to be expressed. Most of them were happy with board meetings, and their thoughts about the major issues were not all that different from what I heard from the leadership. But the process was invigorating for them. Board members may have filled out questionnaires or talked about corporate governance as part of some sort of annual self-evaluation, but this was the first time they had an opportunity to really discuss one-on-one, in depth, how they felt about the way the governance process was operating. That gave me the means and the information I needed to change the structure of board meetings and, therefore, to start building my credibility and relationship with the board.

At Merck, I avoided a mistake that I made when I became CEO of Becton Dickinson. I thought then that the test I faced in dealing with the board was to always have an answer, no matter what the question. In fact, there is nothing wrong with admitting that you don't know the answer. The board is there to provide advice. It makes sense to seek it.

The second thing I learned was to never drop an issue that a director is concerned about until I had driven it to the ground. A CEO may be focused on several priorities, when suddenly a director raises an issue that may not seem all that important in the hierarchy of things. But if it's an area of concern for a director or a group of directors, the CEO should pay attention to it right away. That, too, is a source of credibility and trust with the board. Boards also bring the perspective of the outsider that you can take advantage of. As a director myself, I know that if I don't have the sense that the CEO is listening, it makes me very uncomfortable and uneasy. Directors recognize that they are not running the business, but if they don't think the CEO is attentive to their concerns, it creates circumstances down the road that could be real issues. I believe that it is important to provide as much scope as possible for directors to express their views. That is why we don't run agenda-driven board meetings. We choose a theme for each meeting, giving directors the widest possible range to express their views and ask questions. If a CEO establishes a relationship of openness with the board, it builds the credibility needed to make it his or her board.

Dealing with Your Predecessor

The third constituent for a new CEO to deal with is the former CEO. At Becton Dickinson, my predecessor was still on the board when I took on the job. When I became CEO of Merck, Roy Vagelos made it a lot easier for me by deciding to leave the board and the company and hand over the reins right from the outset.

Having gone through both experiences, I am convinced that the best process is for a retiring CEO to leave the board voluntarily, knowing he is giving his successor more room. My own intention upon retirement, by the way, is to do just that. That's my decision. But in most circumstances, the board has to be a key factor in this very sensitive issue. Ultimately, the board has to provide direction about what role the outgoing CEO should play and whether it is appropriate that he or she play any role at all.

But if the previous CEO expects to play a role, in and of itself that is not necessarily a problem. I have seen situations in which the new CEO pushes the old CEO aside, and I think that's a mistake. It's a matter of performing a balancing act between running the company and keeping the former CEO informed and engaged.

It's important for a new CEO to pay respect to his predecessor and acknowledge the successes of the company. But in a subtle way, it is also important to get across the idea that management must now take the company to another level and deal with new challenges and issues. I always made the point that we faced "new demands and new challenges" but that we would address them in a way that would build on the achievements of the past.

A former CEO will almost always want the new CEO to succeed. The difficulty is that very often the current and former CEOs will have different approaches. At some point, the CEO and the former CEO will have a difference of opinion. How that difference gets resolved will be a function of how well the CEO performs the key part of his job: building support within the company, getting a clear sense of the changes that need to be made, and building a management team that has wide support.

Winning Trust and Respect

A new CEO from outside the company also has to make it clear that some things will not change—including basic values and ethical standards. When I came to Merck, I felt it was especially important to make it clear that I was totally in line with the values and traditions of the company. This was a matter of personal principle for me—and something that was recognized by the board while they were recruiting and hiring me. I didn't want to impose new traditions or abandon old ones simply because I was coming in from the outside.

Soon after I arrived, someone showed me a statement that George W. Merck made in 1950 in a speech at the University of Virginia Medical School. He said, "We try never to forget that medicine is for the people. It is not for the profits. The profits follow, and if we have remembered that, they have never failed to appear." That was embedded in the fabric of the company, but in recent years it had not been highlighted. That was a cultural principle I wanted to revive. It was a way of emphasizing important values without departing from company history. Now, whenever we talk about strategy and where we are taking the company, we make sure this idea is integrated so that this original guiding principle governs our current and future behavior.

The second thing that I did was to make it clear to the organization the importance I placed on integrity and ethical behavior.

Public trust is especially important in the pharmaceutical industry, particularly as it is so heavily regulated. The first place to start, of course, is having the right people on whom you can count to do the right thing. But while that is necessary, it is not sufficient. When companies get into ethical trouble, the source of the problem usually isn't bad people—it's good people who intend to do the right thing but don't. Sometimes they are acting under the mistaken belief that they are helping the company. But part of the problem is that ethical dilemmas are gray. Therefore, it's not enough to simply tell people that we want them to do the right thing. It is important to help them sort out what that is. I took some concrete actions. I appointed a chief ethics officer who reports to me. Together, the management team undertook a global corporate-education program to raise ethics awareness. We conducted workshops that covered the entire company—from a research scientist in New Jersey to a sales rep in Turkey—covering how to recognize and deal with an ethical dilemma. That included examination of case studies, to make the discussion as specific as possible. We also published a code of conduct in multiple languages and made sure it was widely distributed and read.

Additionally, to help set the tone and also to create a channel that is essential to ensuring compliance, we set up ombudsmen. That has been very effective, as have our own compliance mechanisms. Finally, we undertook leadership evaluation that emphasized both leadership development and ethical behavior as being essential elements of leadership. At the end of the year, we conduct a performance evaluation, which includes not only how the business results were achieved but also the leadership attributes and characteristics that were demonstrated in accomplishing those results.

We care about the new medicines we introduce. We care about how fast sales and earnings grow. And we care a lot about how our stock price does. But we also care a lot about how we go about achieving those results. And in achieving those results, we also ask ourselves: Have we conducted ourselves according to the highest standards of ethics and integrity? Have we treated everyone with dignity and respect—both outside the company and particularly those people that report to us inside the company? In that way, we expect to inspire confidence and trust among the people who regulate us, the patients who use our medicines, and the physicians who prescribe them.

Did being an outsider ensure that I would be able to bring these perspectives to the job? No, but it did force me to look at the company from the outside, and that is an essential first step.

CHAPTER TWO

Strategic Shifts at a Turnaround Company

John Dasburg, chairman and CEO of DHL Airways and former chairman and CEO of Burger King and Northwest Airlines

John Dasburg spent nearly a decade as a senior executive at Marriott before becoming CEO of Northwest Airlines during one of the airline industry's most turbulent periods. At the time, the industry was still absorbing the shock of airline deregulation, and many companies, including Northwest, were struggling to remain competitive and deal with the rising costs of union labor. In 1989, a California investment group purchased Northwest for $3.65 billion. Dasburg is widely credited for managing a turnaround that saved the company from bankruptcy. The turnaround required intense negotiations with Northwest's labor unions in the early 1990s, asking them to take wage concessions. His success helped the corporation re-emerge as a public company and become profitable by 1994. "It trained me in negotiating and reaching a common goal," Dasburg told the *Financial Times* after announcing his resignation, "but not always in the most elegant way." In 1994, *Travel Agent* magazine named Dasburg "Man of the Year" for revitalizing the airline.

In 2001, he was named chairman, chief executive officer, and president of Burger King, the world's second-largest restaurant chain, owned by the British food-and-drinks conglomerate Diageo. During his tenure there, he introduced a new marketing campaign and fourteen new items to Burger King's menu as fast-food restaurants continued to face intense head-to-head competition from their rivals and other low-cost casual restaurants. In early 2003, the Burger King chain was sold to the Texas Pacific Group, and Dasburg turned the reins over to a new CEO. A few months later, Dasburg resigned as chairman and accepted an offer to be CEO of DHL Airways.

THE KEY MOMENT in a corporate rescue mission can happen in unusual ways and at surprising times. Soon after taking over as CEO of Northwest Airlines in 1990, I got a call at home from a young executive describing the core of a turnaround strategy that he was convinced would work. It had been a long day, but the young man insisted I hear him out. I was impressed by his confidence and commitment.

He came to my home and presented his ideas in my library. We talked for almost four hours, late into the evening. His proposal was very compelling; he convinced me that we could turn Northwest around by abandoning the prevailing strategy of developing or acquiring as many hubs as possible (at the time referred to as "ubiquity") and instead focusing on only three hubs: Minneapolis–St. Paul, Detroit, and Memphis, Northwest's historic hubs. We put the plan into effect and also created an alliance with the Dutch airline KLM, which meant we no longer had to fight for landing rights in the major hubs of Europe. Such partnerships to extend the global reach of a U.S. airline are common in today's industry, but at the time it was a completely new approach. When we launched the three-hub strategy, it was ridiculed in the industry—the conventional wisdom was that an airline was required to serve every market. But this new strategy saved Northwest. We increased revenue per seat mile, reduced cost per seat mile, improved service dramatically, and reduced administrative costs. By 1994, Northwest was re-listed as a public company, and by 1998 it was earning record profits. All as a result of the change in strategy. Ubiquity had been an inefficient and costly strategy. The company needed to be turned around if it was to survive.

Turnarounds have existed as long as there has been business. They typically involve a specific company whose poor performance makes it an outlier within an industry. In business terms, the company is failing to earn its cost of capital.

When I arrived at Northwest, the company's failures were already recognized. In 1989, the airline had been purchased by a well-known leveraged-buyout firm, and most of the senior executives had resigned. I was brought in by the LBO firm to act as CEO. The development of the three-hub concept is typical of a turnaround: It starts with an idea, triggering what is known as the three S's—strategy, structure, and staffing. Once a strategy is adopted, an organizational structure, usually tight command-and-control, must be adopted. It is the organizational structure that allows for attracting the skilled personnel to execute the strategy. The proper structure also is essential to the execution of the new strategy.

Shaping a Strategy

The first step is strategy. Without a strategic alternative to the current failed strategy, it is difficult to attract skilled people and to ascertain what organization structure is appropriate. A turnaround usually requires a strategy that is different from the one the company has been following. I use the term "usually" because, on rare occasions, the strategy is correct but implementation has failed. Be suspicious if this is the opinion of senior board members or a lead director; to paraphrase, "It's the strategy, stupid." It comes down to this: When a business is failing, there is a reason. The turnaround CEO has to assess what is wrong with the current strategy and what should replace it.

That does not necessarily mean that the company is the only one pursuing the wrong strategy. At the time of my Northwest experience, for example, many competing airlines—excluding Southwest—were pursuing the same strategy we were, trying to build hubs in every major market. And they were also failing. When an entire industry is pursuing the same wrongheaded strategy, it takes boldness to depart. Therefore, the board must believe in the new strategy.

While the idea for a new strategy for Northwest was aggressively promoted by one individual, it was eventually the product of an extensive process. We were searching for a new strategy, a process that involved gathering together the most skilled executives in the company and engaging in wide-range thinking about alternative strategies. The alternate strategy was developed by insiders, people I had identified as high-potential innovative thinkers by searching through the Northwest hierarchy. And it included people who came to me because they wanted to tell me that they believed the company was on the wrong strategic course.

Once we had a strategy that I was confident would work for Northwest, I was able to take on one of the most important tasks for a CEO in any turnaround: selling the new idea within the company. During a turnaround, there must be extensive communication within the company, particularly with the board of directors. Given how radically you are changing the organization, the amount of time you spend with directors has to increase by severalfold.

The relationship between the CEO and the directors is dramatically different during a turnaround. In a non-turnaround company, the directors have a tendency to relate to the CEO with a sense of continuity and comfort. A sense of business-as-usual prevails. But in a turnaround, the relationship can be very tense and fractious. In some ways, it is easier for an incoming CEO, because there is a "honeymoon" and the directors recognize that a fix is needed. On the other hand, significant time must be spent building a CEO-board relationship, and inevitably some board members, as odd as it may seem, believe in the previous strategy and blame failure on execution. Moreover, board members and the CEO must learn one another's eccentricities, which is a further complicating matter. At Northwest, I had a previous relationship with a number of key directors, and this greatly facilitated the change-in-strategy process.

At Northwest, selling the new three-hub strategy to the enterprise took about three months. I nudged it through the decision-making process, educating board members and bringing them along. During that time, I met with members of the board, one-on-one and with groups of key executives. We developed a consistent message for the strategy, with a consistent vocabulary that was shared by all of us, hammering home the message: Serving every major market—"ubiquity"—had failed. We needed to concentrate our flying at our three historic hubs. By the time we formally brought the three-hub strategy to a board meeting, all the questions had been answered.

Getting the necessary support for a turnaround is always going to be time-consuming, even if a board of directors isn't directly involved. At Burger King, which I joined after leaving Northwest, I was dealing with the CEO and CFO of a parent company, rather than with a board. My mission was also a little different. The parent company of Burger King had already made it public that it intended to "separate" Burger King from the company, and my job was to improve its fortunes. Still, moving from airlines to burgers was relatively easy. In a turnaround, a new CEO is permitted to examine the "first principles" of the business. There is no historic attachment to a previous strategy. Additionally, I had worked at managing Big Boy restaurants, which had been owned by Marriott, where I had worked before going to Northwest. But that familiarity was not critical. The key in a turnaround is the ability to identify the strategic assets, figure out what isn't working, and use the assets you think will work.

The CEO and CFO of Burger King's parent company effectively played the role of a board for me. When I arrived, they had already been searching for a strategy, because the company was not producing adequate returns on investment and customer activity was not improving. I reviewed all the existing strategic material. It was clear to me that we had to deal with the problem of overinvestment. In the fast-food industry, 75 percent of all business is from either take-out or drive-through orders. Overinvesting inside the individual restaurants—where only a quarter of the business really took place—had prevented them from earning a reasonable return. Our belief was that every restaurant had to earn a fair return. Additionally, we had to alter the strategy of continually discounting Burger King's premium product, the

Whopper, while still finding a way to compete on price. Wendy's had enjoyed considerable success by never discounting its premium brand but still offering a 99-cent everyday value menu. I thought that was the right marketing strategy.

We moved very quickly on a radical new investment policy, reducing capital investment in individual restaurants. At the same time, we introduced the new marketing strategy, matching Wendy's and our other competitors' key price points without discounting our premium product.

Because Burger King is a franchise business, a lot of one-on-one persuasion was needed in the field. We conducted road shows with the objective of explaining the new agenda, including a new operating strategy focused on the customer.

Building a "Conditional" Strategy

There is a world of difference between strategy in a turnaround situation and a non-turnaround situation. Most important, in a non-turnaround situation a CEO has the time and opportunity to shape a consensus around a strategy and match the strategy to the existing corporate structure. The company can proceed in a logical order, first developing a strategy, next tuning the structure that serves the strategy, and finally tuning the staffing that fits the structure and the strategy. In short, the process is evolutionary, not revolutionary.

In a turnaround situation, a CEO doesn't have that luxury. In a turnaround, the CEO is pursuing all three simultaneously. As early as possible, there has to be a strategic objective to believe in—what might be called a conditional strategy. It is the conditional strategy that allows you to proceed, to build some confidence in the organization. In recruiting new executive talent, for example, it is essential to have something to invite them into. It is difficult to hire good people if there is not a reasonably clear organizational structure to hire them into.

Quite simply, the CEO must land on a strategy. You can't go

through the normal tidy processes, because you will never get the business turned around. Stay flexible—you may have to alter the strategy along the way. But it is necessary to set up at least a conditional strategy and put together the best organizational structure to attract talent as quickly as possible.

You cannot insist on perfection in a strategy before getting it off the ground. You have to anticipate making mistakes. At Northwest Airlines, for example, we knew we had to abandon ubiquity and go for a limited-hub approach. But that opened the question: What do we do with aircraft at the other hubs? As we proceeded to withdraw from hubs, where would the planes go? We also were not sure whether Memphis would work as a hub. These were important questions, and we could have let them hold the strategy up. But then we would not have been able to go forward at all. We dealt with those important issues later, without confusing 50,000 employees. So we built a conditional strategy: We decided to go to three hubs and sort out the scheduling problems later. We put together a team to schedule Northwest under the new strategy and moved on.

At Burger King, we knew we wanted to copy Wendy's value-proposition strategy, but we weren't sure whether the franchisees would accept it. So again, we began by constructing a conditional strategy—in this case, five regional strategies—even before we launched a national value strategy. These five value propositions acted as stepping-stones, easing the path to a wholly new strategy and one national value proposition. It was a halfway measure, but one we had to take to get the turnaround process moving forward.

The important thing is to abandon the losing strategy, adopt a new one, and begin the process of selling it into the organization. It isn't always possible to have the luxury of doing a doctoral study of a new strategy. If you don't have all of the facts and assumptions, you have to use your best judgment in order to create something to work from.

But at the same time, one cannot forfeit credibility. There is a difference between building a straw man and grasping a straws. It is important to understand what is wrong with the current strategy—such as overinvestment in individual restaurants and deep, unpredictable discounting of the premium brand but not matching other discounts. Keep in mind that the more one invests in a conditional strategy, the more flexible it has to be.

The Importance of Organizational Structure

Every enterprise has an organizational structure. It guides decisions about hiring, management, leadership, and implementation. So when the turnaround CEO arrives at a new company, he has to identify the company's organizational structure and then decide whether to stick with it.

When I arrived at Burger King, the structure was decentralized. Decision-making was performed in the field, and franchise owners and restaurant owners had enormous autonomy. We concluded that as much of the structure as possible had to be centralized.

I'd like to say that the decision was a result of a long process of deliberation and consultation. But it never is in a turnaround. You have to settle on a structure that seems to match your strategy—even your tentative, conditional strategy—and the demands of your industry.

My decision to centralize the structure was driven only partly by my desire to rein in some of the decision-making. I also recognized that I had limited time in which to terminate many senior managers and hire, retain, or promote others. The kind of organizational structure I would choose would largely determine what type of people I could attract. I thought I had a better chance of getting the best people in a centralized system. I decided it was easier to hire a senior marketing person who would report directly to me. Since pricing and marketing was so important to the strategy that I wanted to pursue, I believed that I should have the head marketing person report directly to me rather than reporting to the head of North American operations.

I reached the same conclusion with regard to operations and real estate.

But my general point is that I could not start hiring without declaring what the structure would be. There is simply no way in a turnaround that you can attract a talented professional unless you can describe the structure of the organization. They, quite reasonably, want to know where they fit. Since every turnaround is already clouded with uncertainty, deciding on the basic structure creates a new foundation. It lets you tackle your next most pressing issue: hiring people to help you fix the company.

Staffing: A New Strategy Needs a New Team

A CEO or any leader taking over in a turnaround situation has about sixty days to reassign the existing human resources and start hiring new members of the team and mentoring those existing members.

I don't mean to sound callous about it. In fact, replacing senior executives is a very challenging and difficult process. But if they had the right strategy and the right structure, the company would not be in a turnaround situation in the first place. That means there are likely to be some significant terminations, and the new CEO will have to start working on staffing immediately against the conditional strategy.

First, it is important to determine who can be retained. The new CEO has to pick the senior executives with whom he or she is most comfortable, the ones with potential, and put them in key positions. This is very time-consuming but also, if successful, provides some institutional memory.

At the beginning of a turnaround, the new CEO's responsibility is to make sure that the senior team buys into the new strategy with enthusiasm. Anyone who does not has to be replaced, because everyone who stays is going to have to be able to sell the strategy.

At both Northwest Airlines and Burger King, I met with each of the senior people frequently one-on-one to determine if they could be effective in articulating and implementing the new strategy. The first thing I asked them is why they stuck with the previous strategy. Had they argued against it? Could they be persuaded to embrace a new strategy and take it on enthusiastically? Given their place in implementing the old strategy, incumbent senior executives have to be able to defend it or explain why they are willing to switch. How they answer makes it clear if they are really on-board with the new strategy—and also reveals the clarity of their thinking.

If they abandon their support for the old strategy too easily, and without being able to articulate their rationale, one has to wonder about the depth of their commitment to any strategy. But if they defend the old strategy so intensely that they cannot depart from it in good conscience, then they cannot be effective in articulating and advocating the new strategy. What a new CEO is really looking for is a unique individual—one who can defend the old strategy and yet be facile enough to support the new strategy.

Very few existing executives end up staying during a turnaround. At both Northwest and Burger King, most of the senior executives departed within six months. That degree of turnover rolls all the way through to upper middle management; in fact, turnover can run as high as 75 percent or more over time in this group. That is one more reason to begin the recruiting process as soon as possible.

When it comes to hiring new executives, a new CEO needs an extensive personal network—what is often called a "good Rolodex" even in the days since we all got handheld organizers. The best radar system for detecting talent is our own instinct, honed by years of working with people in different circumstances and great recruiting firms. The senior management ranks of any successful company isn't just a collection of talented people—it has to be a team. Of course, most anti-poaching clauses restrain most CEOs from being able to hire out of their previous company. But a turnaround leader doesn't have time to develop senior executives. So he has to look higher up the talent ladder. The people who are brought on have to be already accomplished in their fields. Above all, the goal has to be to shape a team that is comfortable with one another and shares a belief in the turnaround strategy.

No one should make the mistake of thinking that by hiring new senior management—or even middle management—one truly has a new team in place. A new team—or any kind of team—has to be aligned in its thinking and share values. It takes years to change a company's culture, but its behavior can be changed in months. In the first year of a turnaround, the CEO has to spend a great deal of time on changing behavior. One of the key ingredients is the incentives that are put in place, to encourage upper and middle management to align with the strategy. I did this at both Northwest and Burger King by spending an immense amount of time with the top executives. I encouraged robust social engagement and encouraged them to socialize with one another. I believed it was critical that this group, which would be working so intensely together, feel completely comfortable with one another.

Creating a team also means making every effort to find a consensus on key decisions. If early on in a process, a senior executive objects to a decision, you have to work very hard to bring him or her along. You can't ignore objections. And because you need to persuade an entire company about a new direction, finding unanimity among your senior team is essential. That's why slowing down to reach a consensus is worth the time, even when you are working in an environment of the utmost urgency. Often you will find unanimity on operational questions, but not on marketing. You can choose to go forward on one but slow down the other.

Look for Ideas—Not Perfection

The most important thing to remember about making a turnaround work is that everything has to be done quickly. Time is of the essence—the essential elements have to be in place in twelve months in order to restore confidence. A turnaround CEO cannot dot all the I's and cross all the T's; a conditional strategy has to be put forward to get the process started. A turnaround CEO can't first shape a strategy, then build the structure, and, finally, fill the key management spots—all three activities must be pursued at once, to create the needed sense of momentum. And no potential idea can be rejected out of hand. When a CEO trying to lead a turnaround gets a late-night call at home from a young executive convinced of an idea, it makes sense to take the time to listen.

CHAPTER THREE

Clarifying Strategy Through Mergers, Acquisitions, and Divestitures

William S. Stavropoulos, chairman and CEO of Dow Chemical

Founded more than a century ago, Dow has become a global leader in chemicals, plastics, and agricultural products. With 50,000 employees and annual sales in excess of $27 billion, it is the second-largest chemical company in the world and the largest in the United States Throughout its history, Dow has expanded into new products and markets, producing everything from polyethylene to herbicides to consumer products such as Saran Wrap and Ziploc bags. William Stavropoulos was appointed CEO in 1995 after having been with the company since 1967. Under his leadership, Dow began a far-reaching plan to restructure its portfolio, making high-profile acquisitions and selling off businesses it no longer regarded as critical to its mission. It sold off its stake in Marion Merrell Dow, its pharmaceutical division, for $5.1 billion in 1995. DowBrands, which produced many of the company's best-known consumer products, was sold in 1998. At the same time, the company acquired a number of agricultural-science companies. It also acquired or forged joint ventures with chemical companies in Latin America, South Africa, and Asia, including the first trading joint venture with a Chinese company approved by China's government.

In 1999, Dow announced a merger with Union Carbide, a deal valued at $11.6 billion. The new combined company was ranked number 50 on *Fortune*'s annual list of the 500 largest companies.

Stavropoulos stepped down as CEO in 2000 but continued to serve as chairman. After the company suffered financial losses over the next two years, his successor, Michael Parker, was dismissed by the board, and Stavropoulos was reappointed CEO in December 2002.

SOMETIMES A COMPANY reaches a point where it has to ask itself: What business are we in? Dow Chemical reached that point in the mid-1990s. When we looked at our history, mandate, and core strengths, the answer was clear: We were a chemicals business. But when we looked at the full range of our businesses and products, the answer was ambiguous: Somehow we had morphed into a consumer-products business and a pharmaceutical business. There is little point in being something you are not, and little percentage in trying to be a bit of everything. We decided that, rather than try to do everything, we would make it our goal to achieve excellence in the things we are best at.

This was not a retrenchment strategy; it was a growth strategy. We saw opportunities to strengthen our own strong franchises, and we recognized a need to go truly global, by acquiring international companies that would fit our core strengths. But we decided that before we got bigger, we had to get better. That became our mantra. A central aspect of that goal was selling companies that didn't advance our strategy, and acquiring companies that were essential to growing our core business. From 1994 through 1999, we divested over $10 billion worth of businesses and added about $10 billion worth. Over the course of seven years, we divested, acquired, merged with, and completed joint ventures for about 165 companies. We changed the face of Dow Chemical. Perhaps a more precise way of putting it is that we made the face of Dow Chemical reflect its soul.

When I say "soul," I am referring to the company's core mission, the business it is in. Whether you are considering buying a business or selling one, the question is the same: Is this the right fit? When you are looking at a business you own, you have to ask yourself: Could someone else run it better than we can? In Dow's case, we had too many businesses that we could not optimize. We also had too many businesses that were growing too slowly; it was necessary to get rid of those as well, in order to allow us to pursue a growth strategy.

Decisions to sell some of our businesses were never easily

made. Many of the ones we had put up for sale had been in our portfolio for many years, and we had worked hard to make them successful. We also had some excellent people working in these businesses whom we would lose as a result of the divestiture. Selling DowBrands, which was responsible for such well-known products as Saran Wrap and Ziploc bags, was a decision that was difficult for our employees and our retirees. In many ways, DowBrands products had shaped our corporate image. Consumers knew us much better through these products than through caustic soda or polyethylene, two of our most successful chemical products. But the truth was that DowBrands was outside of our competency. We really couldn't add anything to it. So we sold it to S. C. Johnson, where the business was a better fit.

When looking at acquiring a business, I believe it is important to follow a conservative philosophy. Look at it this way: When you are selling a company, you already know everything there is to know about it. When you are buying one, the learning curve is steep. At Dow Chemical, we made it a point to learn as much as possible. For example, when we wanted to enter the Thailand market, we spent a considerable amount of time looking for a partner in that country. We researched potential Thai partners and found one whose leadership and way of doing business we admired, a company that had been in business for many years, called Siam Cement. We devoted a year to getting to know the company's management, by working on some joint initiatives. That was the way we made a number of relatively small acquisitions. Sometimes it makes sense to start with just a distribution agreement at the local level.

At the other end of the scale was Dow's acquisition of Union Carbide, the largest acquisition in the history of the chemical industry up to that time. Few would describe that deal as conservative. But it, too, was subject to the most careful consideration and scrutiny. In fact, because of the size and implications of the deal, it had to be even more intensely scrutinized. As CEO, I was involved from beginning to end.

Any significant transformation of a company—merger, acquisition, divestiture, or strategic alliance—must be based on an overall strategy and backed up by comprehensive reasoning. Making the deal is just the beginning; the tough part is making it work. And convincing everyone in the organization to get behind it.

A corporate executive making an acquisition or entering into a merger can expect to face a lot of questions. There is nothing wrong with employees examining the course their company is taking. Anyone trying to change a company has to be prepared to answer them. If your company announces a merger or acquisition tomorrow morning, here are some of the questions you can expect to be hit up with—repeatedly—by tomorrow afternoon:

- What is in it for me? If you cannot answer that question—if you cannot explain how the action will benefit the company's workforce—you can expect to have a lot of people sitting on their hands.
- Why do we need to change? We're doing okay. (If the company hasn't been doing so well, a rider is usually tacked on to that question: "We've been through this before—the cycle will come back.") This is why it is so important to know exactly how a merger or acquisition will benefit the company strategically before you make the decision to go ahead, and to have a consistent message.
- Isn't the financial cost too high? That's why it is so important to have the financials nailed down and easy to explain, and a clear message shaped regarding the long-term value of the move. You have to be able to ask: How much could it end up costing us *not* to do this?
- What happens to my turf? How do I get a promotion if the organization is going to be flattened? That brings us back to the first question. If people fear personal downsides, you have to be able to demonstrate upsides.

There are no standard, pat answers to these questions. But the approach to answering them ought to be consistent. Our approach was to be open and honest with all of our communications. A merger can create a lot of organizational and emotional turmoil for employees. Our goal was simply to make employees from Dow and from the acquired company feel that they were being treated with respect, not merely as pawns in a large corporate game. After every merger, we explained very early that there would be significant changes, fewer layers in the organization, more empowerment for employees, but, ultimately, fewer people. Our commitment, stated at the outset, was to let employees know their employment status within six months. In the Union Carbide merger, we began telling some employees that they would not be needed in the new company as early as a week after the merger closed. Essentially, our policy was that bad news was better than silence, and we applied it with every merger or divestiture. Bad news travels fast inside a company, so it is much better to be totally transparent at the start. Needless to say, many employees who have been let go after a merger don't like the message we gave them. But they never complained about the process. Indeed, what I consistently heard from Union Carbide employees who departed was that they appreciated the fact that management was open, honest, and timely in communicating with them.

The Three Elements of Corporate Transformation

Visualize any corporate transformation—M&A, divestiture, or strategic alliance—as a pyramid. The top layer is strategy, which includes establishing the vision and values of the new entity. The middle layer is implementation, which includes processes and culture. At the base is integration, which includes information technology, organization, and human-resource policies.

The important thing to keep in mind is that each of these elements is integral to the successful transformation of a company.

You can't pick and choose. Failure to pursue all three successfully leads to confusion and sends out mixed messages. Moreover, all of them have to be achieved with a sense of urgency and speed. Every day in which issues are not resolved is a day in which the company drifts a little bit strategically.

Vision, Values, and Strategy: The vision must be clear, simple—and actionable. Just about every company has some kind of statement of values hanging on a wall in a frame or posted on a bulletin board. But whenever I read one, I ask: Is it actionable? Can an employee incorporate it into his or her performance? Will the stated values be usable as part of his or her performance review? If the values are violated, will decisive action be taken? If a company's statement of values is not actionable—if it is not seen as something that is part of the daily corporate life—then it just becomes an open window for cynicism to drift into the company.

Our mission at Dow—"to constantly improve what is essential to human progress by mastering science and technology"—was supported by a set of six values. The values are pretty straightforward—integrity, respect for people, unity, outside-in focus, agility, and innovation—but what is more noteworthy is how we tried to embed them across the company after each merger. After the Union Carbide merger, this proved to be relatively easy. We quickly realized that the two companies had much in common in terms of culture and outlook. That wasn't entirely surprising. We both had long histories in the chemical business; we had similar shareholders who had helped shape our business priorities. Plant safety, environmental sensitivity, and a rigorous decision-making process were deeply embedded concerns for all of us. For these reasons, the awkwardness that often characterizes relationships between the employees of two newly merged companies was not prominent after the Union Carbide deal.

The strategy must set the context for everything the organization does. Whether it is communicating the reasons for a divestiture or a plant closing or a research project, the initiative should be framed in the context of the strategy, to constantly reinforce what the company is trying to accomplish. After we announced the Union Carbide merger, we were very up-front about the strategic reasons that we believed justified such a large acquisition. We emphasized three major points. First, the merger would immediately double our portfolio of performance chemicals. These are the higher-margin, less cyclical products that are widely used in food, drugs, and other everyday products. Second, the merger strengthened our basic commodity business, such as polyethylene and polypropylene. Finally, the Union Carbide merger gave Dow access to low-cost hydrocarbon feedstocks in the Middle East and Asia Pacific—the raw materials we depend on to make our other specialty and broad-use chemicals. We made sure that these three messages were communicated not only to Wall Street but also to managers and employees. We wanted the entire company to have a consistent message about the thinking behind the merger strategy.

It is easy for senior executives to remember their company's strategy. When people are working seven days a week to advance any strategy, it's hard for them to keep in mind that the overwhelming majority of people are less familiar with it. I am reminded of a story I once heard—it may have been apocryphal—about a CEO whose company was launching a print-advertising campaign. One day he called the agency that was handling the campaign to tell them that it was time to pull the ad—everyone else must be getting as sick of it as he was. The people at his agency were surprised to hear that, since the ad had not run yet! It turned out that he was sick of the ad because it was hanging on his office wall. The truth is: When you get sick and tired of hearing your own message, that is the point when everyone else is about to notice it.

Culture and Work Processes: The most difficult part of any transformation is the cultural adjustment. Shaping the right culture is critical to any restructuring effort, and that is the part that causes many mergers and acquisitions to fail to achieve their full potential. Not enough attention was paid to the culture, at least not until too late in the game. Preparation for shaping the right corporate culture should begin the day that negotiations are entered into, and the effort should go proactive the day the announcement is made. At Dow, on the day a merger or acquisition was announced, we assigned people at the key sites of both companies, explaining why the initiative was being taken, and what it would mean for them. We made it clear to top management how the company was going to be run. After the Union Carbide merger, we assigned more than a hundred company leaders to every Union Carbide site around the world so that these new employees could establish a personal relationship with the Dow team.

The purpose of those initial contacts was to help spread the Dow culture. We identified eight cultural attributes we wanted to instill—initiative, leadership, market focus, teamwork, and so on—and put processes in place to implant those characteristics. In a merger or acquisition, one of the first priorities has to be to "connect" people—get them linked to the rest of the company. That includes connecting them literally: On day one after an acquisition is completed, every new Dow employee gets a Dow workstation, connecting them to Dow news and Dow e-mail. It is also important to connect them figuratively. Every employee of an acquired company is given what we called "learnagy maps," explaining Dow's processes, financial metrics, benefits, and everything else they need to know about the company. Basic processes are put in place right away, with Dow people to manage them.

IT, Organization, HR: IT can be critical to any transformation because it can allow a global business organization to become very flat. At Dow, we went from fourteen layers to five—that was the gap from the CEO to the newest employee. IT made that possible. We were striving for every Dow employee around the world to have the same information at the same time. It's an expensive tool, but it's an essential one if you are going to be able to pull a company together, especially if you are trying to build a global enterprise.

In addition to delayering the organization, we centralized services and put speed and transparency into our systems. We consistently increased our investment in training and development and tightly linked all of our training and development programs to our strategies and the values we were trying to instill.

The Merger Dream Team: The Right Mix of Expertise

How well a merger or acquisition will work depends largely on how soundly it was conceived and negotiated. On an effective merger team, what you need more than anything else is diverse expertise and perspectives. The team has to include someone who is familiar with the specific business, someone who understands finance, a legal person, and someone who is expert in the most complex issues. It is especially important to have someone from finance who is dispassionate. The business-operations people always want to make the move, so it is important to have an objective voice in the group, someone who doesn't have a stake in the deal other than ensuring that it advances the strategic and financial goals of the company. What do you want to see on the other side of the table? A direct link to leadership. It is important to make sure you are negotiating with someone who speaks for the company.

At Dow, in the case of a major merger, the negotiating team was always assembled by top management. In smaller mergers, the head of the relevant business would put together a team and call on the CFO or head of research to flesh it out. In any large acquisition, such as Union Carbide, I would be directly involved from the beginning.

During the due-diligence process, a reason may always turn up to change your mind. It may be that the right technology is not there, or what was represented to be there may turn out not to be. Of course, that doesn't mean that you don't do the deal; it might just be a matter of doing it at a much lower price. But those are the easy decisions. How to prepare for the tougher ones?

First, know in advance what the critical deal-breakers are, and the factors that can change the valuation. Second, always have an expert available on every aspect of how the business operates. At Dow, we would fly people in from all over the world. If the best expert we had was based in Argentina, and we were considering buying a business in Illinois, we would fly him up to Chicago to examine the plant. We would bring experts on all subject matter. That allowed us to do a much more accurate due diligence.

The accuracy of due diligence can make the difference between a good deal and a bad one, and between doing a deal or letting it slip between your fingers. For example, Dow was about to bid on a specialty chemical company dealing with an environmental problem that carried cleanup and other potential liabilities. Not only were our bankers looking at it—so were our top environmental people. We assessed the cost precisely and built it into our bid. A rival who was trying to acquire the company ended up estimating the cost of the liability and cleanup at a rate four times higher than our assessment. Obviously, based on that cost-estimate differential, they didn't acquire it. We did, and the costs came out close to our estimate. I was certainly glad that we had gone to the trouble of putting our most qualified specialists on it.

The Integration Process: Quick, Clear, Comprehensive

Even in a major merger or acquisition, the core integration process should take no more than a year to complete. The second year should be devoted primarily to mopping-up exercises, such as the introduction of new systems.

One can't debate the transition process—that would take too long. It has to be decided at the top and announced to both companies. That sounds undemocratic, but what people want is clarity. They want decisions, and they need them quickly.

Looking at the big picture: At Dow, in any merger or acquisition we would set up a parallel organization of the two companies. At the top level would sit an Integration Executive Committee made up of the CEO and a few senior executives. That committee would decide the big questions, such as governance issues, what processes to use, and what to do with headquarters. This kind of top-level group was set up for every significant acquisition.

Making Major Recommendations: Reporting to the Integration Executive Committee would be an Integration Program Team, which would deal with 10 percent of the issues that came up—important ones. They would decide quickly, something that was possible because it was a small group not laden down by bureaucracy. This team would always include the vice president of operations for manufacturing and supply chain, to ensure integration of relevant processes. They would make recommendations to the Integration Executive Committee.

Dealing with lesser issues: Below the Integration Program Team, we set up a Program Management Team. It made 90 percent of the decisions—less strategic decisions, down to the design of the stationery.

The clean team: As the deal is about to close, it is valuable to put together a "clean team." This is a group made up of two to five people who know the companies but are not currently part of them. Typically, they are retired executives from both companies. They examine policies—such as purchasing processes at both the acquired and acquiring companies—looking at specific overlaps and how to deal with them. They have to be independent, so they shouldn't report to anyone, other than the legal team. On day one, they present their findings and recommendations, such as how to deal with transportation issues. For example, Union Carbide owned barges, while Dow leased its fleet. We compared the costs and determined that the Dow approach was cheaper. One week later, we sold the Union Carbide barges, leased them back, and saved $2.5 million.

The lockdown: In a truly major deal, it is a good idea to hold a lockdown after the merger is closed, in which the leadership of both companies is assembled in one place. The purpose of a lockdown is to share confidential business information with officials from both companies that, prior to the closing, could not legally be shared. This includes everything from customer lists to pricing information and strategic plans. When Dow acquired Union Carbide, we made the closing announcement on Wednesday and had a lockdown on Thursday. About twenty leaders from both companies met for three days to share information about finance, manufacturing, research, our supply-chain processes, and our commercial business. It is a fascinating and critical meeting. After all, before the merger, Dow and Union Carbide were fierce competitors. We both had major polyethylene business franchises, but very little information about our practices and customers had ever been revealed to each other. The lockdown exercise made it possible to quickly understand each other's business, identify issues that needed immediate attention, tell top management both the short-term and long-term game plans, describe the integration process, and announce the leaders.

What I have seen after dozens of acquisitions and divestitures at Dow is that transformation should not be seen as an event. It should not be seen as a decision of a lifetime. Rather, it is an ongoing process. The world is changing all the time; every industry is changing all the time; consumers are changing all the time. What company should see itself as exempt?

Instead of seeing major transformational moves as something

to be minimized or avoided, companies should see them as something to be strategized. The question is not whether a company is undergoing continual change. The question is whether its leadership is strategizing change, and how it is implementing it. It comes down to the questions: What kind of business do you want to be, and what does it take to become that?

CHAPTER FOUR

Dealing with Market Reality: What Should a Leader Do When Markets Disappear?

C. Michael Armstrong, chairman of Comcast Corporation and former chairman and CEO of AT&T and Hughes Electronics

Few CEOs have seen as much upheaval as Mike Armstrong. After a thirty-one-year career at IBM, Armstrong accepted the job as chairman and CEO of Hughes Electronics. He arrived as this defense-electronics company was going through a significant transformation at the end of the Cold War, when Pentagon budgets were shrinking. Under Armstrong's leadership, the company refocused on commercial satellites, creating DirecTV, today the largest broadcast-satellite provider in the United States.

After six years at Hughes, Armstrong moved to another industry in the midst of tumultuous change: telecommunications. He became chairman and CEO of AT&T in 1997, a year after the landmark Telecommunications Act launched an unprecedented period for competition within the industry. Armstrong pursued a new strategy for the company, cutting costs and making large-scale acquisitions that would move America's telephone icon into the cable and wireless-communications business. AT&T's purchase of TCI and then, later, MediaOne transformed it into the largest cable provider in the country.

With falling stock price values, accelerating industry price declines, and considerable debt, Armstrong unveiled a capital structure of three separate AT&T businesses: wire, wireless, and cable. In July 2001, AT&T Wireless was spun off as a separate company. Nearly six months later, Comcast purchased AT&T Broadband, as the cable and data business was known, for $47 billion in stock and $17 billion in debt. With 56% of the new company owned by AT&T shareholders, Armstrong became chairman of Comcast.

JOHN F. KENNEDY was once asked what personal quality gave him the strength of character to become a war hero. His response? "It was easy—they sank my boat."

Sometimes the most difficult decisions are those with no alternative. I cannot compare the transformations of Hughes Electronics or AT&T to Kennedy's heroics captaining the *PT-109*. But there was one similarity: We had no other choice. Hughes had to face the fact that defense expenditures were being cut dramatically. AT&T had to deal with the reality of local telephone companies entering the long-distance business and rapidly replacing AT&T's core revenue and profit with "any-distance" calling.

That made the decision to transform each of the companies seem relatively easy. But actually achieving the goal was anything but.

Corporate transformation such as Hughes's and AT&T's risks intense change in a concentrated period. But corporate renewal that plays out over a long period of time requires the same kind of change leadership. And in this era of market, regulatory, and technological upheaval, risking and leading such change is a fundamental CEO responsibility.

Although business change invariably presents new and unfamiliar situations, leading successful change depends on fairly traditional business principles: understanding your market, solidifying your base, leading from strength, getting the right capital structure, strengthening your management team, and following through on strategy with operational excellence. But the first step is to embrace the very risk of change.

Facing Reality and Embracing the Risk of Change

Any change is risky. Transformational change is a bet-the-company proposition. It's for neither the timid nor the daredevil. It requires a clear-headed assessment of reality and a deliberate, balanced determination to deal with that reality before it deals with you.

When change outside the company moves at a faster pace than change inside the company, the end is near.

When I arrived at Hughes, I certainly wasn't planning to redefine the company. I had come there after thirty-one rewarding years at IBM. During my last few years at the company, I led their vast international operations. I was in my early fifties and content with the idea of spending the rest of my career with IBM. Yet when the opportunity came to lead a great company such as Hughes, it seemed to me that seizing the opportunity was what life was about.

My initial expectation was straightforward: I would manage this aerospace and defense company to improved profitability. That was not without its challenges. For much of its history, Hughes had been motivated by things other than financial success. When Howard Hughes initially ran the company, it was completely at his direction and laden with his interests. Later, when it was under the supervision of the Howard Hughes Medical Institute, the company did only well enough to meet the Institute's annual budget.

Hughes was acquired by General Motors in 1985, and its board wanted someone who would bring about better returns.

But something happened as I was joining this aerospace and defense company: America won the Cold War. That was wonderful news for all Americans, of course. But for Hughes, it also meant that our potential government market was going to be cut significantly.

Now, it's human nature to think that bad news will mostly affect someone else. Many in the defense industry seemed to think that the industry consolidation and cuts would hit the other guy harder.

But the assistant secretary of defense at the time, Bill Perry, called the department's principal suppliers to a meeting in the basement of the Pentagon, where he and his staff made thoughtful presentations about our country's two-concurrent-conflicts defense strategy, the subsequent future of defense spending, and the impact on defense-procurement programs. It was a classified briefing, and the CEOs of all the major contractors—Northrop, Lockheed, Raytheon, McDonnell Douglas, and Hughes—were there. By the end of that session, it was clear to me that Hughes Electronics had been hit by the equivalent of the Japanese destroyer that sank Kennedy's PT boat.

Of course, all of us in the industry knew that defense spending was going to be cut: We had seen the budget submissions. The questions that remained unclear until that meeting were where the money would be spent, which programs would survive, and how quickly others would be abandoned. Secretary Perry's message confirmed that the defense industry was going to have to consolidate. As for Hughes, it became clear that we needed a new direction. We needed to shift from putting things in orbit for the government to selling things on the ground to the rest of the country.

We were able to make that transition in large measure because someone at Hughes had already begun to think about the post–Cold War future. Tony Iorilla and Steve Dorfman, leaders of the company's satellite business, saw the potential of the commercialization of space. I quickly teamed up with them and Eddie Hartenstein, who we asked to run DirecTV, and we brought our vision to the GM board for funding.

But executing a new strategy for Hughes brought with it new challenges. Focusing on the private sector meant changing our business and our culture. Suddenly, we had to move from a known market of several government customers to new markets serving thousands of businesses and millions of consumers. Working under government contracts, we were accustomed to the cost-plus system, in which the markup was part of the negotiation. Now we had to adjust to a competitively earned fixed price business in which the risk of losing money on a contract was always real. On top of that, we needed new products, new distribution, new marketing—new *everything*. We had to become a market-driven culture with a capital structure to fund our new commercial space strategy. That change, while huge, was not impossible. Hughes's culture was rich in intellectual capacity. In some respects, it operated like a national laboratory within the private sector. At one point, the company had 50,000 engineers, technicians, and advanced scientists on its payroll. Installing a market-based culture was much easier because of the sheer number of smart people there.

A comparable dynamic demanding change took place at AT&T. When I arrived in 1997, the company's business was essentially the middle of the phone call: long distance. It had been that way ever since Judge Harold Greene had overseen the historic separation of long distance from local telephone calls back in 1984. In fact, long distance represented about 80 percent of our revenue and 100 percent of our profit. But the Telecommunications Act of 1996, which gave the local Bell Telephone companies a clear path into any-distance calling, was the obituary for stand-alone long-distance service. The long-distance business was going to evaporate, and I knew it when I took the job at AT&T. But how we would create a new business was a little less clear. At my first board meeting, I asked the directors what they thought the company needed. Someone said: "A future."

We had to create a new strategy to restore the direct connection with customers that we had lost in the court decision of 1984. But it was clear that we needed to offer customers video, data, and voice services. The revolution in digital communications technology meant that these services would no longer be separate functions. And we needed more than the narrowband copper connections that the Bell Telephone companies had depended on for decades—we needed broadband digital connectivity into the millions of homes and businesses we served.

We didn't just stumble onto this strategy. I joined AT&T as CEO on November 1, 1997. There was certainly press attention about my arrival, but I ruled out any interaction with the press or even the investment community until we had agreed on our problems and developed a strategy. For the next three months, our senior team met continuously, working every day in a windowless conference room. It was not until January 25, 1998 that we outlined our new strategy for the Street and the press.

The challenge we had was more than acquiring or building new capabilities to provide three different services to customers. We had to do it at the same time that we significantly cut our costs and redesigned our systems to remain competitive. For years, AT&T assumed that it could charge a price premium because of its brand, service, and reputation. That environment no longer existed. Becoming cost- and price-competitive was a critical component of our strategy.

This was no small matter. AT&T was always benchmarking itself to our competitors, primarily WorldCom. The media and financial analysts made the same comparisons. Every quarter, for example, we would look at scatter diagrams of communications pricing. Almost every quarter, WorldCom was leading the industry price declines. Not only were they pricing down their services, but WorldCom was increasing their margins and expanding their revenues at the same time. We were confounded and frustrated. When we looked at their numbers and saw that depreciation as a percentage of revenue was rising, way above the industry standard and their capital expenditures, it didn't make sense to us. We could only assume they were managing better and avoiding cost. We didn't realize they weren't really leading the industry. They were destroying it.

None of us understood at the time that this major competitor was operating off what we now know to be false books. Their fraudulent accounting over three to four critical years added to our already difficult challenge of changing a company while trying to maintain market competitiveness and investor confidence. But it also drove us to take out $7 billion in costs over four years, enabling AT&T to earn industry-leading margins as we executed our transformation.

What we achieved at both Hughes and AT&T was a fundamental redefinition of the companies. In both cases, however, our change was based on the management team and employees recognizing the new marketplace realities that were thrust upon us. At Hughes, it came from a Cold War victory; at AT&T, it came from technology and regulatory change.

Develop a Market-Driven Strategy: Know Thy Customer

What should a company do when it has faced up to reality, however ugly, and embraces the need for fundamental change, however risky?

It had better develop a strategy that is market-driven. There are many forces to harness in transforming a business. Technology, brand, price, distribution, financing, competition, and time must all be thought through. But nothing is more important than understanding where the market is going and how customers can be better served.

There is not a business value more important than one of the oldest: Know thy customer and thy market. In redefining Hughes with its satellite and defense businesses, we realized that market size was more important than transponder size. We made a multibillion-dollar bet that consumers would pay to get better picture quality and more choice in their TV programming. Admittedly, we had the advantage of looking at the market results of existing competitors. The cable industry and subscription television were already in the field, and their market penetration demonstrated market potential: Customers were willing to pay for more programming choices and better-quality video. To tap that market, we had to not only build new space technology and ground systems but also acquire new content, implement new distribution, and enable new service and support. None of that investment would have paid a cent if the market did not want what we had been developing.

To understand what a difference market acceptance can make, consider the results: Compare the recent bidding war for DirecTV with Iridium's bankruptcy filing and Globalstar's recent sale for $55 million. Both companies invested billions to serve people who didn't have access to wireless infrastructure and provide them with satellite phones. Both misread the market. At Hughes, we had looked into investing in Iridium—after all, we were in the satellite business. But we concluded that the market for people who couldn't use the existing wireless network wasn't large enough. Indeed, the market without cell coverage rapidly diminished at the end of the 1990s, and callers were just not ready to pay relatively high rates to make calls on satellite phones several times larger than what they had become used to. This was a strategic market mistake, not a problem that could have been fixed by better management, technology, distribution, financing, or brand.

Change Needs a Foundation: Build on Your Strengths

To be credible, and therefore doable, change must draw from institutional and individual strength. Change needs a foundation. The greater the change, the deeper the foundation needs to be. To depart from the past, you must also take advantage of the past. It is not enough to just point to the "promised land." The changes required to reach it must be based on things that people believe they can do. Change must have institutional and individual roots.

At Hughes, we knew we could deliver government communication services from space. We also believed we could commercialize space if we got the consumer and business services right. We changed what we were good at to serve new markets, but we didn't try to be good at something we didn't know from experience how to do. For example, we didn't try to produce original content at Hughes, even though some argued that video vertical integration from production to distribution made sense. Our change quotient was metered by the range and depth of our strengths.

We took the same principles into consideration when we set out to transform AT&T from a domestic voice long-distance company into a global provider of any-distance broadband services.

For all its challenges, AT&T had an enviable market opportunity. Ironically, while standalone long distance was disappearing, the overall communications industry was growing as networks became digital, fiber-optic cables were stretched through neighborhoods and under the seas, and the world simultaneously went wireless. Voice, video, and data would no longer be relegated to separate networks. Customers would no longer be tethered to wall outlets. Businesses could operate globally with seamless communications.

To capture these opportunities, over a three-year period from 1998 to 2000, we acquired and began building three new networks: A nationwide digital wireless network, the largest multiservice cable network in the world, and the most sophisticated business IP network. We then bundled services on each of these networks and began scaling the businesses in 2001 and 2002.

Bear in mind: We did not have the luxury of introducing these changes in neat, sequential steps. That surely would have been more orderly, less risky, and financially appealing. In each market—wireless, cable, and wireline—technology was moving rapidly, capital deployment accelerating, and competition fierce. We had to be swift in our build and timely in our execution in all three markets.

We built and bought a national wireless infrastructure, introduced the first local–long-distance wireless bundle with "AT&T Digital One Rate," and successfully scaled the business to millions of subscribers. We bought and integrated cable companies TCI and MediaOne. We accelerated their upgrade from an analog-video broadcast-cable system to a digital-broadband interactive-fiber network. And we began scaling the new cable services of digital video, data, and telephony on our fiber co-ax network. In the long-distance business we built 67,000 route miles of state-of-the-art fiber to serve business customers as we extended our reach globally and increasingly connected locally. It was as determined a strategy to connect customers via three networks—wireless/cable/wireline—as it was a determined execution to operationally scale these businesses.

Making all three elements of our strategy work demanded an enormous amount of energy and time. The very nature of the changes we were introducing to the business demanded that the CEO be involved operationally as well as strategically, while I was constantly balancing my focus across the three separate projects. I was fortunate to have a strong CFO, Chuck Noski, who was my partner and confidant at Hughes and AT&T. The fact that we continued to execute even as investor confidence declined and the WorldCom fraud grew was a credit to the AT&T management, which performed with remarkable purpose and integrity. Yet we realized that continuing to act as a conglomerate was not a viable long-term strategy. We just couldn't match the market-value multiples generated by our biggest mainline competitors, WorldCom and Qwest, or our wireless and cable competitors. Nor were our changing core cash-flow projections—a result of accelerating wire line price declines—going to be able to fund our strategy and balance sheet going forward. We had to ask ourselves how we could deliver shareholder value and at the same time fund our future. This challenge is what ultimately led us from one AT&T company to three companies.

Adopt a Structure That Serves Your Strategy

A CEO is charged with increasing long-term shareholder value. To achieve that goal, whatever the hand you have been dealt, requires not only a sound strategy but a long-term capital structure (that is, access to capital from debt or equity) to fund the strategy. That would be challenging enough if capital markets were predictable, access to them stable, and cash flows uninterruptible. But that's not our world.

Strategy is how you deploy your people, products, and markets. A company's capital structure should adapt to make that strategy work. If the structure is the strategy, it's probably financial engineering.

The transformations of Hughes and AT&T did not initially include capital structure changes. In fact, we set out to transform both businesses using their existing capital structures. But as market and capital forces changed, so did the need for capital structure redefinition. We ended up changing the capital structure so AT&T could achieve its value potential by funding its future.

We did not have a strategy to sell Hughes's defense business to Raytheon, a merger that was completed in January 1997. In fact, before America won the Cold War, our strategy was to build Hughes's defense capabilities. But with the Cold War victory, consolidation within the defense industry drove us to a new structural conclusion.

We also shaped a distinct organizational structure for the DirecTV business—including its own buildings, infrastructure, and incentive system. We wanted to get around the cultural and operational implications that DirecTV was just a department of Hughes's satellite business. So we organizationally separated DirecTV and made it a *customer* of the main company; Hughes provided the satellites, but DirecTV was its own unique business. That was a lesson I learned at IBM, which ensured that its start-up PC business was not simply an outgrowth of the mainframe business by establishing a truly separate business unit with its own balance sheet and income statement. Divorcing DirecTV from the mainstream of Hughes was crucial—in fact, the DirecTV success became the mainstream of the Hughes business.

At AT&T we didn't set out to form three companies from the core AT&T. But as each business executed its strategy and scaled its business, we could no longer satisfy their capital needs from our common balance sheet. Nor were we creating shareholder value relative to our industry peers. It's hard to just blame conglomerate discounting for our equity value, or unexpected declines in core cash flow, or the telecom/dot-com meltdown, or too much debt, or our competitors' massive fraud for forcing us to reassess our capital structure in the fall of 2000. It was a combination of these factors that drove us to conclude that restructuring into three balance sheets would permit each business—wireless, cable, and wireline—to fund its strategy, fulfill its future, and bring shareholder value. Many in the industry who didn't face these realities in this time frame and adapt a capital structure to serve their strategy simply didn't make it.

Obviously, I believe that capital structure should serve strategy. But restructuring is such an all-consuming undertaking that it should be considered only if it is necessary to implement the long-term business strategy. However, it should also not be denied if the alternative is to "wait and see." That could result in eroding share price, higher eventual risk, and/or shakier financial viability.

Probably the important question amidst the telecom turmoil of bankruptcies, fraud, and market dynamics is: Did the restructuring of AT&T actually work to fund its future and deliver relative shareholder value? I believe it did. By the time we split into three companies, the data shows AT&T was undervalued compared to WorldCom, Qwest, our wireless and cable competitors, and the major stock indices. We had a "conglomerate" discount in the market. Additionally, the more we invested to grow, the more we diluted our current earnings, added more debt, and affected our stock price. We had, in short, a capital structure that could not fund its future. When we made the decision to restructure, the stock continued to fall, as the dot-com and telecom bubbles had begun to burst. However, as we implemented the restructuring, AT&T stock performed better than the market, the industry, and our peers from October 2001 to November 2002. It appeared that AT&T, AT&T Wireless, and ComCast had made it possible for the original AT&T shareholder to have a future.

To be sure, the new companies were still facing significant challenges. Restructuring AT&T into three companies was hardly a public relations victory for our proud American icon, but given what we hoped to do—build a future for AT&T—it enabled a long-term victory for our shareholders. During this transition, I faced criticism that our execution was lacking. But restructuring to fund a future in the face of massive telecom market fraud, building three state-of-the-industry networks concurrently, and introducing market-defining services was quite an execution by a tough and dedicated team. Indeed, during a period in which most companies in the telecom sector wound up in bankruptcy or scandal, AT&T executed to deliver strong balance sheets, excellent market positions, our integrity intact, and our future unfolding.

Solidifying the CEO's Internal Base

Even when leading from strength, a CEO undergoing fundamental change must prepare for the long haul. The legendary film producer Samuel Goldwyn once quipped, "Give me a couple of years, and I'll make that actress an overnight success." Similarly, a CEO has to realize that real transformation takes real time to accomplish.

The biggest reason that corporate transformation is so difficult is that while it is easy to get agreement on what the problem is, the solution is seldom so obvious. People persist in trying to keep part of the old strategy alive, even if that gets in the way of implementing the new one.

At Hughes it wasn't difficult to explain the impact of winning the Cold War on our government satellite and defense business. Everyone understood the challenge of being a government contractor at a time when the government would be dispensing far fewer and less lucrative contracts. But it was quite a challenge to convince people that what we had to do was nothing less than commercialize space.

At AT&T it wasn't difficult to recognize that our long-distance business was disappearing and that our company would soon follow it. The real challenge was overcoming the perception that all we needed was a partial fix, such as bundling on the bill, rather than building new networks to bundle the services on.

Recognition of the need for change must start at the top, but it can't stop there. It has to spread quickly through the ranks.

At both Hughes and AT&T, defining the problem was just the beginning of change. True change required winning agreement from the people who made up the company from top to bottom.

That points up the value of one of the most important lessons I experienced: A CEO must solidify his or her internal base. People make change happen; achieving successful change depends on winning people over. It is especially important to pay attention to your three internal constituencies of people—the board, management, and employees.

The Board

The board gives the CEO the job. But you shouldn't assume that the board knows the full dimension of what the CEO is facing. Bring them fully into the problem. They should know the risks. Keep them informed and involved. That means the CEO has to invest more time than ever in the board.

At AT&T, board meetings had traditionally been carefully choreographed affairs, lasting only a few hours. But we asked ourselves: Can we honestly expect to deal with the critical issues involved in transforming this American icon in the same amount of time we spent when AT&T was a regulated monopoly? We expanded the length of the board meetings, conducted tutorials, and scheduled committee meetings the afternoon before board meetings. We made sure that board members understood both the challenges we were facing and the changes we were introducing. If they were to be fully supportive, they had to be fully knowledgeable.

The situation at Hughes was somewhat different, because the company was actually owned by General Motors. While Hughes had its own sub-board, the GM board made most of the important decisions. Convincing GM that the shift made sense could be even more difficult than dealing with an autonomous board, because GM's culture was four-wheel-driven in the 1992–93 timeframe and quite concerned with the company's declining position in the auto industry. But GM's board turned out to be both interested and, in the end, effectively involved. And the key to this was the same board approach of time, tutorials, and business-plan involvement.

In the end, both Hughes and AT&T had supportive boards that knew what they were supporting.

Senior Management

When a company undertakes an expedition into new strategic territory, the CEO should not expect all members of the senior management team to make the trip. What made some of them successful may actually inhibit the changes you need to make. A Hughes senior manager who was good at managing a cost-plus government market, for example, might not be right for a commercial fixed-price business. That is why transforming a company requires the best of what you have coupled with continual upgrading with new blood, recruited internally and externally. You should always be in the midst of team-building, especially making room for people who are willing to test your ideas candidly and openly. That kind of independence is fundamental to effective decision-making. Change leadership requires trust and teamwork at the top.

Front-Line Employees

Somebody once asked the coach of a losing football team what he thought of his squad's execution. "I'm all for it," he said. While I don't subscribe to that wholesale theory of management, a good strategy cannot be substituted for bad execution; people who don't measure up should be replaced. But that won't be your biggest problem. Your biggest challenge will be getting everyone to execute the same strategy. Whether you lead an organization of 1,000 or 160,000 people, you have to ensure that the people on the front lines understand your strategy, your game plan for delivering it, and their personal role in making it happen. You should drive middle management to communicate, but don't depend on them exclusively. Middle managers are often the most threatened by change. Supplement them with whatever you can think of to get yourself in front of the people on the front lines—skip-level and "town hall" meetings, a company newspaper column, videotapes, e-mails, site visits, and earnings reports. In fact, I have a sign on my desk that reminds me of one of the most important rules of corporate leadership—"assume nothing." Assume that if you are singularly accountable, you owe it to yourself to ensure that the people who are supposed to execute your plan know what it is and how they fit into it.

But remember: Actions speak louder than words. Discipline your calendar to make time to constantly "show up." People may skip your memos, but they will watch every move you make. That's why getting out of the office and spending time with customers and employees will always be a critical part of the top manager's job.

Criticism: When to Ignore It—and When Not to

In leading a company through big change, it is easy to fall victim to a couple of common mistakes.

First, it is easy to make the mistake of putting off a decision because all of the information is not in. The fact is that all of the information is *never* in. If you wait for all of it to arrive, you will never make a decision. You and your company can suffer more from consistently late decisions than occasionally wrong ones. It may make more sense to take the risk of making a wrong decision but making it in a timely way—and then using your resources to make sure that decision turns out to be the right one.

If you have undertaken a program of risking transformational change, it's because you see no viable alternative. For the most part, you should act with urgency, learn from failure, and celebrate progress.

Second, while no CEO should feel immune to criticism, it is important to keep it in balance. In addition to what your customers tell you, be sensitive to the views of internal critics among the board, senior management, and front-line employees. These are the people you must always answer to. It is important to realize that no one, not even the chief executive officer, is always right. The boss should admit privately and/or publicly when he is wrong. It's the right thing for everyone, including you.

But it is equally important to be skeptical of external critics and the press of the day. You will tend to read everything that is written about you and your company. No one else will. Keep your eye on what really matters: satisfying customers and maintaining your employees' passion for serving them. And as you work to keep a sense of balance through all of this, above all, keep your sense of humor. In the end, you will do the best you can. And in so doing, you will enjoy it.

CHAPTER FIVE

Emerging from Turmoil at Tyco: A New CEO Prepares for His Second Hundred Days

Dennis C. Carey, vice chairman of Spencer Stuart, US

In the summer of 2002, Edward Breen, the former president and chief operating officer of Motorola, stepped into one of the most contentious business stories of the year by agreeing to become chairman and CEO of Tyco International. The business world had been shocked just weeks earlier when Tyco's former CEO, Dennis Kozlowski, abruptly resigned and was then charged with more than $1 million in tax evasion. In the ensuing investigation, Kozlowski would be charged with stealing $170 million and nearly half a billion dollars in fraudulent securities sales.

In the business press, Tyco seemed to be another example of corporate governance gone awry. The massive conglomerate, which included businesses in health care, electronics, flow control, and home security and fire safety, had grown rapidly during the 1990s after making more than 1,000 acquisitions. At one time, some had suggested that it would become the next General Electric. But in the wake of the Kozlowski scandal, the stock price had plunged and new questions were raised about Tyco's accounting, as the company faced a liquidity crunch. Breen's arrival seemed to reverse the company's apparent free fall. Tyco's stock rose 46 percent on the day his appointment was announced. He then began one of the most far-reaching transformations of a corporation's leadership and governance ever undertaken.

Dennis Carey had a front seat at this remarkable transition. As an occasional advisor to Kozlowski and one of the country's leading executive-search experts for chief executives and corporate directors, Carey was asked by Tyco's board to find a new CEO. Over the next several months, he and his colleague Dayton Ogden not only recruited Breen but helped to replace both the senior management team at Tyco and its entire board of directors. Carey also became a part of Breen's close circle of advisors.

In this chapter, Carey argues that Breen did the most important thing for a CEO surrounded by turmoil: move quickly to create a new management and governance structure in the first one hundred days. By putting in place an entirely new team that had no ties to the past, Breen would be able to cope with the company's ongoing restructuring even after his initial "honeymoon" period was over.

Carey is vice chairman of Spencer Stuart US, an executive search firm. He has worked directly with dozens of CEOs and their boards at the largest global companies, providing both strategic advice and intelligence on human capital at competing firms or corporate takeover targets. He is the founder of G100, a private group of global CEOs, the founder of the CEO Academy, and co-editor of this volume. He is coauthor of *CEO Succession* and, most recently, *The Human Side of M&A.*

ON JUNE 17, 2002, I received a call from the board of directors of the most controversial company in America. Two weeks earlier, Tyco International chief executive Dennis Kozlowski had abruptly resigned his post. With its stock price plummeting and rumors circulating that the company would soon face bankruptcy, Tyco's board wanted to prevent the company's problems from spiraling out of control. They asked me if my firm would lead a search for a new CEO and continue the work I had done in the past recruiting new directors for the company.

Tyco was not unknown to me. For more than three years, I had been advising Kozlowski and the company's senior management on a variety of deals and internal personnel issues. We called the work "Global Intelligence," and it typically involved assessing the efficacy and skills of the management team of a company that Tyco had targeted for acquisition. I worked as part of a team assessing potential deals, and, over time, I became familiar with the company's strategy and the kinds of deals Kozlowski and his senior advisors looked for. When he considered, for example, acquiring ADT, one of the country's larger home-security companies, I researched a report for Kozlowski on the company's top executives, corporate organization, and culture.

Like almost everyone else in the business world, I was shocked at the revelations about Kozlowski's possible wrongdoing. I had great respect for what he had accomplished—turning a $5 billion company into a global powerhouse—and, at least from my vantage point, he appeared to be a shrewd if aggressive CEO. In all my dealings with him, I found him to be thoughtful, considerate, polite, almost shy. He was always eager for information about companies he was planning to acquire and never was bitter if I challenged him or disagreed on company strategy. Like all consultants, I made recommendations; some were followed, some were not.

Suddenly, however, Kozlowski was no longer my client. Indeed, what made the Tyco assignment unusual was that I was working directly for the board. In almost all other executive-search work for a CEO's successor, the current CEO is often involved, at least peripherally. The other difference was that information about the company was limited, and a haze still hung over Tyco following Kozlowski's departure. Jeff Fort had been appointed as interim CEO and, given the circumstances, did a tremendous job providing information that could be given to candidates. But there was no hiding the fact that, in the summer of 2002, Tyco's continued viability was in doubt. The Securities and Exchange Commission was delving into Tyco's accounting records. Both the board and I wondered whether getting a world-class leader for the company was even possible.

My Spencer Stuart colleague Dayton Ogden, the co-chairman of our firm, and I decided to search for a new CEO in an unconventional way. We recognized that Tyco was in a state of crisis. While most top-level executive searches can take up to four months, we committed to finding someone in thirty days. We had about twenty names on paper but almost immediately narrowed that down to five or six serious candidates. That list was quickly winnowed to just two people, one of whom was Ed Breen.

Breen appealed to the board for several reasons. He had been a

CEO himself at General Instrument, a technology firm that had been acquired by Motorola. But rather than leaving after the acquisition, he stayed on at Motorola, moved up the ranks, and had recently been named president and chief operating officer. He clearly felt comfortable in a large, global, and complex business. After a few conversations with contacts on Wall Street, we discovered that his reputation for credibility, integrity, and toughness was superb.

It was hardly surprising to learn that Breen didn't jump at the offer. He had been named to his COO role at Motorola at the beginning of the year and clearly was not seeking a new job. More important, Tyco was, at first glance, hardly an inviting opportunity. We knew that and consciously developed an internal team to provide any candidate for the CEO job with all the information about the company we could. We told Breen to use whatever information we could provide to do the proper due diligence so he knew what he was walking into.

Breen took advantage of our offer in a deliberate but quick manner. He spent time with Tyco's accountanting firm, PricewaterhouseCoopers, and with Boies, Schiller & Flexner, the law firm investigating the activities of the management. His goal, understandably, was to hear from the experts that there was nothing monumentally wrong at the core of Tyco's business. Clearly, he saw that there had been a lot of apparent impropriety at the top of Tyco and that, as an incoming CEO, he would have to deal with that lingering problem. But our goal was to convince him—as the board was convinced—that the company's finances were salvageable.

We didn't want him to rely exclusively on Tyco's inside team. As part of his due-diligence exercise, Breen wisely turned to investment bankers who had followed Tyco closely, and to a few trusted business leaders who had a good sense of Tyco's business. From all these discussions, he became persuaded that Tyco remained a sound collection of businesses, even though much needed to be done to restore its reputation.

My often-repeated argument to him was to see the upside that was now clouded by controversy. The fact was that coming into a company on the heels of a disgraced CEO had clear advantages. In many ways, Jeff Immelt, the new CEO of General Electric, had a bigger challenge in succeeding Jack Welch, whom some had called "the manager of the century"—not an easy act to follow. The situation at Tyco couldn't have been more different.

More important, Breen was avoiding much of the corporate politics that typically greets a CEO brought in from the outside. The biggest challenge new CEOs face—even those who have been recruited from within—is the ability to create their own senior team and their own agenda. That is especially true when there is a need to forge a new strategy that takes a different path from the one blazed by a predecessor. Even dealings with a board of directors can be delicate at first, since those board members will have been appointed by someone else and be fully invested in a previous strategy.

As Breen quickly realized, his first hundred days in office would be something of a honeymoon. Indeed, the day his appointment was announced, Tyco's stock price soared. The problem, as all of us recognized, was that after a few months, the easy transition would be over. Lingering problems that at the outset could be blamed on a predecessor would soon become the new CEO's responsibility.

With that in mind, Breen sought to build a new infrastructure at Tyco as quickly as possible: a new senior management team, a new board, new governance processes, and a new level of transparency. As he saw it, the quicker that was in place, the easier it would make his "second hundred days." For him, that was a real test—and, in a sense, the test of every new CEO. A company that goes through any leadership transition soon reaches the point at which the new boss has to take full ownership of the company. If observers continue to assess the company based on the actions and decisions of the former leadership team, the new managers have not done a sufficient job of taking charge. The first hundred days is the time to build a foundation of new leadership. The second hundred days is when that new leadership becomes more fully accountable.

Moving Quickly

Breen didn't waste time on the personnel front. On his first day on the job, he met with the company's chief financial officer and, soon after, asked for his resignation. He was a Tyco executive closely affiliated with the atmosphere of scandal, and there was no question that he had to be replaced quickly. That was a critical step but by no means a sufficient one. Over the next few months, Breen would replace most of the senior team at Tyco. My firm began searches for a new CFO, a new general counsel, a new head of Human Resources, a new treasurer, a new comptroller, and many other key posts. Such a thorough shakeup is not easy, especially when many senior people were as surprised by the allegations of malfeasance as outsiders were. Yet Breen approached the problem in a way that made the most sense for shareholders. It wasn't clear who knew what, who should have known what, and who should have raised their hand, and there was no way to figure this out quickly. So he wasn't going to take any chances.

All these decisions were going on at a time when turmoil was the daily routine at the company. Breen put together an ad-hoc team of outside advisors that met regularly to sort out the daily crisis. David Boies was the outside counsel who dealt with the legal issues and the regulators. Linda Robinson, the seasoned PR veteran, dealt with the press and the mammoth task of reconstructing Tyco's image. I was part of that strategy group; my assignment was to help recruit a new group of managers and communicate with some outside executives and leaders who could provide strategic counsel to Breen.

Breen was facing so many tasks at Tyco that it was appropriate to treat his first few months as ongoing crisis management. He needed to learn a lot about the company's major businesses.

Budget reviews were starting soon after he arrived, which required a deep understanding of Tyco's finances. Regulators and activist shareholders were circling the company, demanding more information. Many of the challenges simply could not be resolved over a short period. But as Breen realized, only so much could be done with a group of advisors. He needed a new team quickly. In his first few months, at least 50 percent of his time was spent on personnel issues.

My instructions were pretty simple: Don't settle for the managers who are available—find the best, most qualified people. No experience in a particular industry was necessary. Tyco needed managers with a solid track record inside complex organizations and, given Tyco's circumstances, a reputation for prudence and conservatism.

With those marching orders, a series of simultaneous searches began. Dave FitzPatrick was among our first recruits. A first-class CFO who came from United Technologies, he fit the profile we were looking for: an established professional from a company with immense scope and complexity. Soon after, Bill Lytton arrived from International Paper to be the new general counsel; he had held the same position at International Paper and was familiar with diversified companies. The decision on Bill was typical in that, although we were moving at rapid speed, Breen got assurances and recommendations from respected CEOs. For example, Bill had served as general counsel at GE Aerospace years back. At a meeting in New York that I attended with Breen, we saw Jack Welch and asked him about Bill. "A-plus" was his answer, an assessment that helped conclude the search.

Perhaps the single most important hire at the new Tyco was someone whom Breen brought in himself to fill a newly created position of senior vice president for corporate governance. For this post, he turned to Eric Pillmore, a superb executive who had been CFO under Breen at General Instrument after more than seventeen years at GE. His task at Tyco was to revamp every procedure in the company, from the boardroom to employee training, in order to strengthen Tyco's governance structure. Together, Breen and Pillmore made the correct assumption that every aspect of accountability and decision-making at the company deserved scrutiny.

During the first few months on the job, Breen also started to push down into the operational levels of the companies, to put in place people who could be trusted and who were willing to make the changes needed to restore investor confidence. He talked to leaders of the core businesses about problems and gave them some tasks to see how they handled them. All the time, he was assessing employees and recruiting new people for key positions. He got to know the staff by walking around the headquarters and visiting operations, in order to get feedback from people deep in the organization and to see things for himself. Given the circumstances, the worst thing that could happen would be a sudden surprise.

Reconstituting the Board

The wholesale changes among senior management during Breen's first months at Tyco were intended to be dramatic. But even more significant were those changes rapidly set in motion at the board level. In many ways, this was a more difficult and delicate assignment for a CEO coming in from the outside. Many directors had been with the Tyco board for a long time and were highly respected businesspeople. But Breen recognized that if the company were to convince shareholders and the public that corporate governance would be reformed at Tyco, a clean slate would be needed. The entire board would have to be replaced—a radical change with few if any precedents in American corporate history.

Breen's job in overseeing this change was made easier when we recruited Jack Krol, the retired chairman and CEO of DuPont, to the Tyco board. At the next board meeting, he was elected lead director and would serve as a point man for governance reform at

Tyco. Krol was the perfect candidate for the role: Not only had he led a very large company through tremendous changes in the 1990s, he was still relatively young, very energetic, and congenial—yet he possessed a steely approach to tough issues. In talking to Krol about joining the Tyco board, I sensed that he saw it as a real test that good corporate governance could work: Done right, you can save a company teetering on the brink.

When the full board met with Breen and Krol present in September 2002, not every director agreed that the complete board should step down. But the arguments that seemed to prevail were that the vestiges of the past had to be removed. The company had to demonstrate in a very public way that it was committed to change. During the process, nearly 40 percent of Tyco's shareholders were polled about the idea of having an entirely new board. They were overwhelmingly in favor of the move. In the end, two members of the board agreed to serve as nonvoting advisors to the new directors, to ensure some institutional memory and draw lessons from the past.

Creating a new board demanded more than just recruiting new directors. It meant an entirely new set of governance procedures. Breen was adamant that he would be the only representative of management on the new board—the rest of the membership would be composed exclusively of independent directors. As lead director, Jack Krol would be immediately responsible for chairing executive sessions of the board, to be held after every formal board meeting. The board adopted a new set of governance principles that spelled out how directors would oversee the strategic planning and operations of the company. It also quickly enacted "delegation of authority" policies that clearly delineated the authority to commit or expend Tyco funds. Additionally, a new guide to ethical conduct was adopted that the company and the board would use to evaluate all senior executives every year—including Breen.

Breen was well aware that the board needed to be actively involved in every aspect of the company. At the first few meetings, directors spent a great deal of time going through new policies and procedures. Breen promised to bring them every relevant piece of information, from charitable contributions to the results of a risk-assessment audit being conducted across the company.

All of this was made easier by having board members with impeccable credentials who were willing to labor long hours to make the process work. During his first few months on the job, I spoke with Breen on almost a daily basis about the makeup of the new board and what we would expect from the directors. Finding the right people was not easily done. Over the last few years, the bane of every CEO has been to find outstanding board members. And as the demands on directors have increased—along with the potential for liability—recruiting board members has become more difficult. A search that might once have taken a month or two was often extending into a several-month process.

But Breen's determination to remake the reputation of a company helped him bring a number of current or retired CEOs to the board. In interviewing candidates, I always stressed the opportunity to help a fallen company regain its credibility and create a new benchmark in ethical corporate culture. It seemed to work. Mackey McDonald, for example, is the CEO of VF Corp., one of the world's largest apparel companies. Jerry York, the former CFO of IBM and current CEO of Micro Warehouse, agreed to serve as chairman of the critical audit committee. These were people accustomed to complex businesses who would feel comfortable at a conglomerate like Tyco. Carl McCall joined the board after he stepped down as comptroller of New York State. Another member, Sandra Wijnberg, is CFO of Marsh & McLennan. We were also lucky to recruit Dennis Blair, the retired admiral who led the U.S. Pacific Command as part of his thirty years of distinguished service in the Navy. He has a sterling reputation for integrity. The other new directors were seasoned corporate leaders who were widely respected and eager to take an active role: George Buckley, chairman and CEO of Brunswick; Bruce Gordon, the head of retail markets at Verizon; and Brendan O'Neill, then CEO of Imperial Chemical Industries.

Laying the Groundwork for the Second Hundred Days

Many new CEOs arrive at their post with the desire to take stock of the situation, huddle with their senior team, and put together a methodical plan for change. Ed Breen had no such luxury. After Tyco's high-profile CEO had left in disgrace, the company appeared rudderless. In the weeks preceding Breen's arrival, the business press was filled with rumors that Tyco might file for bankruptcy.

Clearly, radical changes to the company were needed in order to demonstrate that the abuses of the past would not recur. But what fire to put out first? This is a problem faced by many turnaround CEOs who arrive when a company is floundering. But the Tyco situation presented a set of questions that few incoming CEOs ever have to face. The most important question a CEO must answer is who is going to face that myriad of problems with him.

Breen correctly understood that replacing Tyco's senior management and its board was the only way to break with the past. Because the possibility existed that new and unexpected revelations about corporate wrongdoing at Tyco could emerge months later, the risk of keeping directors and managers who had been embedded in the company's history was unwise. Indeed, none of Tyco's major investors questioned Breen's intention to clean house. And by replacing so many people, he freed himself from directors and senior executives who were still devoted to the old regime.

The good news for Breen was that Tyco's many businesses were fundamentally sound, despite the accounting irregularities. Unlike the dot-com companies, Tyco was involved in long-established business lines such as electronics, health-care products, plastics, and home security. The company was a conglomerate, and it certainly had too much debt. But its deepest problems were not directly related to its business.

What was needed was an emphasis on human capital and leadership. In this area, a new CEO can exercise more influence, more quickly, than in almost any other part of the company. Tyco has more than a quarter of a million employees. What they needed most—and needed right away—was a signal that the people at the top were determined to make the company perform at the highest level of integrity. The demoralization of the workforce would have grown deeper had Breen decided to restructure personnel over a two-year period, or even if he had waited a few months before making any bold moves.

As I write this chapter in the spring of 2003, Tyco's recovery is far from complete. Some questions remain about its accounting, and Breen himself has been the subject of press criticism. That was perhaps a predictable development, but one that also shows that the transition from the old team to the new has been complete. What Breen wanted to avoid was an evolutionary process of transformation at Tyco in which responsibility between the old team and the new arrivals was unclear. By devoting significant time at the start of his tenure putting in place an entirely new infrastructure of governance and personnel, he was laying the groundwork for the "second hundred days"—a time when Tyco could begin to re-emerge as a responsible company, operated with integrity and determined to reclaim its business success.

PART II

Governance: The Board of Directors and Its CEO

No topic has received more attention in the last few years than the way corporations govern themselves. Once a topic reserved for corporate lawyers and the handful of management students, "corporate governance" has emerged as one of the highest priorities for corporate leaders, investors, and business journalists.

The reason for the sudden interest is obvious. Enron, WorldCom, and other companies provided us with the most egregious examples of how corporate leaders could abuse their power, mislead investors, and defy laws intended to protect their employees and the public. The events of 2001–02 will surely be seen as a watershed for all future corporate leaders and those who serve on boards. At a minimum, they can be certain that they will face stricter rules about conduct—some now enshrined in federal law—and much more aggressive scrutiny of all its dealings, accounting, and disclosures.

To be sure, serving on a corporate board was not always so demanding. As some of our contributors to this section remind us, board members were once excessively deferential to management. Board meetings were pro forma affairs, and directors tended to be friends or fellow business leaders who did not see themselves as independent watchdogs guarding investors' interests.

Yet the recent surge in interest in corporate governance is not an entirely new phenomenon. John Smale, who contributes the first chapter of this section, was a pivotal figure in what surely was the most startling event in corporate governance in the last few decades: the decision by the board of directors at General Motors to fire the CEO. In the months that followed, the board invited Smale to act as non-executive chairman, a highly unusual decision at the time that greatly increased the profile and power of the board.

Smale describes a new culture emerging at GM following the directors' rejection of management. Board meetings became more substantive, and directors held management accountable and insisted on clearly visible results.

Those practices are now widely embraced by American corporations, the extreme examples of Enron and WorldCom notwithstanding. Indeed, we have in this section two very full portraits of how a CEO interacts with board members, using them for feedback, ideas, expertise, and criticism. Stephen P. Kaufman, the retired chairman and CEO of Arrow Electronics, describes using the board as a set of informal consultants—people to whom he could turn for advice on one aspect of the company or another. Kevin Sharer of Amgen argues that a CEO must be able to give directors the right kind of information so that they can make truly independent judgments and criticism. The relationship between the CEO and the board members is one of the most complicated there is, he writes. He also argues against the separation of the CEO and chairman roles, insisting that uniting the two positions allows the company to speak with a single voice.

Ira Millstein disagrees. In his contribution, this veteran writer, attorney, and advisor to corporations describes what he believes will be the new era of corporate governance after the Sarbanes-Oxley Act, aimed at the reform of corporate practices. He makes the case for separating the functions of CEO and chairman, as is widely done in Europe, and argues that the day of the all-powerful CEO is fading.

Nell Minow, the shareholder activist and prolific writer on corporate-governance issues, offers the case for being wary about corporate practices that still don't serve investors. She points to a number of areas in which she believes that shareholders must continue to remain vigilant in order to keep management in check.

For his part, Harvey Golub, the retired chairman and CEO of American Express, believes that the tense or confrontational relationship between a CEO and the board is misplaced and unnecessary. In his chapter, he explains that most often the board acts as a ratifying body, because decisions brought to them should already fit into a strategic context with which the board has been deeply involved.

Three general impressions emerge quickly from these chapters on governance. First, the CEO relationship with a board demands considerable time and frequent communication. Second, while there is broad agreement about the need for many of the governance reforms recently adopted by Congress and the major stock exchanges, there remains considerable disagreement about whether it is the role of the board to provide what Ira Millstein calls "creative tension" between the board and the CEO. Finally, we are at the earliest stages of a significant turn in the history of corporate governance. The changes that have been adopted and the new prominence of governance in the life of a corporation will continue to produce new issues and questions for public companies in the years ahead.

CHAPTER SIX

The Board as the Boss: The Relationship Between the CEO and the Board

John G. Smale, former chairman of General Motors and retired chairman and CEO of Procter & Gamble

Although many look at the recent wave of corporate-governance reform as unprecedented, others will argue that the turning point in the relationship between American corporations and their boards occurred at General Motors in 1992. After a decade of losing market share, the world's largest corporation was losing an estimated $11 million a day. In what was described by the press as a "boardroom coup," GM directors ousted chairman and CEO Robert Stempel and company president Lloyd Reuss, both company veterans who had risen through the ranks. In their place, the board appointed insider Jack Smith as CEO and former Procter & Gamble CEO John Smale as GM's first independent, non-executive chairman since 1937.

Smale had recently retired after nearly forty years at Procter & Gamble, the last nine as chief executive. During his tenure, he led P&G's global expansion while reforming and modernizing its pricing and brand strategy. Although he spent only three years as chairman of GM, he is widely credited with reasserting the role of an active board, insisting on a steady flow of information about major issues to the board and pushing management to report on progress toward stated goals. In large part due to his efforts, vehicle quality, market share, globalization, and labor costs became regular discussion items at company board meetings. Through the 1990s, GM began a steady financial turnaround.

The events at GM in the early 1990s sent a strong signal to boards across the country; in the years that followed, activist boards forced the resignation of CEOs at Kodak, Apple, and IBM—actions that would have been unimaginable a decade earlier.

In 1997, when GM announced that Smale would remain on the board even though he had reached the ordinary retirement age of seventy, it was considered a rare but understandable exception. As Ira Millstein, an advisor to GM's board, explained to the *Wall Street Journal*, "This is not your ordinary corporate director."

THE HIGH-PROFILE COLLAPSE of Enron, WorldCom, and other companies that once seemed healthy and promising leaders of our economy has led to a wholesale reexamination of corporate-governance issues. Among the key questions that has puzzled investors, legislators, and regulators are: Where was the board of directors? Why on earth didn't it do something?

There is a general sense that members of the board of directors ought to have enough knowledge about the company's operations to anticipate and even prevent business mistakes or corporate misconduct of the magnitude that crippled Enron, WorldCom, and others. This is an unrealistic assumption. No board, on its own, is going to be able to develop enough insight into the details of a company's activities to prevent corporate misconduct. Nevertheless, these scandals have generated and will continue to generate demands for enhanced oversight responsibilities by corporate boards of directors and greater accountability by management to the board for the company's performance.

I feel confident in this belief because I feel, in part, that I have seen this all before. In the early 1990s, GM faced serious cash-flow problems, a plunging credit rating, and the need to eliminate several production plants. At the nation's largest corporation, the board had begun to lose confidence in management. In January 1992, just over a year after I had retired as CEO of Procter & Gamble, the GM board asked me to assess the company. Specifically, they asked me to conduct a series of in-depth interviews with the company's top managers to get a sense of their attitudes about the company's problems and what changes they felt needed to be made. I did this over the next three months and, in that process, spoke with some twenty-two executives. Each interview lasted two to three hours and was conducted on a confidential basis, with the understanding that the interviewee's comments would not be quoted or attributed to them in my report to the board. To this day, I've never publicly discussed what I heard from those executives. But they gave me enough material to present a formal report to the GM board. That report led to major management changes. A month after submitting my report, the board asked Jack Smith, then the head of international operations for GM, to replace the existing president. But they believed more changes were necessary. After a number of conversations with senior management, Jack Smith was elevated to CEO, and I was asked to be non-executive chairman of the board. At the time, it was seen as one of the most startling assertions of boardroom power. I believe it was good for GM, good for GM shareholders, and a victory for sound corporate governance.

Until that time, it is fair to say, there was very little public debate about how corporations are governed. Today the call for corporate reform comes from many places outside the boardroom or the executive suite. Congress has already rewritten the rules providing for the independence of the accounting industry. Stock exchanges, including the New York Stock Exchange and NASDAQ, are forcing companies to change their corporate-governance provisions or risk being de-listed. The Securities and Exchange Commission and state attorneys general are examining possible conflicts of interest that compromise the work of investment analysts. Many are questioning the influence of stock options on executive decisions.

Despite all of these forces coalescing for reform, the responsibility for strengthening the board's oversight and advisory roles and the extent to which the board will be successful in fulfilling these duties still rest with one person—and that is the company's CEO. A good board can judge a CEO and—as was the case at GM—remove him. But sound corporate governance cannot exist without an active CEO who is committed to shareholders and their representatives on the board.

Today's Board: A Far Cry from the Past

This evolving structure will be a far cry from the director-management relationship of twenty or thirty years ago. Back then, a seat on a board was more like an honorarium than a serious duty. Boards met more frequently—sometimes as often as once a month—but the meetings were generally shorter, usually starting in the late morning, breaking for lunch, and then continuing for an hour or two after.

The atmosphere was mostly collegial; there was very little open dissent or hard questioning of the CEO or other executives. Most of the outside directors, in fact, were strongly inclined to accept the CEO's views without question. Today, many are puzzled by this complacency. After all, board directors were largely senior executives and CEOs themselves—assertive, confident people not known as shrinking violets. Yet one must understand that, in those days, the board saw their role as an advisor to management, providing helpful counsel to the CEO and management. They assumed that their chief constituency was management, not shareholders, and acted accordingly. This put a different tone on board activities than one that calls for oversight of management activities.

Additionally, the structure of the meetings and the process by which they were run also discouraged activism by the board. Board members received no advance distribution of the material relevant to the day's agenda. In fact, board members usually didn't even know the agenda ahead of time. Often, the first exposure the board had to an issue was during its presentation at the meeting—a fact that surely limited directors' ability to challenge a strategy or suggest well-thought-out alternative courses of action.

By the mid-1980s, significant changes began taking place throughout corporate America, with the board taking a more active role in shaping the future direction of the company. There were two main forces driving these changes.

First was the advent of hostile takeovers—a relatively new phenomenon that cast a spotlight on management failures at many very large companies. The threat of outsiders wresting away control at some companies tended to raise the profile of the board of directors generally and at several companies led to comprehensive management changes. These acts were a dramatic exercise in corporate governance by the board and permanently enhanced directors' roles in helping to guide the company.

None of the boards on which I served faced a hostile takeover. Nevertheless, the threat of hostile takeovers in the 1980s was very real and did create changes in corporate by-laws. At GM, for instance, a by-law was created that would prohibit greenmail, the practice used by unfriendly shareholders to force a company to repurchase its stock at a premium to ward off a takeover. At P&G, several by-laws were adopted by shareholder vote that would affect the process of any hostile takeover, such as a staggered board and a supermajority of shareholders to authorize a change in corporate control. Some of these by-laws at P&G have since been eliminated.

The second force was an increased level of activism and greater demands for accountability on the part of large institutional shareholders. Today, 65 percent of equities are owned by institutions such as CalPERS, the Florida State Board of Administration, and other funds that control billions of dollars in shareholder assets. These giant conglomerations of shareholders have been increasingly bold in exercising their rights in ways that are often at odds with management.

Largely as a result of these forces, today's board meetings are far different from those of just two or three decades ago. Boards are smaller now. Meetings are fewer but far more substantive. Board material is distributed ahead of time, and independent board members are expected to put significant preparation time into the meetings.

I certainly noticed those changes taking place after the shakeup at GM. After Jack Smith became CEO and I took over as chairman, six inside directors resigned. Over time, the size of the board was reduced by the deliberate decision not to replace retiring board members. When I joined, there were twenty-five members. Eventually that dropped to fifteen.

But those weren't the only changes. The whole character and tone of board meetings changed. The kind of information that directors received and the depth of it were significantly different and better. The meetings were more open, and there was greater focus on genuine problems. Directors received much deeper financial reviews, and they played a more active role in shaping the agenda.

As chairman, I would sit with five or six key members of management—a team we called the "president's council"—and work up an agenda in advance. We engaged in a sifting process designed to maximize the use of the board's time: Are these topics important enough to merit board consideration, or could they be handled in some other fashion? Is the advance material being distributed relevant, and will it obviate the need to have the same material repeated again in the board meeting itself?

I also tried to improve the process by creating a very clear agenda that emphasized certain important themes for the corporation. For instance, at GM we instituted a practice of always placing a product-quality item at the top of the agenda. Our goal was to send a message that quality in the 1990s was a key priority for the company. We institutionalized this message by establishing and monitoring improvement goals at the board level and by benchmarking the company against our competition. In another break from the past, board members themselves would sometimes prompt a subject to be a regular topic. At General Motors, one of our directors was very focused on plant safety, and it soon became a regular item on the board's agenda. That focus yielded results: Over the next number of years, there was a significant decline in lost time due to accidents at the company. GM clearly became the safety leader in the automotive industry, in large measure because it adopted objectives for specific safety or injury reductions by plant, by year. Progress against those objectives was reported regularly to the board.

In 1994, the General Motors board formally adopted some twenty-eight governance guidelines, ranging from the selection of the CEO to the tenure of independent directors. These guidelines formally outlined the specific actions for which the board and the board's committees were responsible in their duty to oversee the conduct of the business. Today, the boards of most large companies have similar procedures delineating their responsibilities.

I should also add that the changes that occurred at the top ranks of management and on the board had a deep and positive impact on the company. With a different set of executives, a different culture took shape, one that was much more open to ideas and criticism from within, and more frank in its approach to problems. Very quickly, more people across the company developed a full understanding of GM's business. And, of course, the business itself began to turn around.

Strategic Advantages of an Engaged Board

While these changes seemed revolutionary compared to the process by which previous boards operated, they have become standard practice. Yet I believe there are additional steps that would further strengthen the oversight ability of a company's board of directors.

Any proper understanding of the relationship between the CEO and the board has to start with one simple fact: The board is the boss. The board hires and can fire the CEO. In fact, the selection—and in some cases removal—of the CEO is the board's most important duty.

The board is the boss because it represents the true owners of the business—the shareholders. And the only way the board can fulfill its duty to the shareholders is to take responsibility for the progress of the business.

The board can't execute the company's strategy, of course.

Business strategy is always developed and implemented by management. But the board can instruct the management of the company. It can make suggestions or observations that might change the company's strategy. And, from my experience, if the board is properly involved, a CEO frequently ends up with an amended strategy.

Let me cite an example from my years at Procter & Gamble. During the first several years after entering the Japanese market in the 1970s, P&G lost money on its operations there. Eventually, these became sizable losses. I took my senior managers to the board to report on our progress. We outlined our strategy and recommended that we persevere in our efforts to break into the Japanese market. Our strategy was straightforward. We felt it was important that P&G be able to compete on the ground in Japan against Japanese competitors. We felt that, in many respects, Japanese competitive products were the best, from a quality standpoint, that we faced anywhere in the world. We felt that if we couldn't prevail in Japan, we would face problems in other countries around the world as time went on. The board asked a lot of tough questions. I don't know that the board ultimately had much of a role in clarifying the policy, and there was not universal board agreement with continuing on in Japan. But there was a clear majority of directors who felt we were doing the right thing and who, in essence, confirmed our strategy. In this way, the process of going to the board was a healthy reality check and made the management both more confident and more accountable. We had set goals against which we measured our progress, and every six months we reported on it in great detail to the P&G board.

In that case, we stuck to our strategy, and we eventually found success in Japan. But there have been other examples in which the board's influence led to significant changes in management's business plan.

At General Motors in the late 1980s and early 1990s, the company had expanded well beyond the business of making automobiles and financing their purchase. GM had acquired EDS, Hughes Aerospace, National Car Rental, and a variety of component auto-parts makers. Many of these ventures, such as Hughes's military-satellite business, were outside its expertise as a car maker.

The board began to question many of these decisions, particularly the relevance of the EDS acquisition. A new strategy slowly emerged—with heavy input from the board—of focusing on just the auto business and moving away from non-core activities. In keeping with this new strategy, we divested EDS and the defense component of Hughes and spun off a new company called Delphi to run all the auto-components businesses.

Ultimately, the board led management to question whether other businesses should be divested and GM should refocus even more tightly on its core business. It was an evolving, consultative process that took place over an extended period of time.

The lesson I learned through these experiences is that intelligent boards with strong, independent members can make significant contributions to a company's business strategy. Armed with sufficient information, the board can be a tremendous resource. But its ability to make an important contribution depends on the CEO. The board will never be effective unless it is informed. The CEO must ensure that the board understand what he wants to do and why he wants to do it. If directors don't understand the CEO's strategy, they have to confront that issue. They have to force their understanding of the strategy, or they must delay the execution of that strategy until they do understand it. The board's position here needs to be quite clear and inflexible. Unless the board and the CEO really understand each other, there can be no real commitment to the strategy.

Why is this commitment so crucial? First of all, as I've noted, CEOs can benefit from the board's insights. Second, some of the strategies that the CEO might pursue won't work. There is a degree of risk involved in any business decision. No CEO is infallible, and no one expects him or her to be. But the board of directors represents the CEO's boss in the final analysis, and a good CEO should want the representatives of the boss on board before embarking on a strategic course. Directors should have a clear understanding of the risks involved beforehand.

Ensuring Leadership: A Unique Board Responsibility

In addition to providing insights into business strategy, the board has several unique responsibilities. One of the most essential is contributing to the succession-planning process.

When I first became a brand manager at Procter & Gamble in the early 1950s, I had the opportunity to attend my first year-end management meeting. R. R. Dupree, who was then chairman of the board and had been CEO for a number of years, made a speech in which he said that the only significant factor that would govern the future growth of P&G was the company's ability to hire and develop new managers. At the time, I thought this was just another standard pronouncement that one expects from management. I now realize that he was exactly right: There is nothing more important to the future of your business than the development of people. They create the pipeline of talent on which a company depends.

The board has a role in developing people. Specifically, it can help by requiring the CEO to periodically review the company's succession plan and its management-development program. The board needs to know the top people in the organization and the plan for developing them as leaders of the company. Where are they going to be moved? How are they broadening their responsibilities? Are they getting international experience?

Sometimes the board can acquire this knowledge by meeting corporate officers who sit in on all or part of the board meetings. The chief financial officer, for instance, usually attends. So does the chief operating officer. Division heads may be called upon to report periodically to the board. P&G's board was exposed to the top talent of the company through a variety of avenues. First of all, there was a review of the top managers in the company—usually the top 100 to 150. The review went through the background of each manager and, importantly, involved the company's forward plans for the manager's training and broadening. What was going to be the next assignment and why? The board then had the chance a year later to go through the same materials and see what progress had been made or what changes needed to be made.

This process was very deliberate. P&G paid very close attention to the entire process of selection and training, because all of the management-track people hired by the company started in entry positions. This careful training at every level of the company got a great deal of attention from the management and from the board, too.

At both General Motors and Procter & Gamble, we held two-to-three-day offsite meetings bringing together senior management and the board so that all of the players could interact socially as well. Whatever the process, the core idea was to expose the directors to potential successors to the CEO on a regular basis. After all, if the board has to go outside the company to find a new CEO, the incumbent CEO has failed at one of his or her primary obligations—perhaps *the* primary obligation.

Independent Oversight Depends on an Independent Chairman

There are other reforms that would strengthen the board's oversight role. The most important would be to select the board's chairman from among the independent directors on the board. This procedure is common in some countries, such as the United Kingdom, but is relatively rare in the United States. And it's an idea that is not warmly received by most CEOs who also hold the dual job of board chairman, because it implies a sharing—and diminution—of some of the CEO's powers.

When I was chairman and CEO of Procter & Gamble in the

1980s, I would certainly have resisted the thought of an outside director replacing me as chairman. Indeed, even in the crisis of GM's affairs in 1992, the idea of splitting the jobs was adopted reluctantly by some board members. And three and a half years later, the GM board decided to return to the conventional structure of its chairman being a member of management. Even so, I think the board made it clear that it wanted to be very much involved in the oversight of the affairs of the company, and that the time for a passive, reactive board of directors was very much in the past.

Despite my own initial reservations, I've since come to the conclusion that the perceived disadvantages of a non-executive chairman are outweighed by the advantages. If the purpose of a board is to represent the shareholders in overseeing management's conduct of the business, such a structure seems considerably more logical than having the board chaired by a manager who is also the subject of such oversight.

Furthermore, it can create a different tone to the board's activities, a more rigorous oversight climate in the board's approach to its responsibilities. The chairman, working together with the CEO, would set the board's agenda, as well as conduct the board meetings. With an independent director as chairman, the board becomes responsible for its own constituency—selecting, with input from the CEO, its own members. It becomes responsible for its own governance guidelines.

That creates a different attitude—one in which outside directors not only see themselves as advisors and consultants to management but recognize their individual and collective responsibility for how well management runs the business. Will this revised definition of the job put off some directors and director prospects? Perhaps, but first-rate people will see this as not a burden but a challenge. And especially now, we need nothing less than first-rate people serving on the boards of America's companies.

It is also essential for board members to meet in executive session without the CEO. In the old days, it was assumed that if the board met without the CEO, they were plotting a palace coup. Now it is standard practice. At General Motors, we made executive-session meetings part of the new governance quidelines. At Procter & Gamble, the board meets in executive session once a year to review the performance of the CEO.

A further change I believe is worth considering would see the outside auditors reporting to the board. In theory, that is the case today. In fact, in most companies the shareholders vote to confirm the appointment of an outside auditor. In practice, however, the real client of the auditing firm is the management of the company. I believe the client should, in fact, be the audit committee of the board. Certainly, the financial staff of the company must work closely with the outside auditor, but the basic relationship and the reporting responsibility should be directly to the board through the audit committee.

Will these changes avoid a future disaster like Enron or WorldCom? Perhaps not. But I believe they can help achieve three important goals that should be shared by every effective CEO. First, they can help restore public (and investor) confidence in corporate America. Second, they can help improve the opportunity for the board of directors to fulfill its oversight responsibility to shareholders. And third, they can help a CEO satisfy his or her ultimate boss: the board.

CHAPTER SEVEN

The Working Relationship Between a CEO and His Directors

Kevin Sharer, chairman and CEO of Amgen

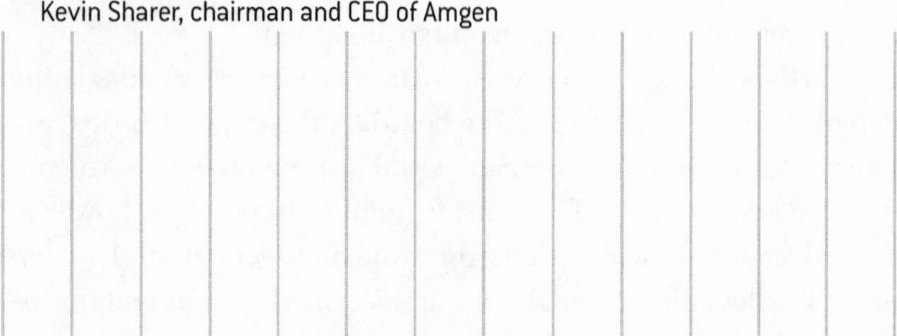

Kevin Sharer served as president and chief operating officer of Amgen, one of the world's leading biotech companies, for seven years before being elevated to chairman and CEO in 2000. While the company has been primarily known for two of its products, the anti-anemia drug Epogen and the immune-system stimulator Neupogen, the company has in recent years expanded its research pipeline and introduced new, promising therapies to the market.

Sharer's career has given him considerable experience in both management and corporate governance. He spent five years at GE in various executive positions and, prior to being recruited by Amgen, was a senior executive at MCI. In addition to serving on the Amgen board since 1992, he is a director at Unocal and 3M.

WE ARE SEEING MORE discussion of corporate governance today than at any time I can remember, perhaps at any time in corporate history. It is easy to understand why. Shareholders—with good reason—are concerned that their interests are not being represented. Management practices and corporate governance have been subjected to unprecedented scrutiny. Most public debate assumes that the relationship between management and corporate directors has been tainted and must be repaired. Unfortunately, I fear, some of the governance measures that have been proposed in the name of protecting shareholders may very well hurt their interests, by reducing the effectiveness of the board and circumscribing management.

The board of directors cannot run the company by itself, of course, and should not try. What the board can do is make sure the company is well run. The real risk in the corporate-governance debate is that boards of directors may be given too much hands-on responsibility and be burdened with far too much detail regarding the operations of the company.

The CEO's job is to report key information to the board and elevate the discussion so that the directors gain a better understanding of the company's core business operations. That doesn't mean deluging the board in detail or offering only the highest-level overview. The CEO's duty is to give the members what they need to know—in great detail if necessary—to execute their oversight and counseling roles.

This is a delicate issue but, increasingly, a critical one. Over the last few years, we have all read about CEOs who have withheld important information from their boards—and the disastrous results. That is why establishing the right roles for the board and the CEO is one of the central challenges of corporate governance. The CEO's task is to make sure the board is getting the right amount of detail, depending on the issue. It has to be a sufficient amount of information, delivered in a timely way, and put in context so the board understands what is at stake. For its part, the board must assert a role, too. In my experience, good directors bring a healthy skepticism to what is presented to them. Directors ought to be responsible for asking probing questions and not just taking everything at face value. Some critics of corporate governance suggest that the board take on an adversarial role. I don't think that's right. But the board ought to have a "show me" attitude toward management and enjoy access to other sources of information about the company who are independent of the CEO.

As a practical matter, how much information can a member of

a board of directors be reasonably expected to absorb? They are chosen because they are bright people who understand business. But their principal exposure to the company is attending four to six meetings a year, lasting four to six hours each. As someone who served as a director of Amgen before becoming CEO and who continues to serve on other boards, I can vouch for the fact that too much information can be as big a problem as too little. Or at least, too much information at a *micro* level can be a problem—in fact, it can make it difficult for directors to fulfill their function. One thing about the experience of serving as a member of a corporate board: You learn the value of focus and clarity.

Case in point: For three years before becoming CEO of Amgen, I served as a director of Unocal, the California-based independent oil-and-gas exploration and production company. It was not our role as directors to decide where to explore or how many wells to drill. But we did have to know enough about the company to assess its major investments. When I first joined the board, we were briefed on the company and its workings so that we could understand it from the perspective of a drilling manager. That meant we were provided with in-depth briefings about the geophysics, the cost of equipment, and a wide range of technical areas. There are a great many corporate-governance advocates who would applaud that policy. There was only one problem with it: It didn't work. The level of information we were being provided was so complex that we couldn't get our heads around it. All it did was cloud the big issues, making it difficult for us to understand what was really at stake and evaluate the business risks.

That is no way to serve the shareholders. The last thing shareholders needed was a group of part-time geologists with no background in geology. It is the managers who need to be in the weeds running the company, while the directors are viewing the operation with enough detachment and just enough information to maintain perspective and judgment.

Directors do not need an explanation of every operational decision. What they need is a thorough explanation of the big bets the company is placing, and why it is making those investments.

When I became CEO of Amgen, the company was in the midst of an exciting transformation in the biotech field. We had been a successful health-care company but, essentially, one that enjoyed a monopoly. The pace had changed, competition had intensified, and our own range of products had expanded. In this new environment, the board could be a major asset. I decided that I had to deal with the members of the Amgen board of directors on three levels—all of which are important, all of which are related, but each of which is different in some respects. An important part of the CEO's job is to give all of the directors the resources they need to perform all three of these roles.

- The CEO's boss: As my boss, they need to know what I am doing and what is working, because it is their job to evaluate me.
- The CEO's colleagues: In this role, they need to be informed about what we are trying to do, because I need their support for new initiatives or ways of solving problems.
- The CEO's trusted counsels and sounding boards: As mentors and counselors, they need a depth of understanding about what is at stake.

Giving Directors the Big Picture

For directors, the most important resource is information—strategic information about the company and its position in the marketplace. I emphasize the word "strategic." If directors are going to concentrate on the big picture, they should not be overly distracted by too many operational details.

But no one should make the mistake of thinking that because the information is being presented at a strategic level, it can be dealt with lightly or quickly. The truth is that providing a thorough and comprehensive perspective on the macro issues facing the company often can take just as much time as a micro-level discussion. The difference is not in the amount of time the CEO and the board spend—it is in its value.

At the beginning of every Amgen board meeting, I spend two hours telling the board about the most important things going on in the company—the things that worry me at that point, and those that make me optimistic. During those two hours, I am the only member of management in the room. It has to be just the CEO and the directors so it is possible to talk openly. The information I share with them typically does not require their approval. Rather, I may simply report on pending personnel changes or acquisitions on which we might soon be ready to move. I'm not seeking their approval, but I do want them to have a full and consistent view of the company. This briefing is formal in the sense that I prepare for it; it is too important to simply adlib. For forty-five minutes in advance of each board meeting, I close my door and think about the points I want to convey.

But my presentation is informal in the sense that it is like sitting around the kitchen table with my family. In some respects, that is how I see the relationship with Amgen's directors. Respect, communication, and openness must characterize our interaction. After all, on Amgen's board and on other boards, directors are typically very smart, highly successful people who collectively have immense knowledge about corporate performance. They can be essential to management. They don't want managed news. But they do want to have a sense that you are giving them a complete and fair picture. I consider a board meeting a success if, afterward, every director leaves feeling that he or she has a clear view of the company.

In considering whether to get into a specific issue or area of operation, my rule of thumb is to ask myself: Does this help the board members fulfill any of their three functions (the CEO's boss, colleague, and counselor)?

I also believe in giving directors a written synopsis of the major issues. But for a memo to be helpful, it cannot be overly long and crammed with too much data. What really brings home the issue is a series of succinct declarative sentences that capture the main points. This was a practice I learned while at GE. A one-page memo with about ten points provides the kind of top-line, overall view of an issue that directors can actually use.

Outside the meetings, I talk to directors regularly, and I send them e-mail on a regular basis. But again, I do not provide excessive detail—what I provide is a high-level summary of what is going on. Directors cannot be given information only when there is a decision to be made. More than anything, managing information flow to directors is a matter of keeping them in the thinking process. I will call a director just to chat about an issue that is emerging and ask him or her to chew on it, because we will be talking more about it at a future board meeting.

Independent Access to Information

It is important that the directors understand the company as the CEO sees it. But they must also have plenty of opportunities to check the CEO's understanding against reality.

The board has to assess the CEO's performance in several respects. And each of them requires direct access to people involved in the company in addition to the CEO. Consider the principal questions that a board has to be able to answer regarding how the CEO is running the company:

- How good is the senior management team, and how well does it work together?
- Is the CEO following good governance principles?
- Is the CEO on top of the issues and being a good leader?
- Does the CEO truly understand the business?
- How is the company performing financially?

- Is the strategy clear and consistent? How well is it being implemented?

To answer these questions, the board needs a wide variety of access points to information. That must include talking to the CEO's direct reports, and to the auditors. I know I would be very worried if I were on a board and my sole source of information was the CEO.

CEO Evaluation by Senior Management Team:

The board needs to hear about how the company is doing from the people who are in the best position to know: its senior employees. That's why my twelve direct reports—who constitute the executive committee of the company—annually provide the board with an evaluation of my performance. They get together for an in-depth session—it usually runs about four hours—to write my evaluation, without me in the room and without any guidance at all from me. Then they have a one-hour session with the board at which they provide my evaluation—once again, without me being present. I find the process to be helpful to me as well as to the board.

After a recent board meeting, the head of human resources met with me to go over the evaluation of my performance that the directors had put together. Most of it was good news: They liked my focus on operations, my articulation of corporate strategy, and my ability to listen to other ideas. But they had some constructive criticism: They found that I tend to take a small amount of data and use that to jump to an extreme position on a complex issue, even if I later back off. I am aware of my tendency to shoot from the hip like that, but the ability of the board to point that out gives me a real incentive to change that behavior.

Board Meetings Without the CEO:

This is another idea that bothers some CEOs, but I have found that at times it can be very helpful for the board to meet by itself, without the CEO or anyone else from management being present.

Of course, the need for such executive sessions depends on how the company is doing. If everything is going well, these meetings might seem unnecessary. On the other hand, having occasional board sessions without the CEO prepares the process for any bad times that might come up. And, of course, they are essential for discussion of CEO succession.

At Amgen at one point, we had a two-day board session, ending with the directors meeting separately. There was no particular problem to deal with; I just saw a need for the board to get a chance to discuss some issues without management being present. After the meeting, they got back to me with ten suggestions, all of which were constructive. For example, in reviewing the company's financial future—on which they had just been briefed—they told me: Don't maximize net income growth if there is a good opportunity for an acquisition or investment. In a sense, they were telling me to not be consumed by short-term results. They were encouraging me to take a broader and longer-term view of the business.

I reported back to them by e-mail on all of the points they made to me, giving them my understanding of their advice. The process was worth going through for several reasons: At a practical business level, it generated some good advice for me. At a corporate-governance level, it provided an opportunity for some informal, face-to-face give-and-take among the directors, allowing them to benefit from one another's understanding of the company and the issues facing it. And it bolstered our sense of collegiality. We recognized that mutual trust was justified. The exercise confirmed that we all shared common goals.

One Job: CEO and Chairman

We are seeing demands from many corporate-governance reformers for splitting up the job of chairman of the board and CEO. The argument is that the chairman has to be in a position to monitor the CEO independently. But if a company were to offer an executive the job of CEO but would not ultimately include the position of chairman as well, I'd recommend that he or she turn it down. Being CEO is hard enough without having to manage the boss of the board.

How one comes down on this issue depends on how one sees the relationship between the CEO and the board. Is it an adversarial relationship, with the board serving as the CEO's judge and jury? If so, then a non-executive chairman makes sense. But I don't look at the board that way, and I am very conscious of making sure that board members don't feel that they have to "confront" me to get the information they need.

Again, the board of directors has three roles: to serve as the CEO's boss, colleague, and mentor. It should not be expected to serve as a policeman as well. There shouldn't be a presumption that the board will catch the CEO doing something wrong.

Does splitting up the two jobs really provide the board with the kind of information it needs to monitor management? Because that is what matters: the quality and quantity of the information they receive. Do they know and trust the CEO? Do they trust and have confidence in the CFO? Is there an internal audit, with teeth? Does the board meet with the outside auditor? Is the audit committee made up of directors who are experienced in corporate finance? With that kind of access to information, a board of directors should be able to ensure that shareholders are being provided with full, fair, and accurate financial reporting. I think that board members at Enron and WorldCom were not getting that kind of information—or they weren't paying enough attention.

On the other hand, splitting up the jobs makes the CEO's role more complicated; the board is part of the company. If the CEO has to worry about managing the chairman as well as managing the board and managing the company, another dimension of complexity is added to the job, without improving its management. Also, splitting the job would create confusion in the company about who is ultimately the boss.

There are times when having a non-executive chairman may help the CEO run the company, but that doesn't remain the case for very long. I know that when I became CEO of Amgen, I wanted my predecessor to remain as chairman for six months to ease the transition. During that time, he was an important discussion partner. But when he resigned from the board, he understood that he was making my job easier. It gave me more room to act. I was in the process of bringing on a new team and pursuing a new direction that the new industry environment demanded. By definition, it required breaking with the past. Those steps are harder to take when your predecessor is still sitting at the boardroom table, and for that reason I think every former chairman should resign from the board. Beyond that, splitting up the job of chairman and CEO only sends out mixed signals. It is critical that senior management see the company speaking with one voice at the top.

Shaping the Board

Many corporate-governance reformers also believe that the CEO should have a reduced role in selecting members of the board. The thesis is that the CEO should not be choosing his or her own boss.

But that argument ignores the fact that the board is not just the CEO's boss but also his or her counselor and colleague. As counselors, directors play a valuable role, and their ability to fulfill it depends on their own strengths, background, and experience. How well does the board encompass all of the distinctive strengths it will require to fulfill its advisory role?

The CEO should have the best understanding of the company's strategy and the challenges it will have to meet in order to execute that strategy successfully. That means that the CEO has a valuable perspective to offer the nominating committee when it is picking the board team.

Of course, the CEO cannot pick and choose who sits on the board. But the chief executive can be a vital source of input. I was fortunate at Amgen to have a nominating committee that gave the CEO's recommendations real weight.

At Amgen, we were entering an interesting transition when I took the job of CEO. The company had long enjoyed a period when few of its biotech products faced real competition, but that had started to change. So as we recruited new board members, we looked for people whose experience would make them real assets in the more competitive environment we faced. During the current effort to reform corporate governance, that experience has sometimes been undervalued. Some, for example, proposed that the chairman of the audit committee must be a professional auditor. Yet I think that there are plenty of former chief financial officers who are perfectly capable of leading an audit committee.

At Amgen, we were fortunate to attract board members whose experience made them a real asset to our business. Here are a few examples of the board members who came to Amgen and what I thought they could bring:

- Fred Gluck was managing director of McKinsey & Co. when we asked him to join our board. I knew and respected him from my years there as a consultant. He had a demonstrated ability to frame strategic issues. When we learned that he was available for a board assignment, we reached out.

- Frank Biondi was president of Viacom, CEO of Universal, and head of HBO. Most important, he had a great mind for finance and for financial deals. When he came on our board, he immediately took a seat on the audit committee.

- Jerry Choate was CEO of Allstate when he joined our board. The insurance business would seem to have little in common with the biotechnology of Amgen. But Jerry had tremendous operating experience. We weren't inviting him on the board to manage the company—we wanted him as a director because of his judgment and his widely respected reputation as a business counselor.

- Serving on the Unocal board, I got a chance to see Don Rice in action as a fellow director. As well as being secretary of the Air Force, Don had been president of Rand and currently acts as CEO or chairman of two small biotech companies. He clearly was qualified. But what made him particularly attractive was his knowledge of the science of biotech. Board members always felt comfortable relying on the expertise of one of their own. Don was a perfect fit.

By the end of this process, the nominating committee had assembled a diverse group of capable advisors. That goes with the job.

The board of directors is too valuable to the company and its shareholders to not be managed effectively. The CEO must ensure that the board includes the diverse range of talent that the company needs and also must ensure that, once that strong bench is assembled, it is given the proper environment to be productive. Directors need the opportunity to focus on issues that require broad judgment; they need that information provided in a form that gets to the heart of the issues the company faces. That is the approach to corporate governance that truly serves the needs of shareholders.

CHAPTER EIGHT

The Board As Consultants

Stephen P. Kaufman, former chairman and CEO of Arrow Electronics

Stephen Kaufman joined Arrow Electronics in 1982, after a tragic event had shaken the company. In 1980, a fire ripped through an upstate New York hotel where Arrow executives were meeting. Thirteen executives perished in the fire, among them five of the top six officers, including its chairman, executive vice president, and CFO. When Kaufman became CEO in 1985, the company had started to recover from the shock of the fire; it had reached the $500 million in annual sales mark, nearly double what it had been a few years earlier. But over the next seventeen years, Kaufman would lead the company through an even more impressive period of growth and global expansion. When he retired in 2002, the company had become the world's largest distributor of electronic and computer components, with 10,000 employees and over $10 billion in annual sales. During his tenure, Kaufman led Arrow through sixty-five acquisitions.

As CEO, Kaufman also carefully reconstituted the board of directors, more than doubling its size and attracting diverse and experienced directors. After stepping down as CEO in 2000 and keeping the title of chairman, Kaufman returned as interim CEO briefly, after his successor departed. He formally retired from the company in September 2002 and began teaching at the Harvard Business School.

SOME YEARS BACK, Arrow Electronics' sales hit a slump. Based on the year's results, none of the salespeople stood to earn any incentive pay. The question before me was: Do we act on the basis of justice or on the basis of mercy? If we acted on the basis of justice, which is my natural inclination, we would have provided no incentives. But was this an instance in which mercy was called for?

I realized that I could not answer this question by myself. I had no experience in sales. My background had always been in operations and finance. I decided that I needed the advice of someone who understood sales. I also needed the advice of someone who was committed to Arrow's overall interests but was sufficiently detached from the company's own internal dynamics to allow for an objective opinion. I called Dan Duval, a member of my board who had been an industrial salesman for ten years before becoming a sales manager, a division president, and eventually president of a large industrial company. I called him my "sales-expert board member." He told me that if I wanted the sales force to be here in two or three years, a little mercy would be a good idea. It wouldn't be necessary to provide incentives comparable to previous years, but a percentage of it—perhaps 30 or 40 percent—made sense, especially for the salespeople we most wanted to retain.

The decision about what kind of bonuses to pay to our sales force was not a board-level decision. Under normal circumstances, it was not the kind of information I shared with the board—nor did they want to know it. But in this case, I used a director as a consultant. In fact, I strongly believe that a CEO should utilize the board of directors as a board of consultants. If the board is properly constituted, it should include businesspeople with proven track records in the areas of expertise that are crucial to the company. Board members are there to provide their judgment on behalf of the shareholders, and the best way to ensure they are able to do that is to see them as a reservoir of experience, and to tap that reservoir.

One of the most effective uses of a board is to syndicate major issues among them, based on each board member's specific areas of experience and knowledge. In one sense, independent directors can be seen as consultants-in-chief. The knowledge and judgment they are able to apply to specific issues is in fact an incalculable resource—incalculable because in most instances they would not be available as paid consultants; if they were available, the value of their advice if translated to a daily rate would be cost-prohibitive.

But for the board's value to be realized, independent directors must be properly selected, effectively managed, thoroughly informed, and appropriately consulted (they should be dealing with major issues and major issues alone).

A Consulting Board: What Skills Are Required?

To effectively use the board as a consulting resource, it is necessary to build a profile of skills that will contribute to and complement the CEO's own areas of expertise, shoring up any areas of weakness that may be important in the exercise of leading the company. When I became CEO, Arrow Electronics was rebuilding itself after a tragic fire three years earlier had claimed the lives of the CEO and twelve other senior executives. Until then, the company had a small board of five directors, including a few of the original family owners of the company. I realized that Arrow needed to build a more traditional board and began a process of seeking out board members who would increase its breadth. I wanted experts available to me in several areas.

I asked myself: What strengths do we need in a director?

First, I felt we needed several people with a broad range of experience in dealing with the issues that come with running a public company—that included several sitting CEOs of public companies.

Because my own background is in finance and operations, I looked to fill the board with members whose backgrounds were in complementary areas. Arrow was a distributor, making sales-force management one of our biggest issues. Consequently, I conducted a search for a couple of strong board members who had started their careers in sales and sales management, providing me with respected advisors in an area I was personally unfamiliar with.

Because our 25 percent growth rate required regular access to additional funding, an understanding of the capital markets was critical, so we sought sitting CFOs, or a CEO who had been a CFO. As we grew, we wanted a distinguished academic to keep ourselves current with the latest management and governance concepts. We invited Dick Rosenbloom, a professor at the Harvard Business School, to join our board, and he provided exactly what we needed. He was very smart, of course, but he was also a strategic thinker. He has a historical perspective on business, and during board discussions he often could link current situations to relevant examples from the past. My other goal in having an academic on the board was to keep us up-to-date with current academic thinking about management, and here too Dick lived up to our expectations. He introduced us to EVA—the "economic value added" financial management and measurement system—long before it was promoted by consultants and the business press. It helped us understand that we should not just look at earnings per share but, rather, try to understand how Arrow created value for shareholders. Interestingly, Dick was also prescient about the importance of corporate governance—he would regularly bring up governance reforms at board meetings. As a result of his leadership on this issue, Arrow adopted a new charter in the early 1990s that codified for us many of the rules—such as the ratio of insider to independent directors and having only independent directors on the key committees—that have now been written into the Sarbanes-Oxley Act on corporate-governance reform.

Finding experienced CEOs from Europe and Asia for our board also became a priority as the company expanded globally. Roger King was a perfect example. He was Shanghai-born and educated in Shanghai and Hong Kong, but he came to America for college. After working as an engineer at Bell Labs, he began a career in business and returned to Asia to be the CEO of a computer-products distributor. He was a perfect fit for our company, and because one of his children was living in the United States, he had a second reason to fly over regularly to attend our board meetings.

I also asked myself what kind of background we did *not* want our board members to have. That too is important. I am a firm believer that a board should never include investment bankers, commercial bankers, or lawyers. A board that includes professional advisors and consultants finds itself with an implicit conflict in its discussions, and an automatic loss of objectivity in several important areas. A company that needs advice about commercial banking, investment banking, or the law should hire the best practitioners it can, consultants who will be responsive to the board rather than serving on it.

Instead of bringing an investment banker on the board, when we needed to engage one I asked a board member with finance expertise for advice on how to assess and select a firm to engage.

In choosing each board member, I focused exclusively on their areas of experience and expertise. In no instance did we seek to include someone on the board as a representative of any one group of stakeholders, whether they be suppliers, employees, customers, or representatives of a particular community or interest group. In my view, when it comes to putting together a board, there is only one kind of stakeholder—the shareholder. I believe that the criteria for selecting directors should be aimed at shaping a board that is best able to represent the interests of all shareholders, rather than any specific constituency.

Removing Board Members—Not an Easy Process

Two of the most difficult tasks of corporate leadership are hiring directors—and firing them. Lining up a director is considerably subtler and more complicated than hiring an executive. When you hire an executive, you conduct extensive and lengthy interviews, reference checks, and background checks. But needless to say, potential board members—particularly other CEOs and COOs—do not expect to submit to that kind of formal interview process. It seems inappropriate to drill a sixty-five-year-old CEO about his qualifications for board membership. After all, the potential director is not applying for the job—you are asking him to consider the invitation. Consequently, a meeting with a potential director has to be focused on sharing thoughts about strategy, positioning, and governance—not asking the potential directors pointed, formal questions about their employment history, successes and failures, or strengths and weaknesses, as one would do to explore and validate the qualifications of a potential senior executive. In my experience, the purpose of this interview is to make an assessment of whether the person "fits" on the board. Is he formal or informal? Outspoken or introverted? What is her view of the role of the board? How comfortable is he with debates at board meetings and free-ranging discussions? Of course, there were some issues that, for me, were a kind of litmus test. Arrow was a strategically focused company. Both the management and the board shared an understanding that in our cyclical industry we would not sacrifice our strategic initiatives just to beat last year's earnings. When I interviewed a potential board member and found that he or she believed that meeting the Wall Street estimates was all-important, I knew right away that the fit wasn't right.

Of course, there are key differences between hiring a senior executive and inviting someone to join your board. In the case of the senior executive, if it doesn't work out, a company can terminate the employment relationship if necessary. But how do you remove a director, and for what reasons? That is a much tougher challenge.

Many companies have a maximum age for directors; at Arrow the maximum age is seventy-two. But that doesn't eliminate directors who are not contributing or who are creating conflicts with the rest of the board. Given that it makes sense to select directors partially based on their full-time position, many companies have a rule calling upon the governance committee to review and recommend whether a director should be removed upon changing his or her principal occupation, such as a CEO who has been fired. At Arrow, we have a rule that requires a director to submit a letter of resignation upon changing principal occupation, giving the governance committee an opportunity to decide if the individual's ongoing primary role and experience still fits the profile our board is looking for. For example, we once brought someone onto our board who had recently become the head of an operating division at his company, because we wanted more operationally experienced directors. Shortly thereafter, he went back to a staff role, and our governance committee received and accepted the required resignation because the person no longer fit the requirements that we were looking for. On the other hand, when another board member retired as CEO of his own company and submitted the required resignation, the committee did not accept it, because he was still very active and current in the issues important to our company

How awkward or difficult it is to remove a board member depends on the issues driving the possible removal behind the situation. If the issue is one of lack of participation—such as a board member who misses too many board meetings, constantly leaves the meeting to answer his or her cell phone, or always leaves early—then the chairman or the head of the governance committee has to take the responsibility of pointing out to the errant director that perhaps he or she is too busy to continue in the position. But that is simple and straightforward compared to a board member whose personality or style in raising questions about business issues is becoming obstructionist rather than constructive and/or is creating dissension on the board or within the management team. The line is very gray between appropriate and well-intentioned questioning of management strategies and performance and inappropriate meddling or obstructionism. I have never spoken to any CEO or board chairman who has a simple formula for dealing with this problem. But certainly one question to consider is: Are you considering removing this board member because of an inability to work well with the rest of the board, or because the board member frequently disagrees with you and the rest of the board? Where does one draw the line between being contrarian and being obstreperous? After all, a CEO should want directors to object on some issues. The tough question is: When does it hinder the board's ability to function effectively?

In one case, we had a younger, less experienced board member who was less financially astute than the other directors. When we entered into a discussion of a particular financial issue, most of the people in the room soon were ready to move on. But because he didn't understand what was at stake, he insisted that he get a full education on the topic at the board meeting. We spent an hour on it, much to the dismay of my other directors. Yet the young director persisted that we flesh out the issue there and then. In hindsight, I realize that it would have been to everyone's benefit if I had simply sat him down with our CFO outside of the meeting.

Most of the time, though, I have benefited from the questions raised by my directors. In one case, I had brought a foreign acquisition to the board for approval. Two directors had deep concerns, suggesting I was buying a weaker company simply to increase our scale in that country—a goal we all agreed on. They pushed me to wait for the right company, and as a result, I didn't bring it to a vote that day and later shelved the idea.

Keeping the Board Informed

It is important to keep in mind that regardless of the board's expertise and commitment, directors will not be able to help a CEO deal with issues if they are kept in the dark about them. Treating board members like mushrooms ("keep them in the dark, cover them with manure, and when a head pops up cut it off") is not a formula for having a truly effective board. Rather than suddenly throwing an unexpected item onto the agenda—or even worse, waiting until the issue has become a newspaper headline—a CEO should be open about the company's challenges, problems, and the tough issues it is dealing with. CEOs must also be frank in discussing the company's and their own setbacks. All of the management-training courses within great companies and leading academic institutions teach that managers need to be able to accept that they will make mistakes, have errors in judgment, and experience failures and that good managers recognize these, confront them, fix them when possible, learn from them, and move on. We need to apply this same philosophy at the board level. One of the best ways for a CEO to build credibility with the board is to be as free describing problems and failures as successes. This also signals to the board where they as individuals might be able to lend a hand to the CEO.

I think it is important to maintain contact on a regular, ongoing basis between meetings. I made it a point to call each board member before each meeting, usually one or two weeks beforehand, to go over the agenda, highlight any unusual or particularly important items, explain the context of these, and share my current thinking on the issues. I was not necessarily lobbying for a particular decision or even looking for the board member's support on the issues; I just wanted to ensure that he or she had a framework and enough time to consider the issue to enhance the board's discussion at the meeting itself. In 1997, I wanted to give all employees except the top hundred a stock-option award because, after two bad years, our bonus plan was not paying off. At the same time, we were going through a restructuring that would cause a lot of dislocation. I wanted something to sweeten the pill for the front-line employees, and that is what I told directors before our meeting. We did have a full discussion of the option award at the meeting, but everyone already understood my reasoning behind it because of our earlier conversations.

Over and above these ongoing conversations, I tried to have an annual one-on-one meeting with each board member, a long dinner or lunch, to give him or her an opportunity to raise with me anything that was on his or her mind and to give me an opportunity to raise any specific expectations. In the ongoing, frequently hectic process of board and committee meetings and pre-meeting preparations, the CEO sometimes does not get the opportunity for deeper discussions of big-picture issues with individual board members, and they often do not have the chance to raise concerns that may not be on the formal agenda.

Managing Board Meetings

Getting the maximum out of each board meeting takes considerable work. Successful board meetings do not just happen.

Successful board meetings require preparation. A board meeting is not meant to be a spontaneous interaction: It has to be planned. CEOs should prepare for each board meeting as they would for a major-customer sales pitch. In my early days as a CEO, I tended to think about the meeting during the previous afternoon and was often guilty of just going into the board meeting and "winging" it. Eventually, I learned that I needed to sit down well in advance of the meeting, consider what the board members were likely to be concerned about, what they would ask, and think about each agenda item from their point of view. (This became easier for me once I joined another company's board as an independent director.) At the same time, however, I do not believe that this process should wind up with extensive rehearsals of each minute or presentation scheduled for the meeting. There is no reason to prepare a detailed script that each management attendee is expected to follow. The goal is to create candid and thoughtful dialogue among the board members and between board members and senior management. As a member of other boards, I am always concerned, and perhaps even skeptical, when I attend a board meeting at which the presentations seem too good, too smooth, and too carefully prepared and rehearsed. I know that in my own company there are problems, disappointments, and areas in which we are not performing as well as we should be or could be. If I don't see evidence and discussion of similar things at the companies on whose boards I serve, I worry that I am not seeing the whole picture. It calls to mind the old saying, "If it looks too good to be true, it probably *is* too good to be true." To carry it to an extreme, I might suggest that the board agenda be structured to spend only half as much time celebrating successes and achievement as looking at problems and challenges.

Successful board meetings require organization. It is important to think through the agenda carefully beforehand and segment the items based on what is actually required from the board. I believe in explicitly differentiating among three types of items dealt with at board meetings: information items; issues on which the CEO would like to hear some discussion and perhaps get some advice but on which he or she will make the ultimate decision; and issues on which the board as a whole has to reach a decision.

Successful board meetings require the appropriate style of meeting management. A board meeting is not just another meeting: A CEO must consciously think about how to conduct it. It is important to think about the format—should it be formal or informal? It is important to think about the length—should it be a half day or a full day? Should it be kicked off with a pre-meeting dinner? It isn't necessary or even desirable to continue the style employed by the former CEO. In fact, it may make sense to deliberately change some aspect of the way the meeting is conducted, to establish that it is not just a continuation of the same process and routine.

I have served on boards whose meetings are conducted both formally and informally. I know of boards for whom the meeting itself is relatively quick, formal, and not very interactive; the real discussion and exchanges occur during dinner the night before, or over breakfast or lunch, or on the side during breaks. And I know of boards for which the meeting lasts all day and the discussion is very interactive and informal. The one criterion that is important to me is that the style be conducive to real, open dialogue at some time and in some way. For me, a successful board meeting is one in which the discussion is intellectually rich and vibrant. In addition to committee reports and reviewing the most recent financial results and forecasts, I believe it is important for a board to focus on current business issues, perhaps by scheduling one specific issue, function, or business group for a detailed review at each meeting. I recall such a discussion at Arrow when we considered exiting the computer-products business in North America. We ended up discussing it over two meetings and made real discoveries about the nature of the business. It turned out that there were really two segments within the computer-products business—one that was attractive to us, the other unattractive. So we decided to exit the low end of the business—mostly PCs and printers—and reconfigured the remaining part so it was focused on high-end computing, which grew to become one of the most profitable businesses in the company. The ability to separate these two businesses was something that emerged only after our extended board discussion. Until then, board members had seen computer products reported as a single business. Because we had the chance to examine it in more detail, the discussion was both energizing and revealing.

Another topic that produced a full and healthy discussion was whether to move our headquarters from New York to Denver. The major reasons were cost savings and being closer to our largest customers and suppliers. But I was of two minds about the move, and I brought it to the board to get advice, not a decision. We spent an hour on it, but didn't vote because the board agreed this was a decision for management to make. But some directors made a point that stuck with me: Relocation would take up essential management time for twelve to eighteen months. It would be very hard to both manage a corporate HQ transition and make an acquisition during that period if an opportunity arose. As a result of this discussion, I decided that Arrow would stay in New York, which proved fortuitous since a very large acquisition opportunity did arise four months later.

Successful board meetings require experience. That includes experience from the other side of the table, as an independent director. I would urge all CEOs to serve on one other board to see what it looks like from that other side. It is very valuable for a CEO to watch how another company runs its board meetings—explicitly seeking or not seeking the directors' advice, providing or not providing advance information, encouraging or discouraging tough questions and discussion. When you serve on a board and watch another CEO, COO, and CFO present that company's situation, you inevitably see the process in a different light. You may get irritated at the use of industry or company jargon and acronyms, you may wish you had more information further in advance, you may ask yourself mental questions about the downsides of a forecast or plan, or you may even ask yourself: "What am I not being told?" Having this experience will give you much food for thought about how to structure and run your own board meetings. However, in the early years of being a CEO, I would not accept more than one other director assignment because a CEO's primary obligation is to his or her own company.

The Need for Interaction

In order to maximize their value to the company, board members must get the chance to truly learn about the company, get to know one another, and get to know senior management—not just the CEO.

Getting to know the company must include getting to know more about its markets—especially its new, emerging markets. At Arrow, we developed a practice that is becoming increasingly popular in corporate America. We would hold one board meeting a year outside of the United States, in a country of importance or growing importance to the corporation. We would heavily involve the senior management team from that region, since typically, managers below the head person in that region would rarely have direct contact with the board. That gives all board members a feel for the company's global operations and how business practices and opportunities may differ in that country or region of the world.

As I mentioned, I believe it is also very important for the board members to get to know one another, build trust in one another, and be comfortable with one another. A board (or any team) with these characteristics will be much more effective, particularly when problems or even disasters occur. You don't want the board members trying to get to know one another *after* the crisis hits. We invited the spouses to our annual international board meeting, building a social agenda around the official agenda. Besides creating opportunities for informal discussion, the goal was to create a bond among the directors around the company and its opportunities and issues. A two-or-three-day meeting with some sightseeing and social activities, as well as business, is a good way to help a board build this kind of bond, before problems hit that require quick and firm decision-making and action.

Long before the current interest in board governance, we believed that it was critical for the independent directors to have a regular opportunity to discuss the issues that affect the company, in executive session, without the CEO or any other members of management present. Some companies have brief executive sessions for the independent directors at the end of the regular board meeting. But a few minutes at the end, when everyone is looking at his or her watch and wondering about travel arrangements, does not create the opportunity for meaningful discussion. At every Arrow board meeting, we would set aside thirty minutes for the board to meet without the CEO or management. At least twice a year, they would meet for a minimum of two hours, under the leadership of one of the committee chairmen (always an independent director). One of these meetings would be the performance review of the CEO and would be led by the chair of the compensation committee. The other meeting would be led by the chair of the governance committee, to discuss succession planning. It may make sense for the CEO to participate in a portion of that meeting, when he or she is presumed to be far from retirement. But starting roughly three years prior to scheduled retirement, the CEO should not participate, unless specifically asked to, presumably to provide information.

Some CEOs feel it is their role to serve as exclusive liaison between the board and the senior management team. I feel the exact opposite. I believe it is the CEO's responsibility to facilitate regular contact between board members and senior managers. One of the best ways for an independent director to become a true resource to the company is by learning about the company's operations from its senior managers. I have always encouraged the independent directors to visit company operations when they are traveling to cities where we have facilities and to each meet annually with two or three senior managers on a one-on-one basis as part of their data gathering for evaluating the CEO. It isn't just an opportunity to find out if the senior managers like the CEO personally or think he or she is doing a good job, but how the company is doing and what that executive thinks the critical issues, opportunities, and challenges are. Along the way, of course, an experienced and savvy board member will also get a sense of how the CEO is performing as leader of the company, and that information should properly be integrated into the annual CEO-evaluation process.

It is also valuable to bring management to the pre-board-meeting dinners, three or four senior managers at a time, so the board can get to know management at an informal level and build networks within the company.

I made clear at the beginning what a valuable asset board members can be to a CEO. They can allow CEOs to expand their expertise and compensate for areas in which they lack experience. But that does not come automatically. Lining up independent directors with a wide spectrum of experience is crucial, but it is only the beginning of the process. In order to make their individual skills of true value to the company, board members must be familiar with the company—its strategy, people, strengths, weaknesses, and markets. CEOs can do themselves a big favor by making sure that board members get the opportunity to become involved in the company. It is the essential precursor to making the independent directors a true board of consultants.

CHAPTER NINE

Keeping Management in Check

Nell Minow, editor of The Corporate Library

For more than sixteen years, Nell Minow has been the leading American voice calling on corporations to improve the way they govern themselves. With her longtime collaborator Robert Monks, she helped lead Institutional Shareholder Services, which counsels institutions on corporate-governance issues. She later joined LENS, a fund that sought out companies that were under-performing and poorly governed and then used its investment to pressure the company to improve its practices and results.

In 1999, Minow and Monks founded The Corporate Library, an independent research firm that compiles studies and critical thinking about the nature of the modern global corporation, with a special emphasis on best practices and standards. When corporate scandals became front-page news, Minow quickly became one of the most frequently quoted experts. "Even in my wildest and most paranoid fantasies, it never occurred to me that there would be this level of corruption and neglect," she told an interviewer.

In addition to her work with The Corporate Library, Nell Minow is coauthor of three books and author of more than two hundred articles about corporate governance, boards of directors, and CEO compensation.

IN DISCUSSING THE ISSUE of corporate governance, it is worth considering the words of a former CEO:

> The responsibility of our board—a responsibility which I expect them to fulfill—is to ensure legal and ethical conduct by the company and by everyone in the company. . . . What a CEO really ex-

pects from a board is good advice and counsel, both of which will make the company stronger and more successful; support for those investments and decisions that serve the interests of the company and its stakeholders; and warnings in those cases in which investments and decisions are not beneficial to the company and its stakeholders.

These were the comments of then-Enron CEO Kenneth Lay, in April 1999, at the Center for Business Ethics at the University of St. Thomas in Houston. Perhaps the most troubling aspect of the quote is that, on paper, Enron met most of the best practices in corporate governance.

Lay's statement was an eloquent expression of what a board should do. But that just illustrates that the key to assessing a board is to look at what it actually *does* do. Is the board prepared to criticize CEO and management policies, or is it content to serve as a corporate cheerleader? Do directors have access to information that is useful to them? How much of a role does the board have in issues of CEO succession and board nominations? What kind of role does the board play in determining CEO pay, financial reporting, and overall strategy? How much time does the CEO spend listening to the concerns of shareholders?

These kinds of questions will be raised more frequently in an era in which investors and the general public have been given reason to feel increasingly skeptical of corporate leaders. CEOs entered this millennium ranked with rock stars as figures of glamour and magic. For decades, *Time* magazine's men of the year were figures from politics and international affairs. In the 1990s, however, three were business leaders: CNN's Ted Turner, Intel's Andy Grove, and Amazon.com's Jeff Bezos. Today, the CEOs with household names are more likely to be avoiding congressional testimony than appearing in laudatory magazine cover stories.

Business leaders need to reclaim public and investor confidence by showing leadership—developing solutions to prevent the next Enron or WorldCom. Much of the responsibility for ensuring that happens must be exercised by truly independent boards of directors.

Independent Boards: It Starts with the Selection Process

It is no longer enough to assess a board of directors simply by the prestige of its members. In judging directors, their résumés are not the issue. The issue is the function they actually perform, and how independently they perform it.

There have been encouraging reports that directors are asking more questions and insisting on spending meeting time without management present. One of the most effective elements of corporate governance is having the outside directors meet regularly, even following every board and committee meeting, in executive session, so that they can have a candid discussion of the agenda, CEO succession, the presentations of consultants and auditors, and other issues that are difficult to raise with management in the room. But there have also been discouraging reports that CEOs are responding by burying board members in the minutiae of financial reports. The board's job is to focus on the big picture and hold management to account for issues that affect investor interests.

Even an ineffective board will often include at least one member who genuinely recognizes a need to stand up firmly on behalf of investor interests. Even one individual on a board can effect change. But too often, CEOs seeking to fill a board vacancy will call their friends or a headhunter, looking for "consensus builders." That is where the problems in corporate governance take root. Take eleven consensus builders and one dynamic leader who controls the agenda, and it is likely to add up to the lowest common denominator: a boardroom in which everyone looks around the table to see what everyone else is saying.

There is a strong tendency for directors to "dance with the one that brung them"—the CEO. To break that cycle, it is crucial that boards include nominating committees led by independent directors. Committee members must take on the responsibility of screening board nominees and recommending names of their own. One CEO told me that the independent directors on his board sometimes turned down his nominees but didn't come up with alternatives. It's important for independent directors to take at least some of the onus on themselves, and even to consult with shareholders about the procedures and criteria for selecting new board members. That is a first step to creating a new cycle of independence, in which boards are continually regenerated.

No matter the process for selecting board members, the value of any director's contribution may change over time, depending on the individual's commitment and the priorities. A company that is changing the nature of its business—say, focusing on service rather than production, or entering an expansion phase—may need a different set of talents and a different base of expertise. For this reason, board-succession challenges are perpetual. But experience has shown that getting rid of a board member is a difficult process. Rather than focus on personalities, outside directors can focus on re-evaluating their needs, working closely with the corporate strategic-planning unit. The re-examined priorities would then form a basis for determining necessary changes in board membership.

Testing Board Effectiveness

How can one determine whether a board is effective? At The Corporate Library, the online repository for corporate-governance research that I co-founded in 1999, we have identified several issues that provide a litmus test of how independently a board represents the interests of the shareholders.

CEO Compensation: How much is the CEO being paid, and how closely is it tied to performance? The 1990s saw one of the most dramatic transfers of wealth in history, as CEO pay skyrocketed both in absolute terms and as a multiple of what the average worker earned. The average CEO earns upward of four hundred times more than the average worker. If the minimum wage had risen at the same rate as executive pay since 1990, it would be over $21 an hour instead of $5.15.

CEOs reaped windfall profits from mega-grants of stock options, made possible in part by the accounting treatment of options. Now that many companies are closing the treatment loophole by expensing options when they are granted, is it not time to switch to a more credible option plan—one that indexes options so that they pay out only if the company does better than its competition?

When addressing the issue of CEO pay, boards should not neglect the question of CEO perks. The employment contract for the former CEO of Global Crossing not only called for the company to buy him a Mercedes but spelled out the make and model. It also provided first-class airfare for his mother to be flown out to visit him once a month. A question to ask of every board: How diligently does it review the perks provided to the CEO, to determine whether they really are helpful to job performance and necessary to attract the right person?

CEO Succession: Perhaps the most important task a board must handle is its responsibility for CEO succession. The future of the company is in the directors' hands, as is the future relationship between the board and the next CEO.

One of the most important things a board must do is establish the right relationship and framework for working with the current CEO in determining the next one. CEOs are often inclined to try to dominate the choice of a successor, especially when their retirement is not on the immediate horizon. Boards should consider putting the responsibility for a successful succession in a CEO's job description. They can make it effective by including an incentive, a bonus in the form of stock that the outgoing CEO must hold on to for, say, three years after leaving the company.

The board has to make it clear that it will not be rubber-stamping anybody. It must determine the kind of successor that is needed and the criteria for reviewing candidates. Board members must get the chance to meet with the potential CEOs, both formally and informally. And boards must—on an ongoing basis—get the opportunity to see potential inside successors in action, as they move up the corporate ranks. One element of evaluating a current CEO is examining his or her ability to attract and retain top talent. Another way of evaluating a potential CEO is to look at what form of compensation he or she wants. A potential CEO who asks for more stock believes in the company; one who wants more perks or a cash bonus is hedging his or her bets.

Financial Reporting: The Sarbanes-Oxley bill made it clear, in case there was any doubt, that auditors of publicly traded companies are accountable to the audit committee of the board. But accountability will be of value only to the extent that independent directors serving on audit committees are qualified and committed to exercising effective due diligence. Recent history is not that promising. What would your reaction be if you learned that O. J. Simpson once served on the audit committee of a board? Or that Cablevision paid its auditor more than $23 million in non-audit fees? Investors may not have paid much attention to these disclosures in the past, but they are doing so now.

Financial reporting is truly a corporate-governance wedge issue—one in which board members must signal their commitment to representing the interests of investors. There is a clear divide between the natural inclination of the CEO and the needs of the shareholders. It is not surprising that the CEO wants the numbers to appear smooth and favorable. The shareholders, on the other hand, want them to be candid and transparent. If the board cannot make sure that the financial reports present a full, fair, and accurate picture of the company's financial position, it is failing in its most basic responsibility.

Audit-committee members must have the qualifications to provide genuine oversight. What is their degree of accounting proficiency? How much experience do they have reviewing financial statements? Are they capable of looking at a balance sheet and spotting the lines that demand inquiry? Boards of directors are fulfilling their responsibility to the shareholders only if the audit-committee members are able to answer "yes" to questions like these.

Strategic Accountability: It is the CEO's responsibility to create shareholder value. It is the board's responsibility to make sure that he pursues a clear strategy for doing that. In that respect, corporate boards are the great underused resource of corporate America. For one thing, they are in a better position than anybody to give the CEO bad news. Too often, a CEO is surrounded by people telling him that he is absolutely right on every issue. For the independent directors to be able to tell the CEO when he is wrong, they need to be intimately familiar with the corporate strategy and how it is being executed. As I mentioned, they need to work with corporate strategic planning and acquire an in-depth understanding of the strategic issues. They need to identify strategic gaps—probing whether marketing needs to be beefed up, or global reach enhanced.

But too often, boards allow themselves to be distracted by granular issues. The directors of one restaurant company spent two full board meetings on the kind of pudding that should be included on the restaurant menus. That's a sign of a board that is allowing itself to be distracted from its real job.

Strategic overview also must include close examination of major expenditures, questioning their real value to the company and its shareholders. For example, if a CEO decides to buy a golf course (as the CEO of Lucent did), the board has to ask: What does this have to do with our business? How does it enhance or unlock shareholder value?

To exercise this kind of oversight, the members of the board must insist on wide access to information—information that will be useful to them in assessing strategy and operations. When my father served on the board of CBS, management continually provided the directors with presentations analyzing the comparative viewership of the big three networks—NBC, ABC, and CBS. My father would always ask for comparative information on new emerging competitors, such as HBO. Finally, at the last CBS meeting he attended as a director, he obtained what he had been seeking for years—a chart with more than three bars.

Board members should have access to resources, including the opportunity to engage outside consultants when necessary. They should be able to find out about outside sources about benchmarking and best practices. If a board does not belong to the National Association of Corporate Directors, an excellent source of information, directors should ask why not—before they are asked that question by their D&O liability insurers or by shareholder-litigation attorneys taking depositions. A board that fails to insist on these tools is a board that will find it difficult to do its job.

Listening to Shareholders

Right now, CEOs and their companies need the confidence and patience of shareholders more than ever before. The fact is that investors have come a long way in evolving from a dispersed group to one that is increasingly organized and active. Some CEOs may find this an irritant. But they should also recognize its potential value, providing them with a mechanism for determining investor concerns and addressing them and for developing a relationship of trust and loyalty to sustain them through business cycles.

Engaging in an investor-outreach effort does require a different mind-set. One CEO, who was very open to talking with shareholders, told me that he did not enjoy meeting with institutional shareholders. This CEO was very excited about the things he and his company were doing in R&D, but he found that institutional investors seemed to want to talk only about issues of corporate governance and accountability. CEOs have to be prepared for that. Shareholders are not analysts or customers, so CEOs have to be prepared to deal with a different set of concerns—issues like compensation, financial reporting, and board independence. On the other hand, building a base of credibility on issues like these is an excellent way of shoring up investor trust at a time when it is in short supply.

In any event, CEOs have little choice but to develop a relationship with their shareholders, because many of them, especially institutional shareholders, are going to be permanent investors. The relationship between the CEO and investors may sometimes seem like a shotgun wedding, but it is for life.

Corporate Governance: Don't Just Check the Box

Of course, not every proposal for corporate-governance reform should be taken as the gold standard. Even some of the most popular proposals should not be seen as panaceas. The British refer to a practice in corporate governance they call "box ticking"—the notion that corporations can simply check all of the boxes of prescribed corporate-governance practices to ensure that the interests of shareholders are being represented.

Some of the specific proposals may make a great deal of sense, others less so. But none solves the problem—they are just tools for boards, and the boards must be prepared to use them.

Some of the most popular proposals are separating the job of CEO from chairman of the board, age limits for directors, and term limits for directors.

Non-Executive Chairman: Companies in the United Kingdom adopt a practice that many U.S. shareholder advocates have been demanding and few have yet received—separation of the job of chairman and CEO. This could be a significant change, if it put in the hands of an independent director considerable control of the agenda, timing, and quality and quantity of information. That could be especially helpful to troubled companies.

But one cannot be sure that such a change would be meaningful. If so many "independent" directors do not demonstrate enough independence, what would lead us to believe that an independent chairman would? Indeed, in the current circumstances it could actually make things worse at some companies, providing a Potemkin chairman to shield the actions of the CEO.

Term Limits, Age Limits: There is nothing like teaching a university class to be reminded of the black-and-white opinions of the world that young people can have. I have taught second-year MBA courses, and one of the things the students get furious about is the age of directors. Of course, when you are in your twenties, just about everybody seems old. But they have a point. Especially for a company involved in new technologies and products, it makes sense to have some younger people on the board—not inexperienced people, but men and women in their forties.

But what about a mandatory retirement age for directors? Some boards have mandatory retirement—usually between the ages of seventy and seventy-five. I described above a proposal for reviewing changing corporate needs and realigning boards based on that. But when it comes to both age limits and term limits, there are a couple of concerns.

- Undercutting the experience curve: We do not want to remove directors just as their depth of knowledge makes them most useful. A board that includes directors who have been serving for ten years or so is a board that has people around who really know what is going on. Mandatory age or term limits could remove someone from the board just when he or she is becoming a real asset.

- Draining the pool: The truth is that there is a very shallow pool of qualified and committed directors. These are people who are offered many more opportunities than they can accept, especially with the new focus on financial expertise and on limiting the number of boards on which a director serves. By attracting directors based on a sense of commitment to the free-market system, companies (and therefore their shareholders) are able to obtain an "expertise premium." We may need to broaden the pool, before we can start calling people out too soon.

For most investors, new processes will ultimately be less important than improved results. In reviewing the corporate-governance performance of boards and their companies, the focus must be on tangibles such as CEO pay, succession, financial reporting, and strategic oversight.

To paraphrase Kenneth Lay, investors are looking to boards for "support for those investments and decisions that serve the interests of the company and its shareholders, and warnings in those cases in which investments and decisions are not beneficial to the company and its shareholders."

But they are looking for concrete results, not hollow sentiments. Increasingly, the assessment of "governance risk" will be a critical element in making an investment decision. Companies that develop and communicate superb systems for independent oversight by capable directors will minimize their cost of capital and maximize shareholder loyalty. Most important, they will create the kind of spirited exchange of ideas that is the best possible assurance of strategic vitality and long-term growth.

CHAPTER TEN

Reforming the Corporate-Governance Process

Ira M. Millstein, senior partner at Weil, Gotshal & Manges

Ira M. Millstein was one of the nation's most influential authorities on corporate governance long before the subject received national attention. During his distinguished career, he has been at the center of debates about corporate behavior and responsibility in both the public and private spheres. In addition to his work for the World Bank and the OECD, he has been an advisor to a large variety of corporations and institutions on corporate governance issues, including General Motors, the Walt Disney Company, Interpublic Group, Westinghouse Electric Corp., Bethlehem Steel Corp., and the California Public Employees' Retirement System. Millstein is also the author of numerous influential books and articles on the relationship between corporate management and the board of directors and speaks widely on the topic. He is a senior partner at the international law firm of Weil, Gotshal & Manges in New York.

WHAT I REMEMBER MOST about the first corporate board meeting I participated in was what *didn't* happen. It was the late 1960s, and I was making a presentation as outside counsel to a client's board of directors regarding a litigation charging the client with price-fixing in a major industry. After completing my report, the chairman thanked me politely. That was it. Not a single director asked me a question.

It was the era of the imperial CEO, a world in which the average CEO had no doubt as to the best relationship with the board: Treat directors as nicely as you can and send them home as rapidly as possible. It was a different world than the one CEOs face today. The power shift has been dramatic.

What will be the nature of the relationship between CEOs and their boards of directors in the years to come? Will increased board scrutiny of the CEO turn them into enemies? I believe that the CEO can make the board a colleague, but it won't be easy or automatic. Boards have a responsibility to shareholders, and the pressures to exercise it are greater than ever. CEOs have to realize they are going to be watched, monitored, and controlled in ways they have never been before in corporate America. Boards will insist on holding CEOs and management to account, because boards themselves are being held to account.

But just because they face issues from across the table does not mean they cannot reach across it.

The trend toward more active and aggressive boards has been gaining momentum for a simple reason. Every day we pick up the papers and read about another corporation misstating or failing to disclose information, at a significant cost to shareholders. People look at the latest example and ask: Where was the board? Every instance is one that might not have happened had there been a board that was watching and paying more attention. Boards are supposed to monitor and observe management, serving as the last stop on the road to address any kind of problem for shareholders. More and more, once people finish criticizing a CEO, they turn to the board and ask: Where were you?

Board Authority: A Legal Requirement, an Economic Necessity

After the news about Enron initially broke, I went back to my own beginnings in economics and started reading Adam Smith again. When people think of Smith, they usually think of an exponent of a tough market system based on survival of the fittest. It is easy to forget that Adam Smith held the first chair in moral philosophy at Glasgow University for eleven years before he founded modern economics. His viewpoint was far from hard-hearted. He believed that the world was made up of people who he hoped would be prudent and virtuous, modest, scrupulous, reluctant to either hurt or offend. That is the society around which he saw the market being constructed. The market he envisioned—the market that works—is not a bare-knuckle, devil-take-the-hindmost market. It is a market that is supposed to be made up of people who also have some moral judgment and don't push self-interest to the extreme.

But not all people match up to Smith's view of the human spirit. How, then, to encourage limits to self-interest? Good economic theory holds that one part of the necessary restraints on self-interest consists of restraints on agents, such as CEOs. That is why the board exists—to monitor CEOs and ensure that they perform in accordance with the wishes of their principals, the shareholders.

The law provides that there are three defining elements to a corporation: shareholders, boards, and managers. Managers are supposed to be accountable to boards, and boards are supposed to be accountable to shareholders. If shareholders object to the way the corporation is run, they need not go to the managers; they can go to the board, and replace management if necessary. If directors don't like the way the corporation is run, they can go to the manager and replace him or her. That is the law, and there are structures to enforce it. Economics and law come together to make the board of directors the focal point in the organization.

But for decades, boards of directors withered from their intended role. What was it that led to weak boards? Strong performance by U.S. corporations. During the postwar period, American companies had little to fear from foreign competition. Our corporations were the icons of the world, globally admired. They seemed to require little scrutiny. Serving on a board may have been prestigious, but it was not considered an important "job" in the active sense of the word. Boards were lulled into doing little other than following senior management. They lacked resources to independently assess the company's strategic options. Handpicked by the CEO from among friends, business associates, and fellow country-club members, the board of directors became less of a decision-making body and more of a social circle.

What prompted boards to reassert their intended role? The rise of brutal international competition in the 1970s and '80s was probably the biggest factor. During these decades, foreign companies recovered the ability to do business. The United States was invaded economically, and the world became a lot tougher and more complicated. In some industries, like steel, boards played an active role in trying to make companies more competitive, but they were stifled by union rules. In other industries, like automobiles, boards were able to contribute to addressing the challenges from abroad.

With the rise of institutional investors, boards of directors found themselves pushed by activist pension funds that demanded improved performance for the companies in which they held shares. At one time, these institutions were not even considered by corporate managers to be shareholders; they were just bureaucrats and stewards. I can recall how difficult it was to get the point across—even to pension-fund managers—that they had to think like shareholders. In fact, the movement to recognize public pension funds as investors didn't even get off the ground until the late 1970s. It was prompted by a case of greenmail, when Texaco paid out $1.3 billion to the corporate-raiding Bass brothers. Fortunately for the cause of corporate governance, 1 percent of Texaco was owned by the California Public Employees' Retirement System. The huge payout drew the indignation of California State Treasurer Jesse Unruh, who set out to launch an umbrella organization of pension funds, called the Council of Institutional Investors. In 1989, New York Governor Mario Cuomo appointed me to head a group to examine the role of state pension funds in corporate governance. Along with Ned Regan, who was then state comptroller and therefore head of the New

York State pension fund, I remember attempting to persuade two groups represented at a meeting—CEOs and the pension funds themselves—that pension funds were, in fact, shareholders. By 1990, the Council became a tool to prod underperforming companies, with the explosive growth of equity indexing.

Now, institutional investors like CalPERS are the voice of the shareholders, pushing boards to closely scrutinize management and, at times, even fire managers. At any setback or failure, institutional investors actively push boards to monitor the agents—the CEO.

The Gatekeepers Resume Their Watch

Many directors seemed to have forgotten that they are supposed to be the system's primary gatekeepers. But who approves the final numbers, and who hires the CEO? In our system, by law it is the board that is ultimately in charge of the company. The law says that the company is managed by, or under the direction of, the board. Boards that have forgotten this recently received a loud reminder.

Laws are being rewritten; new systems are being implemented; new entities for public oversight are being established. Directors bear burdens they did not bear before. In this new environment, boards are going to start to act like the primary gatekeepers. With new stock-exchange listing requirements that require companies to have corporate governance guidelines and new codes of conduct and best practices, they will have no choice.

Every board of every listed company in America has no choice but to do what GM did ten years ago: come up with a set of guiding principles for the board of directors—tough requirements that include definitions of independence, the role of committees, board operations, agenda flow, information flow, board evaluation, executive sessions, and lead directors. Boards will have to adopt a series of new practices or else explain, in their proxy statements, why they have not. These requirements will be mandated through legislation or SEC rulings or under new listing requirements. Directors will have to protect themselves, and the way they will do that is through the CEO. If the CEO is doing well, they will be seen as doing well.

These developments will put CEOs on the hot spot more than ever before. They must begin to cooperate with their boards and set priorities as they pull against a tighter rein. They need to work with their boards rather than resist them and recognize that boards are going to seek a lot more control than in the past. And conversely, boards are going to take considerably more interest in the CEO's strategy. Gone are the days when directors came in every month or two to spend a few hours in a board meeting and then headed home. After all, directors have their reputations to worry about.

CEOs Beware: It's Zero-Tolerance Time

CEOs need a new modus operandi to match this new world of governance. Anyone who needs proof of that need only look at the new listing requirements that the stock exchanges have put out.

CEOs have been given the duty of certifying to the shareholders that, to the best of their knowledge and belief, the company's financial statements and disclosures fairly present the information that's necessary for a reasonable investor to make an investment decision. CEOs must attest to this standard, as well as to the fact they are not aware of any violations of the stock-exchange listing standards—standards that include requirements for governance codes, codes of conduct, independent boards of directors, executive sessions, and a designated presiding director.

In fact, being able to meet these new needs will be part of the basis for hiring CEOs. Boards are now forced to look for people who have a commitment to corporate governance, people who are aware of the way corporate America appears to the world, people who are committed to improving the corporate image.

When it comes to failure to disclose, we are entering an era of zero tolerance. Let me relate a story that gives one board member's definition of that phrase. Not long ago, the chairman of the audit committee of a prominent company asked me to sit with him as he talked to his CEO about the approach the audit committee would want to take in the future. I think he was afraid for his life, but he said to the CEO, plainly and clearly: "This is now zero-tolerance time." The CEO asked what that meant. The audit-committee chairman replied: "If anything turns up resembling a preventable fraud in this company, you are fired—that very day."

That's zero tolerance, and under the new corporate governance process, zero tolerance will not be unusual—it will be the norm. Boards will have zero tolerance for CEOs regarding anything that resembles fraud, and they will expect CEOs to demonstrate the same attitude to the people who work for them. Quite simply, that is the only way they can all protect themselves. Board members also have fiduciary duties, and they must demonstrate that they are exercising them. They are going to be concerned about conveying their seriousness about their fiduciary duties to their CEO. They don't want to have to ask themselves later: Did I communicate clearly enough that this was really the new order of the day?

The Nineties Are Over—Bursting the Salary Bubble

What can CEOs do? They can start by recognizing that the nineties are over. For example, CEO-compensation expectations must decline. Gone is the era when a CEO could walk away with many millions of dollars in a year when the company wasn't doing particularly well. Boards will increasingly be structuring compensation arrangements based on performance rather than competitive market comparisons. I was sitting in a compensation committee meeting with a representative of a well-known compensation expert. He pointed out that the company's CEO was in the 14th percentile. The compensation committee was unimpressed. Rather than try to match other CEOs' packages, it took a different tack: We are not going to base compensation on market comparisons, the committee said. We need to base it on performance.

One thing is clear: CEO compensation is being brought under control. Options may still be part of the compensation mix, but options increasingly need to be designed to generate performance, not simply to encourage CEOs to push the envelope to get market price up. CEOs need to work with their boards on the rules governing when they can exercise their options. Should they be exercised during their tenure? Should they be exercised later?

Whose Board Is It, Anyway?

CEOs often talk about how they created their board and what criteria they use for choosing directors. Again, they have their heads in the nineties. Although the CEO will be consulted on board appointments, increasingly board nominating committees or governance committees—not CEOs—will drive the process of selecting new board members. More and more, we are seeing the same attitude that was expressed to me by John Smale, former non-executive chairman of GM and CEO of Procter & Gamble—and a pioneer in corporate governance. John told me that there was one thing he was going to do when he became non-executive chairman of GM: He was going to work with the board to pick the new directors and make it clear that they were being invited onto the board by the board—not by management.

Being a member of the board and being part of management are two very different jobs. Increasingly, it is the board that will profile potential board members and decide whom they need. At the same time, the pool of potential directors is undergoing considerable change. Under pressure to perform, CEOs are limiting the number of boards on which they serve. Meanwhile, boards are putting a premium on what a potential member can contribute, rather than seeking trophy directors.

Aside from the changes in how board members are selected, we are seeing renewed discussion of how they should be removed. To my knowledge, this is something that has never been done gracefully. The notion of term limits has been proposed by some but has drawn little support because it requires getting rid of people who are useful. A few companies have introduced a practice under which directors are required to submit their resignation automatically when they change jobs, leaving it up to the board to decide whether or not to accept it. This makes sense, as most board members are appointed because of their job and the expertise it encompasses. Unfortunately, past practice has shown that any policy aimed at removing nonperforming directors tends to collapse because nobody wants to tell a fellow board member to go away. I have yet to see a successful mechanism for getting bad people off the board, other than a strong leader—either the head of the governance committee or the chairman—who evaluates the board or acts on a board self-evaluation and can sit down with the board member in question and explain that it's just not working.

Separating the CEO and the Chairman

As boards become increasingly engaged in monitoring management, the issue of splitting the job of chairman and CEO is commanding more attention. After all, how do you monitor yourself? I always wondered how one could seriously manage this dual role, and it is becoming only more difficult. It is one thing to manage a weak board—but how about a strong one that's monitoring you? If the jobs are not split, it will be extremely difficult to determine when you're the chairman of the board running the board and when you're the CEO running the company. How do you take off your CEO hat and say, "Now I'm the chairman of the board—whom would I like to have come in and criticize me? Whom would I like to have come in and set my compensation? From whom am I willing to take criticism when things go wrong?"

The notion of requiring a non-executive chairman is unpopular among many corporate CEOs in the United States, but it works well in the context of the British system. Sir Adrian Cadbury, who conducted a landmark study of U.K. corporate governance, has pointed out that the job of leading the board is not the same as running the company. But one thing that is absolutely essential is that the relationship between the chair and the CEO has to be right. It worked at GM with John Smale as non-executive chairman and Jack Smith as CEO—well enough that they were able to resurrect the company together and never got in each other's hair.

While the chairman and the board must engage and scrutinize the CEO, the two need not be enemies. If a CEO looks at the board as a necessary evil, that is what the board will be. But most of the members of the board want the CEO to be successful. They hired the CEO, and they didn't do it to fail. The CEO cannot ignore the board, and it doesn't make sense to fight. The best strategy is to make the board a colleague—without ever losing that sense of creative tension that comes from remembering that the board works for the interest of the shareholders.

CHAPTER ELEVEN

A CEO Looks at the Director's Role

Harvey Golub, former chairman and CEO of American Express

Harvey Golub retired from American Express in 2001 after seven years as chairman and CEO. During his tenure, the company reached record earnings and the price of its shares increased sixfold. At the same time, American Express became one of the most respected service brands in the world. The outstanding performance of the company continued after his retirement.

Golub joined American Express in 1984 as president and CEO of IDS Financial Services (now known as American Express Financial Advisors). In 1990, he was named vice chairman of American Express and elected a member of the company's board of directors. He was named president of American Express in July 1991 and CEO in January 1993. His detailed knowledge about the role of directors comes from his service on the boards of Campbell Soup, Dow Jones, and Warnaco and as chairman of the board of AirClic, ClientLogic, and TH Lee Putnam Ventures. Shortly before his retirement, he was asked by *Business Week* if the job of CEO was getting harder. He responded that the job is "as hard today as it was two decades ago. . . . The difference is that today measures of CEO performance are much clearer than they were two decades ago, and boards are more willing to act on the basis of those measures."

WHAT IS THE ROLE of a board of directors? Obviously, it must represent the interests of the shareholders. But how to do that well in a modern, complex corporation? How to balance appropriate oversight with meddling? How to get the most out of a board? I'll offer some observations on these points.

Some argue that the complexity of today's large companies demands that board members devote more time to their role. And the job is obviously becoming more time-consuming. But one reaches a point at which the more involved a director becomes in the details of the company, the less able he or she is to maintain the independence that is crucial to his or her role. A company can allow more time (and pay for that time), but to ask independent directors to take all the time that would be required for in-depth understanding of every important element of the company, and then pay them based on their true market value, would turn them into highly paid employees who would be all but impossible to attract. Rather than part-time directors able to exercise independent judgment on behalf of shareholders, they could become virtually full-time quasi-managers.

A Board's Proper Focus: Strategy and CEO Performance

Let's take a step back and consider what shareholders actually need from board members: independence and mature judgment. Rather than expecting independent directors to master the details of a business, we need them to be able to see the big picture—and apply that knowledge to the decisions they are required to make.

What implication does this approach have for the way that boards actually function?

It means that boards must be sufficiently familiar with overall corporate strategy—and engaged in shaping it—that specific applications of the strategy may not even require significant board debate. Some may be surprised to hear that, but it is important to keep in mind that corporate decisions are most often not made in an ad-hoc fashion; they are made within a reasonably clear framework. Board members have to understand the strategic concepts being dealt with, so that the actual decisions that spring from the concepts flow logically.

Let me illustrate from my own experience at American Express. Early in my tenure, it was necessary to restructure the company, including divesting elements of Shearson, Lehman Bros., and other units. But board meetings never became a debate forum over any individual divestiture—except for some of the details. Before it ever came to approve a specific move, we had engaged the board in detailed discussions regarding our brand strategy and its implications on what we would buy or sell or own. When it came to the point of making a specific divestiture, such as Lehman Brothers, there was no need for a detailed discussion of that specific decision. The strategy was already in place; it had been reviewed and understood, and we did not have to rehash it.

The same principle applies to other issues. A good example is executive compensation, an important area for board oversight. Most executive-compensation plans are complex, with incentives carefully calibrated to align senior managers with corporate goals. Of necessity, executive-compensation plans are detailed, and the implications of all of those details are not often obvious on the surface. It would be very difficult for part-time corporate directors—or, for that matter, even full-time senior managers—to keep in mind each and every individual detail when reviewing each compensation decision and understand all the nuances and implications. Instead, what is important is that they understand the theory of the company's compensation plan, help shape it, support it, and hold executives accountable.

Very soon after taking over as CEO, I devoted a substantial part of a board meeting to explaining the theory behind the company's compensation plan, in relatively straightforward terms, to allow for understanding of the principles underlying the plan. Directors needed to understand what I was trying to achieve, so that when we reached the decision-making stage of any initiative, little or no debate was required on structure. We were simply implementing a strategy that had already earned common assent.

If a CEO and a board of directors are working properly together, the board should not be a decision-making body so much as a ratifying body. I viewed it as a failure if the board of American Express rejected a specific decision, such as a divestment or acquisition. That is certainly not because the board was in any way less than diligent in exercising its responsibilities. Quite the opposite. We made an extensive effort to select board members based on judgment, maturity, and intelligence as well as collegiality. The board was consistently independent and diligent. But we never made a specific decision that did not fit into a broad strategic context—and it was the strategic context in which the board was heavily involved and on which most of the debate centered.

For example, I never was in a position in which I had to explain that we wanted to buy a specific business because it gave us entrée into a particular kind of lending, and the importance of that move. The board knew why it was important and did not have to review the strategic goal. When it came to individual decisions, the board was actually ratifying the execution of elements of an overall strategy on which they had already been heavily consulted.

Directors: Why Limit a Good One?

Some argue that board members would be better able to immerse themselves in the details of running a company if they served on fewer boards; some corporate-governance experts propose limits on the number of boards on which a director should serve.

In my view, any arbitrary limit would be a mistake. In fact, one should be wary of any list of corporate-governance procedures, with all companies expected to simply check the boxes. The notion of a limit on board memberships is a good example of the shortcoming of check-the-boxes governance.

The reason that some individuals are directors of several companies is that they bring the most important qualities a board member must have—judgment, maturity, intelligence, and an ability to work in a collegial fashion. Why would we want to restrict people with these qualities from serving on a large number of boards and spreading their talent as widely as possible in corporate America?

A good example is Vernon Jordan, a former Washington lawyer and currently a senior managing director of Lazard. Some corporate governance gadflies would look at the number of boards on which he serves and conclude that he spreads himself too thin. Apparently they have never heard the old saying, "If you want something done right, ask a busy person." Vernon serves on a lot of boards because he provides valuable advice, which is why he has been recruited to join the boards of such companies as Bankers Trust, Dow Jones, Revlon, J.C. Penney, Xerox, and Sara Lee, as well as the Ford Foundation and Howard University. The fact that so many companies want Vernon Jordan on their board simply proves that you cannot dilute good judgment.

I served with Vernon on the board of Dow Jones, and he was also on the board of American Express. Based on his range of knowledge and judgment—and on the fact that he will say exactly what he thinks (diplomatically)—he quickly became one of the two or three directors with whom I consulted most often at American Express. In fact, I found that his service on other boards provided him with even greater insight on how corporate policies would likely be perceived and what people would want to know about them. If he serves on a dozen boards, that simply makes for a dozen lucky CEOs—and millions of fortunate shareholders.

The Need for Limits—Age or Term

Of course, not every board member is as effective as Vernon Jordan. Sometimes a board member just doesn't work out. He or she does not focus on the major issues, or fails to devote sufficient time, or is unable to work with the rest of the board in a collegial fashion. How to deal with the problem?

More often than not, trying to remove a board member smoothly is the corporate-governance equivalent of *Mission: Impossible*. It is one of the more divisive steps that one can take on a board, one that can poison an atmosphere so as to make it not worth the effort. The one time I found that the American Express board was having a problem with a director, I discussed the issue with a senior board member. We talked about the options for dealing with that director, and both of us concluded that seeking his departure from the board would not be worth the internal difficulties it would cause.

As a result of the difficulty in removing directors, companies sometimes end up living with directors who are not filling the role effectively. That is why I think that either time limits or age limits on board service are essential. Every so often, that means a board will lose an invaluable performer. But no single figure is indispensable, and there should always be enough experienced board members at any given time to ensure a smooth transition. Perhaps age should not be an automatic disqualifier. After all, age does not diminish wisdom; in fact, it may enhance it. Term limits would make more sense, but I am not aware of any company that imposes them. Age limits are the next best thing.

CEO-Board Relations: Three Pieces of Advice

Different CEOs have different ways of working with their board, and I would not try to prescribe one set of rules to apply to all companies. But I believe that a few principles are of value:

- The elements of a board's schedule should be set well in advance. At American Express, I set the key elements a year ahead of time, including where and when the off-site meetings would be held, and what strategic issues would command significant blocks of time and when.

  For example, in November I would give an assessment of how the company did over the year and review overall performance. In

January, we would conduct an extensive review of strategy. Obviously, some issues had to be dealt with as they emerged. But the goal was structure, planning, and consistency. These characteristics tend to provide discipline and focus. They also are essential to attracting good directors and getting the most out of them, given that the best board members tend to be busy people who need to be able to plan ahead of time.

Directors were interested in individual topics. I would take their concerns into account and always schedule discussions of those topics.

- It is helpful for a board to meet from time to time without the CEO present. In fact, it may be a good idea for a company to make it an internal rule requiring the board to do that. That would serve as a device to force the board to think about major issues as a group and provide an opportunity for board members to discuss issues privately without the risk of offending the CEO or creating bad relations. In my view, a CEO should prefer board members to meet by themselves from time to time. By encouraging directors to discuss issues that are gnawing at the back of their minds, it could head off issues before they reach a critical point.

Of course, board members don't always want to meet without the CEO. Early in my tenure, I arranged for the board to get together for a dinner meeting without me. Two weeks before the dinner was scheduled to be held, several directors called me and asked me to be there. They felt that the meeting would be more productive with the CEO present. But it makes sense to at least set up the opportunity. I should note that in today's environment, I would have encouraged the board to meet without me and would continue to do so on a regular basis, although I did not do so then.

- The next piece of advice I would offer is that the CEO should not try to be board members' best friend. Some believe that by keeping up an extensive schedule of private dinners and special events with directors, a CEO can build an atmosphere of rapport

> and friendship that will carry over into the boardroom. But the board is not the CEO's friend—it is the CEO's boss. The board of directors is not just a collection of individuals—it is an institution with a responsibility for representing the interests of shareholders. Friendship should never allow a CEO to get concurrence when it otherwise wouldn't be coming.

I would occasionally seek advice on specific situations from some of the members of my board. Other than that, I would not communicate with them a great deal between board meetings unless there was a critical, unexpected matter to review. Once a year or so, I would get together with each of them or get in touch to ask if there were any specific concerns they would like to raise or anything they felt they needed to be better informed about regarding the company.

The last piece of advice I would give a CEO is to be completely open and honest. Be careful to discuss the failures as well as the successes. Never surprise the board. Never ask it to vote on a complicated issue without explaining its nuances and risks.

The important challenge for the CEO is to keep the board on track. It is essential that directors be able to focus on the overall strategic issues and understand the company's strategic goals and how the business processes help advance them. On a good board, there is too much experience and judgment sitting around the table to waste it on anything of secondary importance.

PART III

Operational Excellence and the Pursuit of Strategy

It is impossible to gauge the success of a corporate leader without examining his or her impact on a company's overall performance. As our authors reveal in this section, a chief executive is deeply involved in the details of how a company improves the way it operates and meets its goals. The need for executive leadership in sparking better performance is especially important when a leader is trying to transform the company. The authors in this section tell us that such transformations cannot occur without a systematic method of motivating and measuring employees. Execution, we see, is not just the responsibility of employees but a necessary obsession of the focused CEO.

Robert Nardelli was no stranger to superb execution after his long career at GE. But, as he tells us, when he arrived as the new CEO at The Home Depot he discovered that the highly entrepreneurial retailer had none of the processes or company-wide practices that make good execution possible in the long run. While he deeply admired the decentralized culture that had made the company the world's fastest-growing retailer, Nardelli and his board realized that a different system of operational management was needed if the company was to set new milestones.

Jack Krol needed to introduce a whole range of new systems when he helped transform DuPont in the early 1990s. As he describes in his chapter, DuPont was a classic example of a highly bureaucratic and many-layered corporation that had lost its ability to be responsive. What was needed was a new structure for the entire

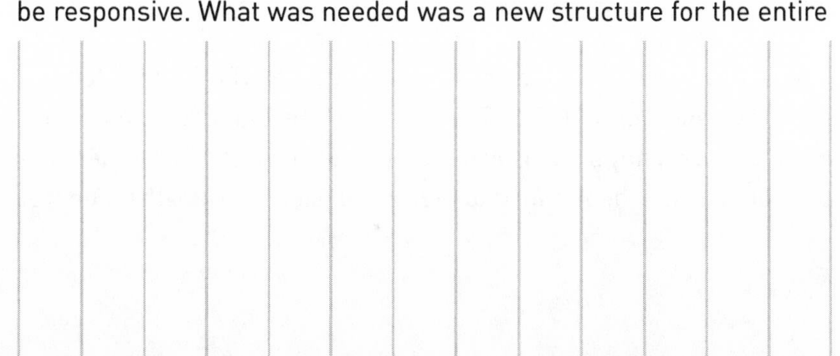

company that replaced dozens of layers of management with a much flatter organization—a step that eventually decreased the chemical giant's workforce by a third. Krol points out that stripping down the structure of the company was only the first part. The next was creating a system of sharing information so that all senior employees could see the numbers that drove the companies. Using these kinds of internal measurements, "the blue book" at DuPont has become an essential element of managing a large, diversified corporation.

How can a company use data? Josh Weston, writing about his long experience at ADP, explains that the proper use of internal measurements is indispensable for instilling peer-group pride—the strongest motivating force that senior managers have for moving employees in the same direction of the strategy. As Weston describes it, once the senior team at ADP understood how to properly measure the things inside their business they cared most about, they began creating metrics and benchmarks for every aspect of the company.

Poor measurements, of course, can be a problem. Weston describes how measuring the wrong things at ADP led to the wrong focus. Lawrence Weinbach, CEO of Unisys, describes how soft evaluations of employee performance led some employees at his company to think they were doing better than they actually were. For Weinbach, who led the company through a tremendous change from mainframe builder to IT consulting, communicating with employees is one of the most important tools for transformation. He makes the case that simple, blunt, unambiguous communication to employees allows a CEO to deliver bad news and make sure that execution is effective because no one misunderstands the company's goals or strategy.

Understanding why execution can be more important than strategy is the reluctant conclusion reached by David Fuente, former chairman and CEO of Office Depot. In 1996, he launched a bid to acquire the company's chief rival, Staples. Soon after the merger was announced, the deal ran into fierce resistance from the Federal

Trade Commission on antitrust grounds. Within a year, the merger was blocked, and the company had to go back to figuring out how to compete rather than integrate. Fuente, now retired from Office Depot, looks back at the mistakes the company made in dealing with the government agency and creating a confrontational environment that set the deal up to fail. His reflections give us not only some basic rules for execution but also some enduring advice on how to deal with one of the most influential agencies of the federal government.

Taken together, the chapters in this section remind us that the work of the CEO is not focused solely on buffing a company's reputation or huddling with senior advisors on long-term strategy. CEOs who are trying to push their companies in a new direction must get deep into the details of operational excellence in order to align the thinking and behavior of an entire company.

CHAPTER TWELVE

When A Company Has to Grow Up

Robert L. Nardelli, chairman, president, and CEO of The Home Depot

Bob Nardelli spent nearly thirty years at General Electric, where he held a number of leadership positions in areas as diverse as lighting and transportation. When he became the chief executive of GE Power Systems, he was one of three internal candidates to succeed Jack Welch as GE's CEO. In late November 2000, when the job went to Jeffery Immelt, The Home Depot rushed in to make Nardelli its new CEO and, a few months later, its chairman.

To both those inside and outside of The Home Depot, the world's largest home improvement retail chain, the choice of Nardelli was surprising. Steeped in the GE culture of process and carefully structured management, and unfamiliar with the culture of retail sales, Nardelli was an outsider entering a deeply entrepreneurial company. Even as it surpassed the $50 billion revenue mark, The Home Depot stuck to its freewheeling style and loose structure.

It became apparent to The Home Depot's board of directors that the company had reached the point where it needed strong, centralized management if its success was going to continue in a much more competitive market. To find a high caliber manager with this kind of experience it clearly needed to reach outside of the company. In this chapter, Nardelli tells the story of how a CEO brought discipline and management processes to a company very much unaccustomed to them. As he explains here, in less than three years he learned a great deal about the details of the retail business and what worked and didn't work at The Home Depot. At the same time, he pursued a strategy that required the company to embrace fundamental changes in its business practices, yet still maintain the entrepreneurial character that made it successful in the first place. The early results have shown that The Home Depot can be a much more rigorously managed company as it maintains leadership of its category and becomes a more mature business.

SOON AFTER I arrived at the The Home Depot as the new CEO in December 2000, I suggested sending an e-mail to all our store managers to share some thoughts with them. I was told politely that I couldn't do that.

My first reaction was puzzlement: Had I breached some unwritten rule governing The Home Depot's culture that discouraged an executive from using such impersonal communication? No, the answer was more mundane. The Home Depot didn't have the technological capability to send e-mail from my Atlanta office to our then-1,100 store managers across the country.

I mention this episode not to point out a weakness of the organization, but rather to emphasize the strength of the company's decentralized culture that greeted me. The Home Depot is, along with Wal-Mart, one of the greatest retail stories in U.S. business history. Founded in 1978 by visionaries Bernard Marcus, Ken Langone, and Arthur Blank, the company helped launch a retail revolution, changing the way home improvement goods were delivered and merchandised to customers.

The company's growth has been staggering. Within its first seven years, the company opened its first signature 140,000-square-foot store—the vast orange-trimmed warehouse-style store that would soon become a fixture across the country. That year, the company had 60 stores altogether, 6,600 employees, and $1 billion in revenue. It never stopped growing. Ten years later, the company celebrated 40 straight quarters of record financial results, the opening of its five-hundredth store, the employment of 98,000 associates, and a revenue base of nearly $20 billion. In 2001, it became the youngest retailer to break the $50 billion revenue mark (having also held that distinction for the $30 billion and $40 billion marks, the company has gone on since then to become only the second retailer *ever* to deliver $1 billion in net income in a single quarter).

Throughout this period, The Home Depot culture was aggressively entrepreneurial. Often described by the business press as a "cowboy culture," The Home Depot leadership consciously encouraged the independence of store managers. These store managers made their own decisions on merchandizing, wages, store layout, and just about everything else. They followed no central rules for hiring or promoting. Nothing better illustrated the decentralized culture than the fact that the corporate headquarters is formally known as the "store support center." The message couldn't have been clearer: Atlanta's store support center's sole purpose was to boost the stores and stay out of the way.

It was in this loose, fiercely independent management environment that an e-mail from the CEO sending advice, information, or instruction from Atlanta seemed out of place. I understood it. I admired it. And I knew it had to change.

The change required for The Home Depot also meant considerable change for me. I had spent thirty years in dozens of different roles in the manufacturing sector. Twenty-six of those years were at GE—the last five as CEO of GE Power Systems—where the affection for process, centralization, and measurement was legendary.

My years at GE were the best education in management anyone could get. Jack Welch had built a system that, above all, produced leaders, and I was lucky to be among them. However, in December 2000 I was making a leap for which even the GE experience couldn't prepare me: moving from an established, process-driven manufacturing environment to one of the world's fastest-growing retailers with a fiercely independent and entrepreneurial spirit. To complicate matters I was also one of the few outsiders ever to take over the reins from the founders of a Fortune 25 company.

Yet in some ways, the challenges I faced coming to The Home Depot were not unique. The company had long ceased to be a startup despite the fact that it continued to act like one. The Home Depot was maturing and dealing with the growing pains that are an unavoidable feature of a successful business. In my view, the company needed to awaken to the reality that it must focus on people, process, and systems in order to continue to expand and grow.

This process of introducing centralized procedures and regular measurement systems into a company unaccustomed to them is a stage that every growing company undergoes. It is a necessary and fundamental part of corporate growth. Business leaders from the CEO level down the management chain all struggle with this challenge. After less than three years on the job, I would never claim that I've surmounted it. But in working with colleagues at The Home Depot and observing how other companies have dealt with the same problem, I've come to recognize a few essential steps required to bring operational excellence to a company that has little experience with formal management process.

This chapter focuses on four of them: getting to know the company; centralizing information and process; making a few big changes quickly; and building a culture based around people.

Getting to Know the Company

I had virtually no transition period into my new job. I had been one of three candidates to succeed Jack Welch at GE, but after Jack let me know that Jeff Immelt would be appointed, I received a call from Kenneth Langone, a brilliant investor who served on both the GE and The Home Depot boards. He had been watching my career closely and helped arrange an introduction to the search firm and the selection committee at The Home Depot. Five days later, I showed up at their headquarters to report for work.

I knew immediately I was on foreign terrain. At GE Power Systems, I had focused on building state-of-the-art turbine engines for utility companies and other large-scale energy projects. We forged partnerships that were months in the making and resulted in multimillion-dollar sales. At The Home Depot, by contrast, the company made nearly a billion transactions a year. Each week, more than twenty million customers walked through the stores and most sales were under $100. In retail, there is no such thing as a backlog of sales. You have to earn it every day.

And, unlike other commercial businesses, retail is heavily dependent upon the biggest variable of all—people.

Nevertheless, the looming challenges for The Home Depot were not unfamiliar. After years of double-digit earnings growth, the landscape was clearly changing. The boom of the 1990s faded into a short recession. New competitors emerged, creating head-to-head contests in some markets. Many of our stores were showing their age, and customer service—once a company hallmark—was slipping.

There were other challenges as well. As the number of stores grew, the sheer scope of the company became harder to manage. Many people close to the company recognized that what got the company to the first $50 billion most certainly could not get us to the next $50 billion. And with the competitive landscape changing, status quo was not an option. As I got to know the company, it became clear to me that only better execution and implementation was going to deliver the improved customer service that was critical to driving sales and growth. Making operations more efficient across the company, spurring innovation, and becoming more attuned to changing tastes and preferences of customers were essential ingredients in The Home Depot's future.

My job as the new, outsider CEO wasn't suddenly to proclaim big changes. I needed to get to know the company from the ground up, taking time to absorb the culture and learn how the stores and the managers operated. In this, I was fortunate to have the partnership and support of cofounder Bernie Marcus, who worked closely with me during my first year of transition. Indeed, the entire board of directors helped me to understand the company better, even as they embraced the new directions I was pushing.

I quickly discovered that we had very little data from which to make fact-based decisions. It turned out that many of our vendors knew more about The Home Depot than we knew about them.

So I started to get to know the company through an ambitious schedule of talking to store managers, calling up suppliers, listening to Wall Street analysts, and meeting with associates at every level. I visited stores constantly, stopping in as many as six cities a week, with six or seven store visits in each location. Most of the time I would show up unannounced. My goal was not to catch associates off guard, but rather to see the stores the way our customers do. After a year of such visits, it would take me less than five minutes inside a Home Depot store to determine how well it was managed.

Store visits also allowed me to learn from the group I wanted to hear from most: our store managers and sales associates who spend their working days in the aisles, many of whom have devoted their careers to The Home Depot. I still commit a big portion of my time to meeting with and hearing from our front-line associates. During a recent 12-month period, I met with every one of our more than 1,500 store managers at least three times through my visits and at a variety of forums and leadership meetings.

My immediate goal was to be visible and listen, learn, and respond. We initiated the company's first-ever employer of choice survey to gauge our associates' opinions and to help us shape the policies and programs that affect them. Eighty-one percent of our 280,000 associates completed the survey. To me, the most telling—and encouraging—news was that 76 percent of our associates said they planned to be working at The Home Depot next year. Although I was making a number of changes at the senior management level (and many executives had simply decided to leave when founder Bernie Marcus stepped down as chairman soon after I arrived), most of our associates showed no great sense of despair.

But they also acknowledged in their answers that the company was due for change. The fierce pace of growth had allowed smaller administrative and management problems to fester, and the associates knew that we needed to make changes.

That was a healthy sign. Spending time in the stores and with associates made me more convinced of a general rule that was as true for The Home Depot as it had been for GE: The rate of internal change has to be greater than the rate of external change. If not, you are moving backward. One of the great strengths at GE was that even average ideas were implemented faster, better, and quicker than the competition, which gave the company a competitive advantage. I wanted The Home Depot to develop the flexibility to embrace change at a similarly rapid pace.

Meeting that challenge required adopting a new way of thinking. The fact was we could no longer operate as a start-up company. We needed to keep our entrepreneurial spirit, but redirect it toward execution. To make that shift, The Home Depot needed the people, processes, and systems discipline of an established company so that we could deliver predictable and sustainable growth.

Creating a Hybrid Organization

My intention was never to try and remake The Home Depot into a GE. Instead, my senior team helped us move toward a hybrid organization—one that gave us consistent execution without losing elements of the entrepreneurial energy that was so important to the culture. One of my first steps toward that goal was to flatten the organization in order to have more exposure to the company's vast operations. The number of direct reports to the CEO more than doubled to 22. I tried to create an executive team that truly sat around the figurative "roundtable." I wanted a group of leaders who interacted with one another and felt comfortable applying their expertise to every part of the company, not just their niche responsibility. Together we established a Monday noontime call where we exchange reports and get a better understanding of what is happening across the company.

This flatter, more transparent leadership style is an essential part of centralization. Often when one hears about a rigorously centralized organization, a common assumption is that it must be heavily layered and hierarchical. That is a myth, or at least a mistake. The purpose of centralization is to collect information, share it, and apply it. The more senior the people engaged in that process, the more effective the centralization.

Because of the bottom-up culture I described, central procedures of any sort were in short supply at The Home Depot. When I arrived, the company had no chief counsel to establish company-wide compliance standards. There was no central merchandising unit; every store manager orchestrated his or her own purchases. Data on aggregated sales and performance across the company were hard to come across.

Anyone who is a graduate of GE's management training can be fairly accused of being consumed with the pursuit of data. But as I quickly learned, data are even more important in the retail game, given the speed with which you need to make decisions to respond to customer preferences or competitive challenges. Solid measurement systems were also needed to understand our workplace, our market, and the communities we served.

To deal with this data in a smart way and make the information part of our short- and long-term thinking, we introduced the SOAR system—a strategic, operating, and resource planning process—which lets my senior team think about our strategy in a more organized way.

In the modern corporation, you cannot adequately sift through the daily data of a business without a serious commitment to information systems. On this front, The Home Depot was behind the curve. Today the company is investing 12 times more on IT systems than it did when I arrived.

We began measuring as much about the company as we could. We had district managers measure whether all customers were greeted as they came in the door. We tracked at what time of the day sales were made and then aligned our associates' work schedules to match the demand. I paid particular attention to out-of-stock data. I learned that "out-of-stock" doesn't necessarily mean that the store is out of stock; the product is likely somewhere in storage, perhaps on a shelf overhead. But what every out-of-stock message means is that a sale has been lost—a critical missed opportunity in a business as competitive as ours.

By the end of my first year on the job, The Home Depot had recruited a new chief information officer. He recognized immediately that we, like so many companies, were handicapped by a stack of legacy mainframe computers that made it very difficult to retrieve and analyze sales data. He is helping lead our effort to bring the company to the cutting edge of the information revolution.

In retail, that really requires two types of technology. The first allows the management and sales team to collect and act on data in real time. To do that requires replacing legacy computer systems with a true data warehouse, which we launched in the fall of 2002. With a data warehouse, executives and store managers have a continuous flow of data on business performance. It permits our senior managers—including me—to keep a computerized "dashboard" in each office: a full screen of real-time data and critical indicators about everything from inventory to the sale of high-profit items.

We also introduced other, smaller technology that helped centralize knowledge. For example, mobile ordering carts—essentially electronic messaging systems—allow an associate working in one of our store aisles to scan a bar code and find out what products are out of stock. We also digitized our certified receiving process so that inventories could be updated constantly.

The second critical technology investment is the one that helps the customers themselves. For example, lines at cash registers at some stores had eroded the company's reputation for fast service. To fix the problem, we began to install self-scanning checkouts, already a common sight in national grocery chains but an industry first for our category.

Not all centralization requires sophisticated high-tech. Some of it is a matter of simple efficiency. When I arrived I learned that the company had more than 150 different associate performance evaluation forms; today we have just one. Training, too, was inconsistent and fragmented. It seemed to me that in a corporation that values its people and its culture, a uniform training system was even more critical as the company grew. For example, on core curriculum development we are able to have a few specialists develop key learning modules and deploy them via e-learning kiosks in the training room of every store. This relatively simple step suddenly meant that associates were getting the same high-quality instruction in a manner that was much easier to deliver than with thousands of trainers creating and delivering material in the field.

We also improved the way we communicated with our associates. In break rooms in every store, we began broadcasting an internal TV channel in a format similar to CNN's "Headline News." The TV broadcasts allowed us for the first time to reach all our stores with timely information about the company and product knowledge selling tips. Smart centralization has to mean never missing an opportunity to share a message and communicate with associates or to give them the knowledge to be successful in working with customers. These are, of course, not complicated things, but they are essential to creating a cohesive company that has a common focus, which is, after all, the real purpose of centralization.

A Few Bold, Quick Moves

As conscious as I was about moving too quickly, I knew some changes couldn't wait. Once you identify a few key changes, my advice is to launch quickly and implement even faster.

Our senior team focused on two ripe targets for change. The first was the way the company purchased the products we sold in our stores. As I mentioned, there was no centralized process for merchandising. Instead, we had nine different merchandising offices with little in common. Some merchandising offices were buying identical products for a variety of different prices. Purchases came with different terms and conditions, depending on who was buying. More troubling was that the confidence level in the merchandising offices varied widely. We concluded that there had to be a central merchandising unit that would be based in Atlanta.

There is always reluctance by managers to make this type of radical change in the way a company does business for fear of tampering with the core culture of the organization. Yet many company practices are misidentified as deep cultural traits when in fact they are just a management habit that has been acquired along the way. That was the case with merchandising at The Home Depot. I believed that the entrepreneurial spirit of the business resided in the ability to meet the needs of customers and complete transactions. A better merchandising system would only improve the sales associates' and store managers' ability to do that.

We decided to make the change on a single day. After several months of front-end analysis at the functional and operational levels, on a Saturday morning in the spring of 2001, our leadership team gathered and in one day completely re-engineered the merchandising function of a $50 billion enterprise. It started with agreeing on the strategy, the structure, the organization, and the new processes we would establish and it ended with selecting the talent and making offers that same day. By the end of that Saturday, we had made decisions and had commitments for 29 new officers to lead this new organization.

The impact on our bottom line was almost immediate. Reducing the inefficiencies of the decentralized merchandising system generated an enormous financial return for the business. It was part of what helped us go from negative $800 million cash a year to posting reserves of $4 billion two years later. Our gross margin also grew to its highest level ever. Centralizing merchandising also let us keep track of where everything was going. The level of our "shrink"—the amount of inventory that is stolen, mislabeled, or misrecorded—was reduced considerably. In a company with 30,000 SKU's, or products, in stock, centralizing merchandising company-wide was a necessary step.

The other large-scale change we introduced in my first six months was our Service Performance Improvement (SPI). Our goal here was to recapture the high-quality service that the company had been losing by setting down a few basic rules and measurements that would apply to every store. The most central one was how the arrival of new inventory would be treated. Until the launch of SPI, arriving inventories would be unpacked in the aisles, often making it inconvenient for customers to reach products. For too long that custom had been attributed to the warehouse style of our stores. But, the fact was that it was taking too much time and pulling associates away from helping customers. So we established a simple rule: All new deliveries could only be packed out at night.

SPI contained a number of other steps to ensure that stores were customer-friendly, orderly, and clean. The goal of this, in combination with our store-remodeling program, has been to make each store "grand-opening ready" every single day.

None of these steps was a revolution. But in the unstructured culture of Home Depot, we were trying to send a clear message: There were certain company-wide policies that, if followed, would help associates focus on the business of serving customers. Store managers would be evaluated on their ability to implement these policies. By launching these policies quickly, along with centralized merchandising, we eliminated the opportunity for second-guessing. The goals were to improve efficiency, establish company-wide practices, and demonstrate that the company could improve its performance. Getting our structure right made that easier.

A Culture Built Around People

The centralization I have described here came about as we began to place more emphasis on the value of our people and in our efforts to respond to them as genuine assets of the company.

The year I was hired, we had 225,000 associates. We would hire an additional 25,000 people during my first year on the job. In the more competitive environment we faced, it was impossible not to conclude that the associates we had on the floor of our stores, their knowledge about the products, and their ability to help customers were important factors that contributed to the core of our business model.

In addition to listening to associates through store visits, surveys, and focus groups, I was determined to create a strategy to develop their careers, improve their skills, and recruit even more experienced and skilled personnel.

One of my first hires was my chief human resources officer—a position that had been vacant for nearly a year. I selected someone whom I not only trusted, but someone whom I viewed as a strategic partner who could help me rapidly implement the needed changes in the organization. As one of the largest employers in the world, we needed a world-class system for managing our human capital.

Of special concern was how we dealt with our people. I felt I had come out of GE with the ability to assess talent, and I wanted to stay intimately involved in personnel issues. I introduced a new process that allowed me to meet and interview every candidate for an officer position in the company. And, with my new chief of human resources, I put together a regular schedule of associate meetings that were heavily focused on getting to know our top people. A typical HR review for me began with a meeting with division or functional leaders and a review of all the senior personnel. I would then meet their staffs in one-on-one sessions, followed by hosting two roundtable lunches with high-potential associates. After completing the HR review in the afternoon, we would host a town hall meeting for all associates, then fly to the next city and do it all over again. During the first six months on the job, I spent at least 50 percent of my time on such personnel issues.

Revamping our training, or learning, as we call it, was critical to our HR effort, not just because I believed in it, but because associates wanted and needed it. Many of our associates on the floor felt inadequately prepared for the questions customers were asking. Just as important, learning is vital to our growth plans. Too many companies have both ambitious plans to expand and plenty of opportunity. But unless you have the right people already in the pipeline and ready to take on responsibility, growth will always be a burden. You simply can't hire to meet all the demands of new business. That is why, while we were cutting costs across the company, we were also investing in our associates to "appreciate" their value for our long-term competitive advantage.

We practically started our effort from scratch. We revamped the core curriculum for all associates. We created a leadership forum that every store manager and district manager would attend for a week. It includes competitive simulations, role-playing, and business diagnostics to help our front-line managers understand their role as business leaders. We put computer-learning workstations into every store so that associates could quickly learn how to use new products in stock.

Executive leadership and the creation of a cadre of managers who would be prepared to become executives one day was another priority of learning. We created both internal and external pipelines to build our bench, including a two-year rotational program for 700 young people with college degrees and an additional 300 former junior military officers to prepare for store leadership. We would recruit experienced leaders from other businesses and industries and put them on an executive management fast track. We began to identify early on high-potential candidates and immediately make them assistant store managers.

Today the company "invests" 19 million hours a year in learning. Our executive training program alone represents an investment of a penny per share. But for that marginal amount, we are growing our talent and teaching them the skills that will allow them to develop from "operating a box" to "leading a business" and ensuring that the company has the future leadership capacity to grow and lead a $100 billion organization.

The Well-Managed Company

Thirty years ago, American business was filled with highly centralized corporations laden with procedures and policy manuals. They were thick with layers of management and bureaucracy. When faced with international competition or the arrival of new technology, they were slow to respond.

Companies such as The Home Depot were created to be the opposite of these organizations. Entrepreneurial, comfortable with taking risks, and built on venture capital, their loose structure permitted rapid growth and complete business flexibility. Over the last decade, all successful companies—even well-established ones—have had to reinvent themselves to be as limber as these start-ups.

At the same time, growing companies have to learn how to maintain their innovation, their customer focus, and their competitiveness. That is a much harder task as a business takes on more associates, more locations, and faces more intense business challenges. Harder, but even more important because it is precisely as companies mature that they risk losing the spark that made them grow in the first place. For that reason, a company that wants to keep growing needs to deploy the right tools and practices to determine not only whether it is on course, but also whether the chosen course is the right one.

Bringing those tools and practices to a company doesn't require a deep expertise in the industry. But it does require creating a structure that allows you to understand how the company operates at every level while, at the same time, building the talent to fuel the future. That structure has shown results. As I approached my third year at the company, The Home Depot was enjoying the highest average sales ticket ever and the stock price was rising. We were building a bright future on the foundation of a proud past.

None of this happened overnight. During my rapid transition to

The Home Depot, I had much to learn about the company's proud culture and the details of the retail world, and I cannot overemphasize how important it is to make a successful transition before you can begin a transformation.

From my experience, about 70 percent of leadership skills are portable across industries. The balance is derived from an intensive and committed deep dive into the new business. Leadership, talent assessment, the ability to measure performance, and the willingness to lead change have turned out to be as necessary to the transformation of The Home Depot as they were in a variety of different businesses at GE.

CHAPTER THIRTEEN

Streamlining the Overmanaged Company

John Krol, retired chairman and CEO of E.I. du Pont de Nemours

E.I. du Pont de Nemours, known widely as DuPont, has been one of the largest American corporations for more than 200 years. The family company started in the gunpowder and explosives business but over time expanded into chemicals, paint, pharmaceuticals, energy, biotechnology, and agricultural products.

Through the 1970s and 1980s, DuPont's breadth and diversity contributed to both its success and its weakness. In an economy that valued speed and flexibility, the company had become highly structured, with separate management structures overseeing a vast array of businesses and products.

Jack Krol knew the DuPont system well—he had spent his career at the company, arriving as a chemist in 1963. After serving in a variety of marketing, manufacturing, and business leadership positions across the company, Krol became vice chairman in 1992 under CEO Ed Woolard. Together they began a restructuring process that dramatically changed the way the company was managed. When Krol became CEO three years later, the company had shifted directions, shedding businesses that no longer made sense for it and continuing to acquire companies that would expand its role as player in the life-sciences industry.

Although Krol retired from the company in 1998, he remains active on corporate boards. Most recently, he joined the board of Tyco International and was appointed lead director.

IN 1991, DuPont received some troubling news from the CEO of a company that had been doing business with us for at least two decades. He told us that the company would have to cut off its business with us. We were not cost-competitive, and that was making his business uncompetitive. He told us that our company had so many layers that we had become unresponsive; it took too long to get an answer from us when one was needed. Quite simply, he was concerned that we were going to put him out of business.

Talk about a wake-up call! This was a client who purchased nearly $400 million a year from us. Fortunately, we managed to hang on to that account. And we managed to absorb a crucial lesson: The problems facing our business were not just the typical challenges associated with a recession. They were the challenges of globalization, the emergence of a new economic order that would require a new level of competitiveness.

For years, DuPont's huge middle management had been very slow to make change. That was not unusual. It is in human nature to see change as a threat, and to resist it for as long as possible. But human nature or not, the company could not continue to fall behind as the world moved forward. I was vice chairman of DuPont at the time, and it was clear to me and Ed Woolard, the chairman and CEO, that we had to drive change or it was going to drive us out of business. Along with a key leadership group made up of a few of our top executives, we shook up the senior management ranks, a task that was made easier by the fact that many were coming due for retirement. We changed the organizational structure and put in place new processes that would lead to lower costs and significantly improve efficiency, and we dramatically improved the efficiency of our capital expenditures. We focused on productivity and innovation, recognizing that would be the only path to growing shareholder value—in fact, to surviving—in the globalized era. We pursued a transformation from a company that was based on fibers, polymers, and chemicals to one that would achieve more than a third of its earnings from the life sciences, such as biotech, agritech, and pharmatech. As part of expanding our agribusiness, in 1999 DuPont bought full ownership of Pioneer Hi-Bred International, the largest seed-corn company in the world (increasing our stake from 20 percent).

We were shaping the message we would deliver to shareholders, but our first task was to bring it to life within the company. Looking ahead in the early 1990s, we had to make a big change in the culture. DuPont had to shift to a culture based on facing reality (recognizing what the world required of us); a culture based on specificity, speed, and accountability; a culture based on anticipating and embracing the need for "step-change"—a term I will explain—rather than responding to it incrementally.

Facing Reality

In trying to change a company, the first thing that has to be changed is its way of thinking. At DuPont, we were suffering from a problem that afflicts many businesses that fail to keep up with the times—a disconnect between the expectations of the marketplace and investors and our capabilities, between the expectations we were raising and our ability to meet them.

Nothing is more demoralizing to employees than consistently failing to achieve their targets for revenue, profit, productivity, and other key metrics. The difference between consistently achieving expectations and consistently failing to is the difference between a winning spirit and a demoralized one. I saw it firsthand at DuPont, and I've heard about it elsewhere: An organization that consistently fails to meet expectations is an organization that will collectively throw up its hands. It is important that a company understand its capacity and focus on improving its ability to deliver rather than inflating expectations.

Obviously, a company that fails to meet expectations will also pay the inevitable price in terms of investor confidence. It doesn't make sense to lowball expectations, but it *does* make sense to put out a message to investors that is in line with reality and shared throughout the company. That is why it is also important to avoid complicating the message and, therefore, confusing the investment community. Nothing can undercut a company's value needlessly as quickly as a throwaway remark. In an informal discussion with analysts, there is always a temptation to make some generalizations about future success or increased performance. Even if true, these remarks become distractions. Everyone from the CEO on down has to understand the message that the company is trying to convey to the market and stick to it. If you appear to promise too little, that will have an immediate negative impact on share value. If you appear—even for a moment—to promise too much, you will pay the price later. Either way, the investment community will remember it—and they won't let you forget it. It is important to shape a message to investors that is accurate, credible, positive, and consistent. It is important to face reality—and convey it.

Of course, it is not enough for a company to face reality. It is also necessary to shape it. This was the key to IBM's success under Lou Gerstner. It was a lumbering giant that developed a clear direction that its competitors had to respond to. GE has been shaping the reality of its business for years. But in a competitive environment these sorts of changes can happen only if a company can meet its customers' needs quickly.

Speed

The incident I described involving a longtime customer that threatened to cut off its relationship with DuPont illustrates the importance of speed. In a global economy with seemingly instant communications, speed of decision-making, execution, and delivery are essential. The experience with the customer that almost fired us made me realize this. Speed had become a major competitive differentiator. Of course, to deliver results quickly, an organization has to be lean. There cannot be too many decision-making hoops to jump through from the point of customer contact to the level in the organization where someone can make a policy decision that will actually ensure customer satisfaction.

DuPont, however, was structured like the military. So were most American companies. That may have made sense decades ago, but it doesn't in today's global economy. We were structured with many layers of management because, without systems or processes and without a lot of automation, there was no other way to oversee thousands of employees doing thousands of different tasks. For example, in our plants we had a supervisor for every five or so people. Today at most companies, one supervisor for every fifty to one hundred people is sufficient.

Prior to the 1990s, layer over layer of management at DuPont made it difficult to respond to the need for change and speed. Our organizational structure effectively built those layers into the system. We had very large departments such as Fibers, Chemicals, and Polymers. Each of them had thousands of employees, and each operated as an independent business with its own infrastructure and internal management structure. The Polymers department, for example, had its own resources—finance, engineering, human-resources, and so on—residing within the business. So did the Fibers department. Within each of these massive departments, there were important products that also had their own layers of management. Lycra, for example, was housed within the Fibers department, but there was a separate HR and engineering staff just for the Lycra business unit. On top of all that, DuPont headquarters contained the central corporate layers of management, each with its own committee structure.

Our decision to "delayer" the company fundamentally changed DuPont. The company had become reminiscent of medieval Europe, carved into duchies containing fiefdoms. Our goal was to eliminate the behemoth departments and focus on the main products—Lycra, nylon, Kevlar, polyester, Teflon, and other major businesses—and turn each into a strategic business unit. The result was the creation of seventeen integrated organizations.

The goal was to have no more than one layer between the CEO and the leader of these units, and within the units no more than one or two layers between its leader and, for example, a salesman. Most of the strategic units reported to me—at the time, I was company vice chairman.

It was a monumental change. The restructuring and other productivity increases meant phasing out roughly 40,000 people—a third of our workforce. We recognized that it had to be done quickly or would never get done at all. Had we proposed these changes to be implemented over several years, people in the organization would have changed careers or moved on, and we would have lost the commitment. We would have also faced the problem of entrenched management dragging its feet and seeing if it could wait out the change and survive—a common tactic whenever these type of changes are proposed. Most important, when large-scale layoffs are necessary, it is simply unfair to employees to extend it over several years. So we moved quickly. In about twenty-four months, we restructured DuPont and created an entirely new way of doing business and making internal decisions. A short while after we implemented the changes, the customer we almost lost came to us and remarked, "This is like a new world here."

Accountability

One thing that an organization has to avoid is soft commitments—forecasts by business units that are continually revised, to the extent that no business-unit assessment is any firmer than a bathroom sponge. In the 1970s and '80s, more often than not, business units at DuPont would make a forecast, then simply revise it, usually downward, as the year progressed. We were dealing with constantly shifting forecasts, and it reached the point at which it seemed easier to put energy into explaining why the forecast had to be revised than to try to actually meet it.

The only way to address that problem is by providing incentives that are clearly targeted to ensure accountability. We shifted the reward system so that 60 percent of a business leader's incentive compensation was tied to performance at meeting his or her specific objectives, measured against metrics such as productivity and profitability. There was still a reward based on overall corporate performance—40 percent of the incentive pay—but the shift to individual and business-unit rewards changed the culture dramatically. Forecasts became real commitments rather than moving targets. Instead of simply revising their commitments, managers focused on how to meet them. If circumstances changed, their goal became to make up the difference by improving performance. A culture that was superb at explaining an inability to meet commitments was transformed into a culture that was superb at innovative thinking to meet commitments even when circumstances changed.

Along with incentives, accountability depends on access to the right information. The CEO and the senior management team have to know what is going on beneath the surface. That is why the computerization and networking of information systems are so important. At DuPont, information was at one time a monopoly in the hands of a few hundred people who exclusively controlled and communicated it in the business units. When full-scale use of computers was introduced, it was like the Soviet Union collapsing. Information that was previously hoarded suddenly became easy to obtain. People throughout the organization could share in it.

I cannot overemphasize the importance of accountability; it should be a corporate mantra. It makes speed and efficiency possible.

Specificity

Accountability demands specific measurements. Quite simply, the numbers have to mean something. Soft commitments have to be firmed up.

We came up with a method for doing that at DuPont. We introduced something called the "blue book." That book became the performance bible for strategic business unit leaders, and other senior people throughout the company. It wasn't too popular at first, because it provided a mechanism for tying managers down to specific performance commitments. But it became widely accepted once its value became clear. It made the benchmarks for performance clear, and all of our business-unit heads were able to understand much better how their own business was performing and why, and also to see how their own unit was doing in relation to them.

The blue book contained all of the key performance-expectation metrics—revenue, fixed costs, productivity—for every unit. The book did not gather dust in a file cabinet. It was used on an ongoing basis.

For each business, the blue book had a page of key financials and the commitments for the year, which had to be updated at least once a month by all responsible senior managers and business-unit heads. On the same page, the book contained the business unit's costs, revenue, and variable costs for the previous year. On one page, I could see before me a clear picture of not only the bottom line profits, but also the key drivers of the bottom line. This allowed for a much deeper discussion of the areas that needed focus. Until we instituted the blue book, there was no central repository of information that could provide for meaningful comparisons. Once or twice a month, we were able to look at how the businesses were doing, instead of relying on how the business leaders *said* they were doing. What the blue book did was give us a tool for measuring performance in real time, instead of waiting until the end of the quarter or the end of the year to find out whether we had hit our targets. What we did was make the company an open book. It was no longer possible to hide in plain sight.

That was an important thing about the blue book: the cultural change it engendered. Senior managers knew that they would have to meet with me or Ed Woolard throughout the year, and they knew that I would be working from the basis of up-to-date data, rather than subjective, secondhand assessments. We instituted that change when I was vice chairman of the company, and I carried responsibility for it with me when I became CEO. I was convinced—and still am—that a company must have specific tools for accountability.

Changing the Evolutionary Mind-Set

New systems to ensure accountability and eliminate layers of decision-making were important, but the crucial challenge isn't only changing systems—it is changing the corporate mind-set. That meant changing the way in which our employees understood our business and even changing the way they worked.

It is necessary to achieve what I call "step change"—jolting a company's leaders out of an evolutionary mind-set in which they believe that change will evolve slowly on its own and making step change part of the company's accepted culture—whether it be in strategy, tactics, or operations.

One example of an important area in which DuPont had to be proactive is its environmental impact. The company had always been focused on compliance with the law. We were determined that we had to broaden our thinking. We could not just focus on compliance; we had to see the environmental issue as a business proposition and take a leadership position. We had to see it as a productivity issue, continually focused on making the next unit of production with fewer resources. We were treating "waste"—or at least what was regarded as waste—from our processes to the tune of about $1.3 billion a year, with the cost rising at a rate of 15 percent. Once we got people thinking about the fact that every ton of waste represents an opportunity to cut costs—once we got people to think creatively—we were able to cut that number almost in half, to $700 million a year. In other words, instead of how to efficiently treat waste, the mind-set shifted to how to minimize the waste produced in the first place.

In our Lycra spandex production capacity, our usable yields had consistently been running at the 70 to 80 percent range. Most of the people involved felt that was the maximum that could be achieved. But when reducing waste became both an environmental and a business priority, our employees started rethinking how to tackle the problem in a different way. By focusing on achieving higher yield with every batch, re-examining the process from beginning to end, we were able to increase our yield to over 90 percent. Not only did that lower our costs and improve our quality, it also resulted in much more first-grade capacity, thereby avoiding the need for the large capital outlay to build another Lycra plant. We achieved it by aiming at no waste at the end of the line, rather than thinking incrementally about treating waste at the end of the line.

Communicating Change to the Street

DuPont had a good message: our shift from a predominantly chemical company to one with a strong life-sciences component. We had to demonstrate how we were achieving it.

There is no magic to dealing with investors. It is important for the CEO to be accessible, and to make other members of the senior team accessible. But the one subtlety involved there is not to be *too* accessible—not to be so accessible that you seem to be selling too hard. It is important that a CEO be heavily involved in investor-relations strategy, both shaping and executing it. I was in constant touch with both my CFO and head of IR. It was crucial that we shape a message that was both accurate and compelling, one that we could back up—and it was just as crucial that we stick to it, down the line.

It was not enough to make changes: We had to be able to explain them to investors, and to explain the changes in a way by which investors would see their value and understand how they were leading to improved productivity and efficiency and ultimately the bottom line. DuPont is in a highly technical business, but our message could not be highly technical. We honed our message down to a simple formula of productivity plus innovation equals profitable growth. We repeated it as a mantra and showcased all of the changes we were making to bring that formula to life.

We emphasized moves such as our purchase of Pioneer and other steps to strengthen our agriculture-related businesses. We emphasized our acquisition of several small pharma companies and initiatives on the genetic-engineering side. We purchased a paint business from Hoechst for close to $3 billion. At the same time, we were divesting businesses that we didn't think would remain competitive. DuPont had a large imaging business that at one time was very successful producing film for X-rays. But when digital imaging emerged, we knew that business simply wouldn't last.

How do you demonstrate a new attitude in the midst of all these changes? That is the toughest message to convey. It is important to be able to point your finger at specifics. The acquisitions we had made in the life sciences and other parts of our business in which we had long-term competitive advantages demonstrated our innovation-based growth strategy. Reorganizing the business units demonstrated our commitment to speed and accountability. One of the most important pieces of evidence to prove our commitment to competitiveness and productivity was eliminating a third of our workforce. We also made significant changes in the leadership ranks. After all, we were changing the company so much that we had to look at each of our people and ask if we thought they could lead a unit in this new environment. Would they be able to adapt to the new principles of accountability and specificity? Would they be able to adopt the commitment to speed and responsiveness? In the end, we moved out about half of the leaders within the company; some were moved to other jobs, while some left the company. It is not easy having to break bad news like that to someone you have worked with, but it would be unfair to everyone else—and to the shareholders—to fail to make changes on the basis of personal feelings.

Dealing with investors takes focus—and patience. It took the analysts six months to a year to start writing about our focus on life sciences. We had to keep demonstrating that the acquisitions and other new initiatives we were taking were not isolated acts but, rather, part of a broad strategy that was leading to something larger.

Getting this message out to investors was a matter of action more than words. We laid out a message—and piece by piece, we redirected the company to bring that message to life. The only way to demonstrate the ability to change is by actually making changes and delivering results.

As I mentioned, DuPont had received a wake-up call from its customers. When a company gets a wake-up call, it has to recognize the need to spring to life, not to push the snooze button.

CHAPTER FOURTEEN

How a CEO Measures Success

Josh Weston, former chairman and CEO of Automatic Data Processing

Josh Weston has been deeply involved in measuring business success for most of his career. He joined ADP, the world's largest payroll and tax-filing processor, in 1970. Shortly thereafter, the company began a significant global expansion, acquiring companies in the United States, Britain, Holland, and Brazil that were involved in a wide range of data-processing businesses, including payroll, computer networks, inventory control, and shareholder services. When he became CEO in 1983, ADP was expanding its role in providing services for the new wave of personal-computer technology that was remaking the way in which most businesses operate. ADP was responsible for installing the first computer workstations in a number of Wall Street's largest brokerage houses.

Under Weston's watch, the company grew from less than $1 billion in revenue to over $5 billion and 30,000 employees. Some of this growth was achieved by a series of high-profile acquisitions in the 1990s, including the purchase of BankAmerica's business-services division, Peachtree Software; Health Benefits America; and the European computing-services company GSI.

In his presentation to the CEO Academy, Weston emphasized the importance of synthesizing and presenting data as a management tool. He overhauled many of the existing measurement systems that had been in place at ADP and used "numbers" to motivate employees and improve performance.

Weston retired from ADP in 1996. He continues to serve on the company's board of directors.

HOW DO YOU ENLIST HUNDREDS, or thousands, of people to share a vision of a company? In my experience, it is not a matter of making impassioned speeches or issuing eloquent manifestos. Like so much in business, it comes down to properly using numbers. How people perform is mostly a result of how their performance is measured and rewarded.

When many people hear about metrics, their eyes roll. But measurement systems can dramatize a company's heartbeat. They can demonstrate to middle managers what makes the company tick and give life to the business model and the business strategy.

To achieve these goals, performance measurement cannot be seen simply as a means by which the corporate center exercises control. Rather, performance has to be measured and reported in such a way that managers facing comparable challenges can share information about the most important indicators, take pride in their own positive metrics, accept responsibility when their metrics compare poorly with the performance of others, and actively learn from their counterparts. I call that "peer group awareness"—managers' knowledge of how they are performing compared to their peers, based on comprehensive and respected indicators. When a company achieves that kind of universal awareness throughout its management ranks, a combination of pride, commitment, and plain old competitiveness kicks in.

Throughout my experience, systems aimed at creating that kind of peer-group awareness, challenge, and pride have been more effective than a system of command-and-control, in which the corporate center sets targets and tries to penalize failure to meet them. It is far more effective for managers throughout a company to learn from one another and to be challenged by their respective performance than it is to try to dictate practices from the top.

But for peer-group awareness to be successful, reporting and measurement systems have to be clear, consistent, reliable, and valid: They have to measure results that are comparable, they have to generate statistics that genuinely illuminate performance, and they have to generate numbers that actually recognize success rather than disguise it.

In other words, what a company measures, how it measures it, and how it displays such measurements to employees, analysts, and the public are vital to the pursuit of its strategy. That means that the CEO has to be deeply involved in the process of designing measurement systems. Just as Georges Clemenceau said that war is too important to be left to the generals, performance measurement is too important to a company to be left to the CFO or CIO.

In fact, if the goal is to shape the peer-group awareness that I believe is so important to instilling a corporate vision, neither the CFO nor the CIO is the right person to be designing the information and measurement systems. Shaping peer-group awareness requires an ability to get inside the heads of the line managers, to understand how they should look at things, because the challenge is to align their thinking with the strategy and the business model. The CIO and CFO usually don't look at things the way line managers look at them. That is a job for the number-one or number-two person in the organization. That's why when I became COO at ADP, I decided it was my job to become heavily involved in guiding the design of our reporting and measurement systems—and translating them into peer-group-awareness systems.

Some may wonder if the CEO of a large company should really be devoting time to what is often seen as a mundane and formularized task—designing systems for evaluating information. But that gets right to the point: It's a crucial task that should be neither mundane nor formularized. The measurement system itself should automatically stimulate decentralized management and also help make important decisions—decisions that display how the company values the factors that determine its success. It is a process that involves examination, debate, and, ultimately, top-level decision-making.

The Real Wealth of Information

Before describing some of the decisions I had to make to shape a performance-measurement system that would bring peer-group awareness to life, I want to put that in the context of the actual value of information. We frequently hear that in today's society, where information is so readily available, it is the most valuable commodity. But the value of a commodity usually declines with easy availability. The same is true of information. The value is to be found not in its quantity but in its quality. There are two kinds of information, and the difference in their value is like the difference between gold and fool's gold. Sorting them out is one of a CEO's most important jobs.

First, there is what I consider the fool's gold of information: raw data. There is nothing less valuable than raw data that is not properly filtered and vetted. It is easy to push a button and drown yourself in outputs that don't reveal much. The same piece of data that is vital to one business unit can mean absolutely nothing to another. The valid time frame for displaying data can vary widely for different functions. The effectiveness of marketing, for example, might be best tested on the basis of data gathered over a period of weeks or months. Customer service, on the other hand, might be better measured over a period of hours or days.

In an information age, the real gold isn't data—it's new knowledge. It's being able to analyze and distill the data properly, extricate what is valuable, and use it to disseminate understanding of how the company is really performing, how well it is meeting its priorities, and where its strengths and weaknesses actually are. Excess data can actually dilute knowledge, by causing you to focus on counting so many dots that you are unable to connect them.

Understanding the difference between data and new knowledge—separating the strategic wheat from the statistical chaff—is one of the most important challenges facing any company.

One example of the chaff of reporting and evaluation systems is the frequently cited metric of SG&A—selling, general, and administrative costs. Why combine the cost of generating sales with general and administrative costs? That is like comparing apples, oranges, and vacuum cleaners. SG&A as a spending subtotal combines costs in areas that have no relationship to one another. If SG&A is up, is that necessarily a bad thing? At ADP, we were anxious to see the productive "S" go up; we were quite willing to invest more in selling expenses so long as they were generating incremental return. On the other hand, the G and A—general and administrative costs—are categories that one always wants to keep as low as possible. What is to be gained by lumping these unrelated categories together? Indeed, there is much to be *lost*. It can become a perverse incentive. A manager feeling pressure to cut SG&A often finds it easier to cut selling costs than to eliminate the jobs of general and administrative employees whose office is right around the corner.

SG&A is a good example of data. But is it usable information? Does it provide any valuable knowledge about where expenses should be increased or cut? True, one can debate the value of any metric. But that's the point. Shaping measurement systems is something that requires evaluation, deliberation, and even debate. The CEO and/or COO has to play an important part in that.

Making Numbers Add Up to Motivation

I came by my interest in turning raw data into meaningful information honestly. I spent eighteen years at the company that eventually became clothing catalog company J. Crew, ending up as COO. As a mail-order company, it was data-intensive. Even fifty years ago, a good mail-order company had to invest heavily in ensuring that it had the best possible information technology. After all, if you get one or two digits wrong, you can end up sending a large red dress instead of a small blue sweater.

It was my focus on large volumes of computer-supported information and data at J. Crew that made it easy for me to make the shift to the payroll business at ADP, which I joined in 1970. That move led me to become even more involved in data management. ADP's CEO at the time, Frank Lautenberg, concentrated heavily on sales and marketing, which is where the bulk of his success had been achieved. As a result, I focused on the key administrative and operations functions.

I spent a lot of time during my first two years with ADP figuring out the right measurements for a reporting system that would reinforce the company's vision. What I sought to create wasn't just a reporting system that would help middle managers run their business. I felt strongly that we also needed a system that would help them understand the overall business, and what made it work. We needed a system that accurately and precisely identified and tracked the factors that were key to our success.

By this point—with all my focus on reporting systems and metrics—you may be wondering if I am an accountant by training. I'm not, and I didn't approach the issue as an accountant would. I wanted to shape metrics for managers—numbers that would help us design, reinforce, and evaluate business strategies and motivate employees to implement them effectively.

As I indicated, I believe that the best motivator for any manager is awareness of how he or she compares with counterparts and with past performance, based on measurements that are both fair and meaningful. Peer-group awareness was especially important to ADP. The company's employees were spread out across the United States. Managers had peers with similar functions all over the country. We needed reporting and information systems that would allow our managers to share information about the most important indicators, compare their own track record with peers, and evaluate their own performance. That would actually get me out of the process and let peer-group pride take over.

To achieve that, we had to revitalize reporting and measurement at ADP, because at the time the system that was in place was rudimentary, to say the least. For example, the ADP accounting department employed a metric that measured total payroll as a percentage of total revenue. That wasn't surprising. Thousands of accounting departments in all types of businesses do the same thing. When businesses want to measure how they are doing, they typically use ratios: finding out what the percentage of sales is, or the percentage of revenue.

The problem is that in most businesses, those raw numbers don't tell managers very much. At ADP, I realized that while the accountants' figures on total revenue were accurate, they could also be misleading. In January and February, the payroll business typically sees a surge of activity, producing W-2 forms for employees. This business creates a significant increase in revenue that virtually disappears after the first quarter. In that sense, any attempt to look at performance based on the total revenue figures from January to March would see a huge distortion due to this seasonal but short-lived source of revenue. Managers know this, and, when asked about performance during the first quarter, they have to explain the data variations caused by certain activities that don't occur every month of the year. Of course, the W-2 business isn't the only thing driving our revenue numbers up and down. Throughout the year, we experience fluctuations that change the revenue numbers but, again, don't accurately tell managers how they are really performing during a given period of time.

What business managers need are a set of financial reports that help them think about their business. Using the GAAP standards embraced by accountants isn't helpful in that regard, and that is what I sought to change at ADP. The changes I wanted applied not just to revenue but to every set of numbers that experience wide variations over time: expenses, sales, capital expenditures, and so on. We created these reports based on extensive conversation with our line managers. What information did they really need to know in order to measure themselves and compare their performance with other ADP offices? What we came up with we applied not just to accounting data but every type of data that told us something about performance and could be displayed in an objective way.

One example of a performance metric that we created emerged when we decided that prompt phone service at our fifty call centers ("help desks") around the country was a priority. We started by determining that we wanted 80 percent of all inbound phone calls answered within twenty seconds. At the time, we were far from that goal and very sporadic within and between call centers. Measuring and displaying actual performance changed that. At every call center, we created a display of intra-week performance at one-hour intervals within each center for internal use by that center. And then we displayed weekly performance between centers, showing what percentage of our million inbound calls per week were answered within twenty seconds at each site. Initially, fewer than 50 percent of calls met that goal in most centers. Then a few centers reached 80 percent, and now virtually all fifty locations top the 80 percent mark; a few even top 90 percent.

That experience reinforced the power of peer-group awareness when it comes to changing and improving performance. We designed a peer-group-awareness system that measured performance across all of our business units not just on P&L items but on areas like client acquisition, client retention, client satisfaction, employee retention, and even employee attitude. We initiated a report to compare business units' candor in employee performance-review ratings, to provide a sense of which managers were handing out top ratings too easily.

We also examined the appropriate measuring intervals for each metric. Left alone, accountants will usually define all reporting cycles to match the need for monthly financial statements. But the optimum interval between measurement reports isn't necessarily one month—the optimum interval is the shortest time during which you have the right to expect something meaningful to happen. For example, our salespeople would have a lot of prospects and be expected to close more than one sale a week.

That made weekly reporting meaningful. The weekly report allowed for effective evaluation of sales personnel, which is something that a young, growing company needs. This was underscored by the experience of our CEO at the time. Frank Lautenberg came from Prudential Insurance, where weekly reporting was the norm for sales.

In some areas, such as the help desk, hourly or daily reporting indicators are useful. For that we adopted real-time software to measure performance on an intra-day basis.

But shaping peer-group awareness as a tool for pursuing corporate strategy is not just a matter of creating a new measurement system. For it to have any effect, a corporate culture has to be fostered that will accept the measurement system, buy into its validity, and use it as a basis for recognition and improvement. That means that the senior executive who is pushing the measurement system—the one who believes in it most deeply and has a true passion for its potential—has to make the case for it. Corporate leadership has to make it clear that the reporting system will be the basis for evaluation and recognition of managers.

In any case, at ADP the system was working because our metrics produced new knowledge that was truly valuable. In less than a year, we had developed and introduced a dozen metrics that provided useful information. Now we have fifty.

What was the impact of all of this peer awareness? Peer motivation. After we introduced the first dozen performance indicators at about twenty operating locations, there was an immediate effect, because they generated reports that could be read across the country. When we release the results of the indicators, the managers who are meeting the goals receive an extra boost of pride, and those who aren't make it their mission to improve their own indicators. The indicators provide a strong incentive to improve because everyone in the peer group gets to see everyone else's results. And the indicators also provide a reference list of whom to turn to for advice. Managers turn not to corporate headquarters but to their peers—comparable managers who are showing better results. Managers will call a peer across the country to find out how to get better results.

Not only do the numbers provide us with a basis for measuring performance—they allow us to measure the effectiveness of the reporting and measurement system itself. We can see the positive impact because over a period of about five years, the gap between quartiles narrowed. When our peer-group measurement system first hit the ground, the difference between the highest and lowest performers was easily 25 percent. Over time, it dropped to about three points. The worst started to learn from the best.

In my view, the basis for evaluating any measurement system is its impact on performance. Companies cannot afford to measure performance simply to obtain static information. For the process to be worth the time and resources invested in it, it has to be dynamic—it has to change operations for the better, align managers to the objectives, and raise the bottom performers closer to the top. Data cannot shape a vision, but properly organized and evaluated—and, most important, communicated—the way a company measures results today can make a huge difference in how it performs tomorrow.

CHAPTER FIFTEEN

Leading by Communicating

Lawrence A. Weinbach, chairman and CEO of Unisys

Unisys was created in 1986 through the merger of mainframe computer makers Burroughs and Sperry. Over the next decade, it would undergo significant changes, spinning off its defense business and focusing on mainframes and data processing. Yet by the 1990s, when the mainframe business began to fade, the company was in trouble.

Its comeback and new focus as an information-consulting firm was led largely by Lawrence Weinbach, who had been the chief executive at Andersen Worldwide, the accounting and consulting giant, for nine years. Weinbach had begun his career as an accountant for Andersen in 1961, and he brought his passion for the service business to the computer-technology company. Beginning soon after he became chairman and CEO, Weinbach began repositioning the company as "services driven and technology enabled." The company discontinued its low-margin commodity business, including PCs. Today, Unisys focuses on high-end services and technology in specific industries, including financial services, public sector, transportation, telecommunications, and the commercial sector. Throughout this process, Weinbach worked steadily to boost employee morale and strengthen the company's image with high-profile marketing campaigns. Today, Unisys is one of the world's largest technology-consulting businesses and enjoys some of the largest service contracts with governments and financial services companies worldwide.

WHEN I WAS RECRUITED to Unisys, the company was a turnaround candidate. It was almost $4 billion in debt, with no tangible net worth. But one would never have guessed that by looking at the employee performance ratings. Despite the company's problems, when I looked at the results of its performance-rating system, I found that most of the employees were receiving top grades. Half the employees were being rated in the top two brackets. I stood before my management team and asked: If 50 percent of our employees merit top ratings, why are we losing money? The answer I was given: We fired all the others. I asked: Then why are we still losing money?

The problem with the easy-grading review system that the company had been using was not just that it distorted the company's pay-for-performance system, although that was bad enough. The worst part is that it served as a symbol of one of the biggest problems that a troubled company has to solve if it is going to turn itself around: failure to communicate honestly. The lopsided performance-review system symbolized a company in denial. To succeed, a company has to be able to communicate—starting with itself. That means that no punches can be pulled. A CEO cannot pull back from delivering bad news; he or she cannot refrain from offering criticism—including self-criticism. A company's vision statement cannot be so wordy that it ends up saying nothing. Communication has to be based on the clear transmission of accurate information and honestly held opinions. As simple as that sounds, it is an essential underpinning of a successful business.

The Need to Communicate Honestly

People will accept the truth, even if it is unpleasant. At Unisys, people accepted—reluctantly at first—the decision to revamp the system of employee assessments. In fact, one of the first changes I made was to introduce a pay-for-performance system based on a bell-shaped curve. The new review policy stipulated that over the next two years, no more than 30 percent of our people would be rated in one of the top two categories. Today, four years later,

28 percent of employees are rated in the top two categories, a meaningful reflection of individual performance, and the process has now been accepted as the norm.

When so many people in the company saw their performance ratings drop, do you think that was easy for them to accept? Let's face it: It hurt their egos as well as their pocketbooks. The only way to prevent that kind of disappointment from turning into deep resentment was to deal with the issue honestly. We used every communication vehicle at our disposal—including our own internal television broadcast—to get the message across that the company had to pay for performance, and the performance had to be honestly and objectively evaluated.

Soon after implementing the new rating system, I went to one of the leadership schools that we hold on a regular basis, in this case for a group of our engineers. One of the engineers raised his hand and told me that he was really upset—his rating had been dropped down because of me. He said that his supervisor had told him that he should have been rated higher—a 1 or a 2 under the old system—but had to be dropped down because of the bell curve.

In his question, I recognized a problem endemic in all employee-ranking systems: managers who tell employees that their evaluation is merely part of a system imposed from above, rather than a frank assessment of performance. You see it often because many supervisors don't like to deliver bad news and confront an underperforming employee. It is easier to blame poor evaluations on a faulty system.

I could have tried to dodge the issue or simply have said, "take the matter up with your supervisor." But I thought it was important to take the issue head-on, by standing behind the policy and demonstrating its relevance. I asked him: "If you have one week to start and complete a project, and you can choose ten people to take part in it, do you know exactly which ten people in your department you would pick?" He said he did. I told him that those are his number 1s, his top-rated people. It suddenly dawned on him that he was not among the top people in his department—and that his supervisor lacked the courage to tell him so.

A CEO has to make a choice—whether to be loved or to be effective. Being loved does not make a CEO effective; being respected and trusted does. If you can get your employees to trust you, they'll do whatever you want them to do. They will go through the wall for you. If they don't trust you, and you say, "Let's go through the wall," they're going to watch you go through it, and you're going to hurt yourself. But if you can win their trust, they will work with you.

How to build that kind of trust? I start with the assumption that all of our employees are smart and want to know the truth. A CEO has to be able to tell employees the truth, without sugarcoating it. If there is bad news, it is necessary to give it to them. Most of the time when there is good news, I give the people who work with me the opportunity to announce it. But when there is bad news to deliver, I'm going to stand up and deliver it myself.

It wasn't long after taking over as CEO of Unisys that I had some bad news to deliver. Our industry as a whole was facing problems, and we had to reduce our workforce significantly—cutting back our 40,000-person workforce by 10 percent. We preserved 36,000 jobs at the cost of 4,000. That would help soften the bad news, but it would still be tough medicine to swallow. I believed that the only way to deal with the issue was up-front and honestly. There were three elements to my approach:

- First, when we had to announce that 4,000 employees were going to have to be let go, I made the announcement myself.
- Second, while it would have been economically impossible to maintain the full workforce, it was quite possible to demonstrate empathy. And it was important to demonstrate empathy in a very concrete form: We gave everyone we would have to let go some time to adjust to the news and look for other work. We let everyone know about the workforce reduction two months in advance.

- Third, I made a compelling business case explaining why we had to take the step. The senior team had thought out the issue, determined that there was no alternative, and was unanimously in support of the workforce reduction as the only feasible option.

Perhaps the most important reason that the decision was accepted throughout the company was the fact that we had earned the trust and respect of our employees. If your employees get used to hearing you tell them the truth—without sugarcoating it—they will find it easier to accept the basis for your decisions, even the ones that hurt.

Of course, telling it like it is includes owning up to your own mistakes. When I took over as CEO of Unisys, there was one part of our business—servicing the federal government—that I was unable to turn around. It was a frustrating experience. I tried changing the leadership several times, but that didn't work. I tried selling it, but the market wasn't there at an appropriate price. Trying to sell it at that point was a mistake, and a year later I went in front of the employees and acknowledged that. The whole experience of trying to turn that business around was costly and time-consuming, and the only good thing about it was the respect it earned me throughout the company.

Telling it like it is includes telling everyone the same thing. When it comes to building trust, consistency is as important a leadership characteristic as honesty. There are CEOs who are influenced by the last person they spoke to, or who give different answers to different groups of people. Telling people what they want to hear may make them happy while they are sitting in your office, but it makes them angry and alienated not long after they leave, as soon as they talk to someone who received an entirely different answer. If ten different people walk into the CEO's office and ask the same question, they had all better get the same answer. The best way to kill trust is to give different answers to different people.

Telling it like it is also includes being able to disagree with people while making it clear to them that their views are being heard and respected. Many of the most valuable people in any company are those who have a high certainty of their own views. It is easy to let people like that get under your skin, because they tend to be prima donnas. But prima donnas are critical to the success of any organization. They have a great deal of self-confidence; in fact, that is what makes them so sure of everything. They are able to sell themselves—exactly the kind of people a company needs if it is going to be able to sell itself.

But prima donnas don't like being disagreed with. Nonetheless, the same principle of honesty has to apply to them as it does to everyone else in the organization. A CEO has to develop the unique skill of giving people like this the sense that they are valued, without giving in to their every whim. They need to know that their views are being taken seriously. They need to know that when they have a point of view to express, they will be given the time to express it. When you explain why you disagree with them, it is important to go over each point, in sufficient detail that there can be no question but that you heard what they had to say, and you recognize the merit of their argument even if you don't agree with it. Ideally, when they leave your office, they will be focusing on the thorough discussion that you had with them rather than on the fact that you said no.

Communication—Keep It Constant, Keep It Simple

In real estate, the three overriding values are location, location, location. In building trust, it is all about communication, communication, communication.

That was especially important for me to keep in mind when I took on the job of CEO of Unisys, because I was coming from outside the company. I had to get to know the organization and give everyone in it a chance to get to know me—as soon as possible.

Over the first three months, I held group meetings in more than twenty locations with half of the 40,000 people in the global company. I made a point of talking to them without notes, so they would know I was speaking to them directly, and I made sure that we always had time for a question-and-answer session each time.

In fact, whenever I visit a company location, I try to have an all-hands meeting. Some might see this as a drag on productivity, because it takes people away from their work. But they'll remember what the CEO has to say, and that makes for a great opportunity to drive home the message.

But nobody can talk to everyone in person, all of the time. That is what makes the Internet so valuable. Once a month, I send a letter to everyone in the organization over our intranet system. It's not a short note, either: It runs two to five pages, depending on what is going on in the company.

It is important to measure the degree to which employees are actually reading or listening to what you have to say. If you are advertising on television or in magazines, you want to see viewer ratings and readership analysis to make sure you are getting your money's worth. It is just as important to measure the degree to which your message is getting out inside the company. One of the reasons I continue to send the companywide e-mail is that our research has demonstrated a 93 percent readership. Similarly, I do presentations on our internal business television network, as issues warrant. We find that just about everyone in the organization watches, either live or, subsequently, on video.

But it is not enough for communications to be constant. What you communicate must also be easy to remember and to repeat. That is why I am a firm believer in the principle of keeping it simple.

I believe that the principle of simple, straightforward messaging has to apply to every communications device the company employs. Take the vision statement. Just about every company has one. As a consultant years ago, I learned something about vision statements: Usually it hangs on the wall of the boardroom, unread. My guess is that, more often than not, only the person who wrote the vision statement knows what it says. Why? Almost every statement I've ever read has the same problem. No matter how beautifully written it may be, it has too many words in it. In my opinion, a vision has to be simple enough to fit on a pin.

The very first day I arrived at Unisys, I did a broadcast on our in-house system. I was asked my vision for the company, and since I hadn't had a chance to prepare, I simply said what I've always believed: There are only three things that are important—customers, employees, and reputation. If you get these three things right, you will be successful. It's like a three-legged stool. If all three legs are strong, you have something solid to sit on.

That concept—the notion of the three-legged stool of customers, employees, and reputation—took off throughout the company. It became something for employees to rally around. We even had pins made up in the shape of a three-legged stool. Everybody in the company wears it when I show up, because it signifies something about the company. I have about twenty three-legged stools in my office that employees have made for me.

The three-legged stool illustrates the most important thing about a corporate vision. It doesn't have to be a work of genius. It doesn't have to be dramatic. But it has to be something that people can remember and something they can relate to.

That is what makes the vision of "customers, employees, and reputation" effective for us. People can remember it—it's three simple words. And people can relate to it—it's three plain and simple concepts.

Corporate strategies have to be kept simple as well. Every year we go through a process in which we analyze our competitive situation and develop strategies for the coming year. One rule is that we can't end up with more than five strategies. When people ask me why, I say that is all I can remember. The truth is that it is important to keep the strategic messages down to a manageable number. More than anything, the annual strategic-development process is a tool for driving home a consistent message every time we get a chance to talk to our people.

The CEO as Teacher

Like most CEOs, I get hundreds of e-mails every week. I read every one of them. If it's a personal e-mail, I'll respond personally. If it's generic, we post the answer on our companywide e-mail.

Through this process, we learned something very interesting: Our employees didn't understand a lot of the metrics that were central to measuring our performance as a company. Many didn't understand earnings per share. They didn't understand P/E ratio. They didn't know why cash flow was so important. As a result, we launched an educational system through our intranet, which gave birth to a new training program. We didn't call it a training program—we just put out information on basic financial fundamentals every week.

That kind of electronic tutorial is valuable. But beyond that, to develop people in the organization, it is important to establish leadership training. And the CEO needs to be doing some of the teaching. It is important that people see that the CEO is investing serious time in the process and rolling up his or her sleeves rather than just saying hello. I also make a point of socializing with the people afterward. They want to get a chance to talk to the CEO and ask questions. Again, it is important to tell it like it is, with no sugarcoating. The goal isn't to be loved—it is to be trusted, to build confidence.

At the same time, it is important for the CEO to set an example by personally spending time with customers. I have a consistent message to country managers: I won't visit your country without customer visits. I focus on all customers, potential customers as well as customers we are concerned about losing. That is a form of teaching by example. If the CEO spends time with customers, it helps shape a customer-focused culture.

All of this is part of fulfilling one of the most important jobs a CEO has: the job of teacher. That includes teaching the senior team. Some senior managers are not natural communicators, as competent as they may be in other respects. It is important to teach by example, and by demonstrating the effectiveness of communication. If you can show them how to have the organization embrace a tough policy, such as a revision of employee ratings—or if you can give them an example of how to illustrate a major point, such as the three-legged stool—then you make it easier for the senior team to communicate. That makes it easier for everyone in the company to get a clear, consistent message.

CHAPTER SIXTEEN

Learning from Failure: When Execution Trumps Strategy

David Fuente, former chairman and CEO of Office Depot

When the Federal Trade Commission voted in 1997 to block the proposed merger between office supply giants Staples and Office Depot, it struck many as an anachronistic return to the age of trust busters. After many years in which M&A deals were a routine part of the business landscape, the defeat of the Staples–Office Depot merger was the most significant action by federal regulators to stop a merger.

No one was as surprised as David Fuente, the chairman and CEO of Office Depot at the time. For years he had entertained the possibility of a merger with his number-one competitor. When they reached an agreement in the fall of 1996, the two companies started moving quickly toward integration. Neither side seriously entertained the possibility of a protracted battle with regulators.

As Fuente now looks back on the deal that stopped in its tracks, he sees it as a case study of how companies need to interact with federal authorities. In this chapter he argues that had the two companies and their legal team assumed a different attitude and posture toward the FTC, approval of the merger would have been possible.

Fuente arrived at Office Depot in 1987 as chairman and CEO after serving as president of Sherwin Williams Paint Store Division. He led the company through considerable expansion in the United States and abroad and expanded its product line. By the early 1990s, it was the largest office supply company in North America. He retired from the company in 2002.

ON JUNE 30, 1997, a judge sided with the Federal Trade Commission's decision to block the merger of Office Depot and Staples, then the two largest office-supply businesses in the nation. That decision ended a vision that I had entertained for several years. It was a personal disappointment but, more immediately, a massive business challenge to pick up the pieces created by a failed merger attempt. In the months that followed, lawyers, economists, and public-policy students exhaustively debated the substance and meaning of the FTC's high-profile decision. Some saw it as a return to an activist anti-trust enforcement that had long been dormant. Others suggested that it was a victory for consumers against the corporate behemoths. Still others suggested it was unfounded federal meddling in the efficient marketplace.

As the then-chairman and CEO of Office Depot, I did not spend a lot of time in the wake of the decision second-guessing the FTC, even though I disagreed with its verdict. I have, however, reflected on what we could have done to make the merger work. Despite all the economic reasoning behind the anti-trust ruling, I believe the Office Depot–Staples merger was, fundamentally, a failure of companies to deal properly with Washington, D.C., regulators. The lessons I learned from a failed merger offer valuable guidance to other executives who may one day find themselves planning a merger and dealing with a similar confrontation with federal authorities.

Seeking to Merge

In the late eighties, there were about two dozen companies in the office-supply business. The industry was changing dramatically, and Office Depot was a leading force in that transition. The company had helped introduce the idea of a supply superstore, and it expanded rapidly in the late 1980s and early 1990s. We deployed first-rate technology to bring down costs and improve customer service. The company expanded across the country and internationally, broadened its product offerings, and entered into the business-services market. By the early 1990s, the company had established itself as the largest office-supply company in North America.

Our chief competitor was Staples, another office-superstore chain that had been the number-two player in the industry. We had talked about merging several times. Discussions went on and off, with the issue of which company would be the lead company changing back and forth. We came very close to acquiring our rival in 1992, and I invested a lot of time with Tom Stemberg, the Staples CEO, thinking through the deal. We never could agree on a price, and in retrospect that may have been a key missed opportunity. But in 1996, we were able to find common ground. One critical thing had changed, however. Earlier that year, Office Depot had missed an earnings estimate, and our price/earnings ratio dropped precipitously. Staples, on the other hand, saw its P/E ratio climbing steadily. As a result, the deal we reached was a $3.4 billion stock swap that allowed them to acquire us. Staples was effectively paying us a 40 percent premium on our shares, but it was still hard for some of our employees to swallow the idea that Office Depot's largest rival was taking us over. When we went in front of the cameras to announce the merger, I wore a Staples baseball cap and Staples CEO Tom Stemberg wore an Office Depot cap, to illustrate our declaration that it was to be a merger of equals. It made for a good photo opportunity, but there was only one problem with the picture: There is no such thing as a merger of equals. There is an easy way to tell which company will be dominating the merged entity—just look at who is going to be the CEO. Giving up the job of CEO wasn't a particularly happy moment for me. But I kept reminding myself that if the merger was a great move for the company paying a premium, it surely must be an even better development for the company *receiving* a premium. Yet as I quickly learned, many Office Depot employees were not happy about the proposed deal, and the events that followed did little to boost their enthusiasm.

Because Tom Stemberg and I had gone down this road before,

the actual negotiations for the final deal were uncomplicated. I spent less than a month in the negotiations, working closely with my chief financial officer, Barry Goldstein, and our investment bankers. We suspected that the FTC would take a serious look at the deal, requiring more than the customary thirty-day review. But during our negotiations, the topic of a carefully coordinated strategy to deal with FTC objections was discussed only briefly. Instead, we focused on how we could prepare to integrate the companies and do so as quickly as possible.

We were not being naive about this. I had led Office Depot through a number of mergers, including the acquisition of Office Club, a California-based office-superstore chain, and Eastman Office Products, a major West Coast office supplier. The FTC had approved each within thirty days. But in this case, we assumed that if the FTC required a deeper study of the merger, we could have our legal team provide information or respond to our objections. Winning broader popular support for the merger would also play a role in the coming months, but during our negotiations, the topic received little attention.

The Confrontation

After we submitted our initial statement and documentation for review, the FTC, as we fully expected, asked for more information. I didn't know it at the time, but the FTC was examining our merger through the lens of what is called the "differentiated products" theory that was increasingly being used by anti-trust advocates. Under the theory, regulators question whether the two firms merging represent each other's top competitors, whose customers would be unlikely to look elsewhere if there were a post-merger price increase. As a practical matter, the theory let regulators define a market for office supplies very narrowly. Combined, Office Depot and Staples had only 10 percent of the office-supply market. But under the "differentiated products" theory, regulators saw us operating in the much more narrow "office-supply superstore market," where we were indeed dominant players.

This distinction between the broad office-supply market and the office-superstore market struck us as obvious. Every day, we were competing against hundreds of smaller competitors. Wal-Mart sold more office supplies at retail than our two companies combined. In 1997, the embryonic market for online office-supply shops was also an emerging competitive threat. As one writer pointed out, the FTC itself obtained office supplies from 105 different suppliers. The idea that we would be limiting consumer choices struck us as easy to disprove once the facts were fairly presented.

But as soon as we turned to our legal team to respond to the FTC request, I saw that we were heading into hostile territory. At the advice of our legal team, we immediately assumed a confrontational posture toward the FTC. The number of lawyers and economists and public-relations staff expanded as if we were girding for battle. Kirkland & Ellis, our law firm, was one of the most experienced in dealing with these types of FTC reviews. But as I came to realize, their experience had also made them antagonistic, even hostile, to the FTC staff. That turned out to be a strategic error. Instead of raising the level of combativeness, that was the moment we should have toned it down.

Unfortunately, the litigation process itself seems to drive up the level of combativeness and hostility. Every action you take has the potential to become a battle; every battle has the potential to turn into a full-scale war. When I gave my first deposition, our attorneys did something that I would have thought was a simple matter of administrative efficiency: They brought in a secretary to take notes. The FTC immediately objected, arguing that we were not permitted to have a secretary in the room. They contended she was a paralegal. That one dispute lasted for forty-five minutes, despite the fact that both sides knew a transcript would be issued the next day in any event. That petty issue set the tone for my deposition; in those circumstances, I was bound to come across badly, no matter what I had to say. Even routine questions about the company seemed to bring with it the mood of a cross-examination during a murder trial.

I didn't realize it at the time, but the FTC staff was not wholly to blame for this atmosphere. After the merger was turned down, I had the opportunity to get to know one of the FTC commissioners and talk to her about our experience. She explained to me that the anti-trust debate behind our merger was a contentious one. The 4–1 ruling against the merger could actually have gone the other way. But the commissioners—who are generally highly erudite and experienced in these matters—felt alienated by the angry and hostile posture of our attorneys.

The FTC wanted a negotiation process rather than a litigation battle, and so did we. In fact, we were doing everything we could to reach an agreement with the federal government. We responded to every request for information, probably swamping their offices with paperwork. When we first started to get signals that the merger might not be approved, we pushed even harder to make the negotiation process work.

But beneath the surface of our negotiating strategy there was always a slight tone of arrogance and overconfidence. In the middle of negotiations, we decided to run full-page ads in newspapers across the country—including the *Washington Post*, where FTC commissioners were sure to see it—extolling the virtues of the merger. It was a move that surely irked them. Additionally, although we were never explicit, our team occasionally conveyed the impression that we were eager to beat the regulators in court, if that's what was required. We never made such a threat, but it was often palpable in the room when negotiations got tough. I suspect that the FTC commissioners we met with individually sensed it.

Indeed, at one point in the process, I received a telephone message from our chief lawyer. When I called him back, the first thing

I heard was the theme song from the movie *Superman*. As the music played in the background, our lead attorney described the sense of fear that the FTC would feel in anticipation of his "flying" into the courtroom. It dawned on me then that the heroes-versus-villains approach that our lawyers (and we) had accepted from the outset might have been deeply flawed.

Failing to Heed Advice

As you might expect in a negotiation process with the government, they often make demands that you believe are unreasonable. That was certainly the case in our merger. But rather than trying to find a way we could comply and get on with the merger, we fought bitterly, ultimately to our own detriment.

The greatest sticking point for us was the requirement that Office Depot divest itself of more than a hundred stores, a move the FTC felt was necessary to prevent excessive market dominance. The only company that could have been a logical buyer—in terms of size and market—was our third-ranked competitor, OfficeMax. That put us in the uncomfortable position of having the FTC's staff draw up a list of stores they felt were acceptable to divest and then go to our competitor to try to maximize the price. Of course, OfficeMax saw all the advantages of this situation. It realized that it didn't need to pay too much—we were under the gun to sell the stores. We were willing to sell them, but OfficeMax was not being reasonable in their offer.

Yet reaching an agreement with OfficeMax was critical to the deal. That wasn't just speculation. We had explicit instructions on that point. Two days before the FTC was scheduled to vote on the merger, we had a meeting with the chairman of the commission, Robert Pitofsky, who was one of the most respected figures in anti-trust circles. He told us bluntly that if we wanted the merger to be approved, we should hurry up and make a deal with OfficeMax before the vote. It now seems obvious, but this advice should have been followed immediately. A large company pays lawyers and consultants enormous fees to provide insight into the thinking of regulators and government officials. When a regulator tells you exactly what he is thinking, he is providing you with invaluable information for free. Yet at that point, we thought that we could beat the FTC at the negotiation game and ignore its requests.

Two days later, the FTC voted to reject the merger and began the legal process to have a judge block it. Suddenly, we realized, we were in a far weaker position. We wanted to renegotiate with the FTC to open up the opportunity for another vote, but the only way the commissioners would consider it was if we completed the sale of specific stores to OfficeMax. It was only after the commissioner's vote that OfficeMax realized it had missed a tremendous opportunity to buy stores at cut rates. We pushed them again, and this time they raised their offer, not as high as we would have liked but to an acceptable level. With that agreement done, a sense of goodwill appeared to emerge betwen our side and the commission. The FTC's staff actually went on to recommend approval of the merger. Yet when the issue went before the commissioners, they voted against the merger a second time—perhaps the only time the commission rejected the recommendation of its staff.

Our relationship with the FTC over several months had apparently soured the deal. Even though we had legitimate differences over its interpretation of antitrust statutes, the antagonism—and, in my opinion, the ineptness—of our legal team did not persuade the commissioners that we took their anticompetitive concerns seriously. Had we spent more time talking to one another and understanding our different perspectives, I think we could have reached an acceptable compromise without the rancor and distrust that litigation invariably produces. It is often necessary to fight regulators who have little understanding of your business. But in general, a company that takes on the FTC, or any other significant federal agency, in court is fighting an enemy with endless resources and very savvy legal professionals. It is a situation that should be avoided wherever possible.

The Perils of Integrating Too Quickly

The unhappy conclusion of our conflict with the FTC produced another important lesson that pertains directly to how companies should pursue mergers. Widely repeated conventional wisdom holds that the best way to make a merger work is by being ready to go on day one with a plan approved and people in place. Regardless of the regulatory and legal hurdles ahead, as soon as two companies have struck a deal, there is a tendency to get on with it and begin the process of turning the two entities into one. Almost inevitably, that involves putting together a staffing plan, hiring integration consultants, figuring out how to link information systems together, and so on. The advantages of this kind of off-the-mark preparedness are obvious—if the merger is approved. But what if the merger is blocked? What are the costs to both companies, in terms of both corporate morale and strategic positioning? As we discovered, the costs are high enough to warrant some prudence about integration.

Capital-investment issues are a case in point. As with many mergers, we had agreed to Office Depot's taking the lead role in information systems because of its vastly superior computer network. I have always believed that the only way to ensure first-class execution is through state-of-the-art information systems. It has always been a passion of mine to have precise systems to measure every aspect of our business, especially customer service. So once the deal was struck, Office Depot continued to invest heavily in computer systems to prepare for integration of the two companies, and Staples left the field clear to us. That meant fairly high expenses for us, but it also meant that, once the merger was blocked, Staples would end up still further behind in its information systems.

The other major investment issue was real estate. Throughout its history, Office Depot had a very aggressive real-estate development operation that allowed us to expand in key markets on desirable properties. But once we decided that Staples was to be responsible for the real-estate activity during the transition process, we discontinued all of its store-development activity and essentially shut down our real-estate operation. Nine months later, when the merger was blocked, Office Depot had no leases in the pipeline, choking off any plans for continued growth. It took nearly another year until our real-estate program was back to its prior strength.

These capital-investment issues are difficult in the wake of a failed merger, but they pale compared to the human capital issues. In developing any integration plan, there is a tremendous amount of office politics involved. Everyone knows that some people are going to lose their jobs, and everyone plots to make sure that they are not among them. It makes for neither a pleasant process nor a happy result. A team that has been carefully assembled over the years is not a team any longer. Senior managers who were told they were being moved out of their jobs feel betrayed, an attitude that will not simply go away when the deal falls apart and everyone can hold on to his or her job again. In our case, many senior people had already received severance packages and moved on to seek other careers. Others had been promised severance packages and made plans. When the merger collapsed, they still wanted the package. One thing was clear, however: Our employees were never enthusiastic about the merger, and the wrenching experience of planning for who would have to leave made the deal even less appetizing. When the news came down that the FTC had voted against the merger, our headquarters building literally shook with whoops of joy and celebratory hollering.

The other human-capital problem when two competitors come so close to merging is that your rival finds out a lot of advantageous competitive information. During our preliminary integration process, Staples was able to assess some of our most skilled managers. But we felt secure because the two companies had signed an agreement with each other at the outset of our merger negotiations that we would not solicit or recruit each other's employees. Unfortunately, I failed to focus on the fact that the agreement lasted only a year. A short while after the merger had been rejected by the court, the agreement lapsed. I was stunned when Staples began recruiting and stealing a number of our leading players. It was a technical failure on my part; the agreement should have been renewed even after the deal was over. But to me, the nonsolicitation agreement was part of the good intentions with which we initially negotiated the merger. To come in after it was over and, using the knowledge they had gained from the process, take some of our best people was unethical and immoral. These problems become obvious to anyone involved in a merger that doesn't pan out. But there is not a clear answer about how to avoid them completely. In several mergers, I've aimed at ensuring that the new company be ready to go on day one and achieved it successfully. But if the deal doesn't go through, the results are so severe that my recommendation would be to tread very cautiously on premerger integration. I have seen the benefits, and they do not come close to outweighing the costs to the organization if the deal should not go through.

There is another hazard of pursuing full-scale integration while waiting for completion of the merger: You could end up paying so much attention to integration that you neglect the tasks needed to getting the deal done. In our attempt to merge with Staples, both companies had agreed to a comprehensive integration plan, but we paid insufficient attention to how we needed to react to resistance at the FTC. We simply put those problems in the hands of outside counsel, never thinking that the companies themselves needed a fully thought-through strategy, with all the ramifications of any move we might have taken.

The difficulties faced by Office Depot and Staples are not unique. In fact, since the FTC ruling against us in 1997, there have been a number of high-profile cases brought by both the Justice Department and the European Commission. The Justice Department's antitrust suit against Microsoft, and the decision of the Brussels competition authority to block both the Sprint–MCI and the GE–Honeywell mergers, do not necessarily reflect a global trend against mergers. But they are highly visible reminders that the architects of high-stakes mergers need to consider not only the possibilities of the newly merged company, but also the possibility that their deal will not go through.

PART IV

The CEO and the Outside World

At each session of the CEO Academy, we make sure that current CEOs have a chance to hear from veteran corporate leaders but also to learn from professionals whose careers put them in close proximity to the everyday work of business executives. These professionals have developed a deep understanding about the role of corporate leadership and management—and often played vital roles in making executives and their companies successful. Most important, we choose discussion leaders who can tell us, based on their own experience, how a CEO best deals with the world beyond the executive suite. As every executive quickly learns, Wall Street, the press, and public perception can have enormous influence on the fortunes of a company and the reputation of an individual leader. In this section, we asked some of the most experienced CEO advisors to share their views more broadly.

Mark Begor had a chance to study one of the world's most celebrated CEOs up close. As head of investor relations for General Electric, Begor was in daily contact with Jack Welch and saw how frequent and how strategic the interactions between a company and its investors and analysts must be. He explains how the interaction between senior management and the financial world should be more than merely cordial—it must be a systematic part of understanding why the company's stock is being bought or not being bought.

On the other side of Wall Street, as it were, stood Robert Hurst, now vice chairman of Goldman Sachs after a long and distinguished career at the firm. He examines the new environment that has emerged after the recent corporate scandals and suggests how it will shape relationships between Wall Street analysts and corporate executives. Transparency, disclosure, and accessibility will be the most important qualities that research analysts and investors will demand from CEOs. And they will be much more demanding that a CEO produce an in-depth knowledge of balance-sheet issues. Storytelling and general observations will be insufficient fodder for the Street. The time when company management could also use analysts as sounding boards has probably gone, too, he concludes. Instead, companies will be required, as Begor also suggests, to know their investor community in a much more comprehensive way.

The new scrutiny of corporate conduct also raises the issue of how a company interacts with the press. Christoph Walther, who for many years served as the chief of corporate communications for DaimlerChrysler, argues for keeping the press at a carefully maintained arm's length. While it has long been the practice of public-relations advisors to court the media assiduously, Walther suggests that press events be carefully chosen and that refining the message, especially in the midst of a crisis, should be done only after complete information is at hand. Without full information, the CEO has no business talking to the press.

Matthew Bishop of *The Economist* takes a different view, naturally. He urges CEOs to dismiss the handlers and public relations people and establish open and ongoing relationships with reporters. The result will not only provide better coverage, he argues, but might also give a troubled company the benefit of the doubt when bad news breaks.

As these writers make clear, the CEO is judged in many ways by many observers. But surely the greatest effect of the corporate scandals of the last few years will be a much higher premium on the integrity and ethics of executives and their companies. The press has understandably devoted the greatest amount of attention to executives whose behavior has shocked and angered shareholders. Yet, as Joseph Badaracco of the Harvard Business School explains in the book's closing chapter, the executive who needs to decide between right and wrong has an easy choice. Far more difficult is when a business or a business leader must choose "between right and right." Badaracco examines the various frameworks that through history have helped guide moral decision-making and suggests how they can be applied to the universe of business decisions that executives cannot avoid.

The unmistakable lesson of the diverse chapters in this section is that the world is watching business behavior more closely than ever before. Corporate conduct must meet not only the higher legal standards that have recently been imposed, but also the much tougher questioning from the press, investors, and employees. In any given circumstance, making the right decision or providing the correct answer has become a much harder yet much more urgent task for business leaders.

CHAPTER SEVENTEEN

The View from the Street

Robert J. Hurst, vice chairman of the Goldman Sachs Group

Corporations are not the only entities that have felt the impact of the recent scandals, investigations, and investor distrust. Investment banks have also been shaken by the recent environment, and the leading institutions have put forth new procedures and rules to eliminate or fully disclose possible conflicts of interest. The role of Wall Street research has come under particularly close scrutiny, in part because regulators have openly questioned the independence of research conducted by investment banks and the relationship between research and banking operations.

Goldman Sachs has been among the most prominent investment-banking firms calling for higher standards across the board in the ways in which companies disclose financial information and the ways in which investment banks interact with them. The delicate relationship between Wall Street and its corporate clients is well known to Bob Hurst. He has spent nearly thirty years at Goldman Sachs, becoming vice chairman of the firm after a decade as co-head of its investment-banking division.

As he explains in this chapter, the relationship between Wall Street analysts and the companies on which they report is undergoing a dramatic change. Many of the new rules will alter the behavior of analysts, but they will also demand more of the CEOs and senior executives, who, he argues, must be more active in telling their story, provide more transparent data about company performance, and remain more accessible to investors.

GENERAL ELECTRIC'S 2001 annual report provided Wall Street and investors with more information than ever before. Sales and income were broken out for twenty-six businesses rather than twelve consolidated segments. The document contained greater disclosure of accounting practices and a large amount of data on GE Capital, the company's finance unit, which provides some 40 percent of GE's revenue. The wealth of information prompted one analyst to comment to *Business Week*, "If this was the way GE reported when I started covering the company, I would have understood it a lot sooner."

GE's 2001 annual report was a sign of a new era in business transparency. It is a welcome and, some would say, necessary change. Many companies are now—or soon will be—providing the same or greater breadth and depth of information to investors. As a result of the recent spate of corporate scandals, the troubled economy, and tough times for the stock market, responding to investors and making them confident about a company's financial data has become a critical corporate priority. We have entered an era in which there is a mistrust of business and skepticism about how public companies are governed. For many companies, the problem of winning back the public trust has been made harder by weak performance and depressed stock prices.

Today's challenge of developing investor trust is not insurmountable. Managing a relationship with Wall Street and the investor community has never been easy for public companies. It has always required corporate leaders to be proactive, credible, fair, and reasonable in their dealings. While those characteristics were always important, they are now essential. They are not, however, sufficient. Because of the greater degree of scrutiny, any public company that wants to enhance its standing among the investor community must focus on five areas: improving the transparency of financial data; expanding the accessibility of the CEO; managing expectations about future performance; understanding and respecting the work of Wall Street analysts; and establishing a focused approach to investor relations and communication. In this chapter, I will try to address each of these topics briefly.

The Importance of Transparency

Dragnet's Joe Friday would feel at home on Wall Street these days, because reports of misleading accounting practices at companies such as Enron and WorldCom, coupled with the rapid collapse of the stock market, have caused investors to demand that senior company officials give them "just the facts." For many company leaders, that will require a change in the communications style they once used with Wall Street. In the past, many CEOs played the role of corporate visionary: They understood their task as providing investors with a longer-term picture of the company's goals and objectives. Today investors have little appetite for "storytellers." To be sure, chief executives must clearly explain a company's strategy and growth prospects, but in addition they are expected to be very knowledgeable about balance-sheet, liquidity, and accounting issues. The chief financial officer will also be expected to play a bigger communication role, but increasingly CEOs will share the duty of interpreting financial data for analysts, shareholders, and business reporters. True transparency, though, extends beyond accounting and financial issues. A CEO needs to be knowledgeable in depth about operating issues, growth prospects, governance, and other conditions affecting the business and the industry.

Expanding Accessibility

The CEO will also have to be more accessible. It is no doubt less appealing for a chief executive to be accessible during down markets and tough times. Yet it is precisely when business performance is lackluster that contentious issues should not be left to a CFO or business-unit leader to explain. A CEO who personally addresses issues consistently through good and bad times will earn respect and a reservoir of goodwill that will help a company through more difficult periods.

Over the last decade, many CEOs have hardly been shrinking

violets. For some, appearances at investor conferences, business gatherings, and on magazine covers became overdone. Going forward, some of that visibility will need to continue, but it should be done judiciously, ideally as a deliberate part of a comprehensive communications plan.

Managing Expectations

The investor community does not usually hold a chief executive individually responsible for a company's valuation. Indeed, a CEO's inability to control valuation is a source of frustration to many corporate leaders. But a CEO can still set expectations. If those expectations can be met consistently over time, the CEO and the company have a much better chance of retaining credibility with Wall Street.

Corporate performance, of course, is the most important driver of valuation. That performance must be reported accurately and clearly but, also, put in the proper context. Investors will increasingly look to a CEO to give a comprehensive overview of a company's environment, assess its performance and progress within its industry, and offer a prognosis for the future. The ability to provide a context for company performance ultimately gives a greater weight and a sense of realism to forecasts.

As one might expect, the most important element of managing expectations is to avoid surprises. Today, both the overly optimistic and unnecessarily cautious forecasts erode credibility. Short of on-target forecasts, a company that modestly underpromises and modestly overdelivers will be rewarded for its predictability. With good corporate news a relatively scarce commodity, clear expectations are the next best thing. Sudden surprises are to be scrupulously avoided. They show that either business controls or communication is weak.

Respecting the Independence of Wall Street Research

The events of the last few years have compelled changes not only in the way CEOs deal with investors, but also in the way the sell-side research analysts will deal with companies and their executives going forward. The most important consequence of the April 2003 settlement between regulators and ten leading Wall Street firms has been the reaffirmation of the need for an independent research community. Even before the settlement was announced, many investment-banking firms had begun strengthening the walls between their research divisions and other parts of their operations to reinforce the principles of independence. Under the new, stricter rules, every research report issued by an analyst must be accompanied by a certification statement affirming that the views contained in the report are those of the analyst. The clear message of the new, stricter rules that will guide research departments is that stock research must act and be treated as an independent function.

This independence must be recognized and respected by senior management of a public company. Clearly, there are circumstances when a CEO can challenge an analyst's findings by pointing out an error or the failure to take account of assumptions made by the company. But in general, the best relationships between a company and an analyst will be based on the willingness of a CEO to accept the research product rather than hoping that they can influence it.

Attempts to pressure an analyst through an investment banker are both inappropriate and futile. In fact, under the new rules, there are no opportunities to apply pressure; a banker cannot talk to an analyst without permission from a central clearing office. If permission is granted, a "chaperone" must be present for all communication, whether in person or through voice mail, e-mail, or telephone. The role of the chaperone is to ensure that there be no pressure applied.

This posture toward the analyst community, even in the face of a negative research assessment, can actually benefit a company in two ways. First, analysts will demonstrate their objectivity, which may enhance their credibility and reputation over time. No one can be happy about a negative or critical report—yet by respecting such recommendations, the company will benefit when it is the subject of a positive report from the same analyst. Also remember that in this new environment it is likely that analysts will change ratings more frequently—today's "sell" may be tomorrow's "buy."

Second, over time analysts will assess CEOs in part by how they treat and respect the research effort. At a time when the entire investor community places a premium on executive candor and a willingness to deal openly, particularly in the face of negative results, the executive who tries to battle every critical research report will only weaken his or her standing.

Senior corporate management must also understand the many changes that have taken place in the research structure and stock-rating systems at all leading firms. In general, even though many firms have reduced the number of rating categories from five or six to just three, the process to make a recommendation has become more complex. That is because at most major firms, these new ratings are not measured against the entire universe of stocks followed by the firms, as was once the common practice, but against the smaller selection of stocks covered by that research analyst. Frequently, a firm will have more than one analyst covering an industry, and then all ratings will have to be overlaid against the firm's industry weightings. We should also expect a higher percentage of "sell" or "underperform" recommendations than in the past. Corporate leaders will need to get comfortable with these new rating systems and understand how they differ from firm to firm.

Understanding the ratings is important because analysts are going to be judged by them. As a result of the April 2003 settlement between regulators and Wall Street firms, a significant portion of analysts' compensation must be based on the predictive accuracy of their investment ratings. Getting those ratings right has, therefore, become a key motivator for the analyst profession.

Other changes in research should be expected. The research product will likely become more cautious and less colorful. There will be fewer analysts willing to make unorthodox interpretations of data as the new framework places a greater premium on purely objective, data-driven analysis. At the same time, relationships between analysts and the companies may become more formal. In order to avoid any appearance of impropriety, corporate executives will shy away from using analysts as sounding boards. The process of publishing reports and recommendations is also likely to be more cumbersome and bureaucratic as the need for more systems of internal approvals grows. Research departments will also cover fewer companies, making it harder for smaller capitalization companies to develop meaningful and broad coverage. Finally, the importance of "buy side" analysts will probably increase as Wall Street goes through dramatic changes in ratings, coverage, and analyst compensation.

Still, the new regulations should be welcomed. They are essential to rebuilding the credibility of the research product. They may make research reports easier to understand, and any potential conflicts of interest between the investment bank and its research will be transparent to the public. But the once-celebrated idiosyncratic writing and unique market interpretation by particular firms or individual analysts will, for better or worse, be a scarcer component of Wall Street research.

Targeting the Investor Base

More than ever, companies need a sophisticated approach to understanding their investor universe. That has become a more complex exercise than it was years ago. The investor base for a given company is frequently shifting. Moreover, the universe of investors can be highly segmented. Even within a single investment group, there can be different funds buying or selling a company stock at the same time.

Given this diversity, how does a company target investors? An investor-relations team should begin with a comprehensive approach to knowing who its shareholders are, who is selling and who is buying. A company needs to understand who is *not* a shareholder and the reasons behind the lack of interest. That requires identifying who is investing in other companies in the same industry, and at what level and proportion, or current shareholders who ought to have a larger stake in your company. A good investor-relations team should regularly compare the ownership of shares held by investors in other companies in the same industry.

It is also important to accept that changes will naturally occur in the shareholder base. For example, as share prices move up, there may be a shift from value to growth investors, or the investors attracted by yield may downsize their holdings as share prices rise and yields decline. Other external changes can influence investor buying or selling patterns. The recent tax-code changes that reduced the taxation of dividends, for example, will certainly alter the priorities of both companies and their investors. All these shifts in the investor base need to be carefully tracked and understood by a CEO and senior management.

For the CEO, knowing your shareholder base also provides flexibility and strength should the firm face a hostile bid or criticism from shareholder activists. Even before a challenge emerges, the CEO needs to know which of its shareholders are potential allies. Similar information is invaluable if the company is the acquirer or plans an equity financing. When a CEO is asking investors to support a significant strategic step, it greatly helps to have an already established relationship with major shareholders.

Developing a smart investor-targeting strategy also requires understanding two important changes in the nature of investing. First, investors are becoming more activist in their attitude toward companies. They are closely monitoring management, assessing governance, and calling for changes when thought necessary.

The second change is that hedge funds are growing in importance. CEOs and their IR departments may not like this trend, because they may expect hedge-fund managers to take a short-term view or simply take short positions. But these funds collectively are now too big to ignore, so companies must get to know them. Respected hedge funds can provide considerable liquidity to a company's stock, and, moreover, many of them take long positions. It is a part of the investor world that simply cannot be overlooked.

The Qualities of an Investor-Relations Department

Dealing with the Street and with investors is a demanding part of the CEO's job. To do the job effectively, a CEO must have confidence in the head of the IR department—the information gatekeeper.

There is no single type of background that is best for a director of investor relations. Investor relations can be performed successfully by career professionals or people with a finance background. Sometimes the public-affairs department handles investor relations in conjunction with a consulting firm; sometimes it is run by the CFO. The important thing is not the structure of the operation so much as its character—it must be credible, proactive, and accessible.

A CEO has to know at all times how the head of investor relations is perceived by the Street. Is he or she viewed as honest, smart, direct, and available? CEOs should seek as their head of IR someone who is willing to stand up to the CEO. He or she must be willing to deliver bad news and, also, to be ready and able to guide the CEO in his or her dealings with the Street. Above all, the head of IR should be proactive in addressing the issues on the minds of investors and should aim to reach an ever-growing number of shareholders.

Since Wall Street conferences take up an increasing amount of time, deciding on which conferences to go to and which to pass on requires good intelligence from the IR department. If, for example, the bulk of other presenters or panelists are below the CEO level, then the CEO might designate someone else to make the presentation. Still, that decision has to be balanced with the need to keep a CEO accessible to the investor community. The best method is to be selective about institutional meetings and conferences while pursuing regular one-on-one meetings with significant investors. Technology also provides some efficient alternatives. Many companies, for example, frequently stage webcasts that attract thousands of viewers.

The new climate of the investing world will force companies to rethink not only their methods for communicating but also the substance of those communications. This is particularly true with respect to quarterly estimates. The corporate and Wall Street scandals of the last few years, combined with the volatile stock market, may have become the events that ultimately change the earnings perspective.

Quarterly estimates have proven to be a problematic measure of a company's long-term financial prospects, and Wall Street's overreliance on quarterly forecasts have led some companies to use questionable or overly aggressive accounting practices in order to meet estimates. But today's emphasis on "just the facts" now applies both to companies as they prepare and frame their financial reports and to analysts who assess the meaning of those reports. Over time, it will, hopefully, produce a greater emphasis on full-year or even longer-term results.

This trend has been helped by the actions of a few bold companies. Coca-Cola announced in December 2002 that it would no longer provide quarterly or annual earnings estimates to investors. Instead, Coca-Cola will provide information that it says will help investors understand the long-term goals of the business. "We believe that establishing short-term guidance prevents a more meaningful focus on the strategic initiatives that a company is taking to build its business and succeed over the long run," said Coca-Cola's chairman and CEO, Douglas Daft.

Intel is another company that doesn't provide quarterly financial forecasts. The company instead provides analysts with key business metrics and range estimates. "We've never forecasted earnings per share or profitability. We forecast a group of factors related to business fundamentals—top-line revenue in a range, a range of gross margin, a range of expenses," Intel spokesman Chuck Mulloy told *Business 2.0* in December 2002. "Taking a long-term approach has worked for us."

This long-term approach and a focus on just the facts are consistent with the other changes that emerged from the corporate scandals of 2001 and 2002. Investors, Wall Street analysts, and the companies themselves will benefit enormously from more transparent financial data, CEOs who are accessible and knowledgeable about balance-sheet issues, properly managed forecasts, a respect for the independence of research, and a carefully focused strategy toward investor communications. Certainly from the investor perspective, these are the areas most in need of attention. If dealt with properly, they will help restore the credibility and confidence that the investment world needs to function and thrive.

CHAPTER EIGHTEEN

Building Confident Investors

Mark W. Begor, president and CEO of GE Consumer Finance–Americas and former head of Investor Communications at General Electric

Mark Begor joined GE after college and had spent nearly sixteen years at various positions in the company when Jack Welch selected him to manage the company's Investor Communications. As he describes in this chapter, Investor Communications has a special role at GE that the CEO watches and depends upon. Working closely with Welch, Begor was able to observe how the analyst and investor community deals with one of the world's most closely watched companies.

Begor quickly distinguished himself as an indispensable source of information for Welch and a widely respected and trusted source for the investor community. The trade publication *Investor Relations* named him Officer of the Year in 1997 and 1998. After two years running Investor Communications, he moved to another part of GE: NBC. There he has served as executive vice president and chief financial officer and since 2000 as CFO and president of NBC Business Development and Interactive Media.

IT COULD HAVE BEEN any time of the day. When I was running Investor Communications at GE and my phone rang, there was a very good chance that when I picked it up I would hear Jack Welch's voice. He might have been just checking in to ask what the big institutional investors or the analysts were talking about, or about who was buying and who was selling GE stock. Or he might have just wanted to make sure that we were getting out the message that we were buying a company in Hungary or had just secured a new order from British Airways. The point is that Jack was engaged, as is his successor, Jeff Immelt. As head of IR, I would have daily conversations with Jack, wherever he was in the world. He always wanted to know what was on investors' minds.

That is a unique feature of GE, and one that explains a lot about the success of its investor-relations program: At GE, the CEO takes a personal and ongoing interest in investor relations. In fact, the CEO *owns* investor relations. On paper, the head of IR may report to the CFO; in practice, it is a continual, direct relationship with the CEO. GE's head of IR hears from the CEO constantly and has ongoing access to the CEO.

It starts with the way in which the head of IR is chosen. Both Welch and Immelt treat the IR position in a special way. Like many companies, GE used to move career communications people into the IR job. Jack Welch changed that a couple of decades ago. Now, at GE, the CEO handpicks the head of IR, looking for someone who has shown potential and has had broad exposure to the company—usually in finance, where one gets the chance to learn about the entire business from an investor-oriented point of view. For example, I was previously in a number of financial roles in GE's plastics business, including three years in Singapore as CFO for the Asian plastics business. One GE IR alumnus, Mark Vachon, became the CFO at NBC; another, Jay Ireland, runs NBC Television Stations.

The Most Important IR Tool: Access

GE's focus on investor relations includes access: At some companies, the IR people are too far down in the organization to get the full picture of the company. The analysts know they are not getting the story from them, so they try to run around them and get to the CEO or CFO. The investor community knows that at GE, investor relations is in the game. I firmly believe that is one of the fundamental elements of a successful investor-relations program. If the head of IR is buried somewhere in the organization and not directly connected to the top of the company, investors and analysts will have little confidence in him or her. They have to know that when they are talking to the head of IR, they are talking to the company.

The close access that Jack Welch gave me included physical proximity. My office was one floor directly below Jack's. Given how often I heard from him, sometimes I thought he would just start banging on the floor when he wanted me! Hardly a day would go by when I was in IR that Jack didn't call me to ask what was the word on the Street—what are the big investors thinking about; what's on their minds? After a specific announcement, he would be on to me to find out how the investment community was reacting to it: What did they think of the big acquisition we just made? Are they worried about our rates?

When we were looking to make an acquisition, I would be at the table, and the consideration would always be how Wall Street would react. I sat on GE's Corporate Executive Council, which is mostly made up of the CEO's direct reports. As head of IR, I participated in shaping the corporate strategy of the company. I sat in all the strategic reviews and budget-planning sessions. I probably spent 20 percent of my time on meetings like that to keep connected to all aspects of the company. What were the benefits of all of this access? When anything was going to happen, I was in a position to explain it to the Street. I was also in a position to get the analysts' attention. Some companies' IR people find it hard to get a meeting with analysts. But if I went to meeting with a mutual-fund firm like Fidelity, there would be twenty people in the room. The reason? They knew I spoke for the company and was involved in all aspects of GE's operations and strategy. I owed that to Jack Welch, and the current head of IR has the same advantage because of Jeff Immelt. The important thing is that the analysts know that GE's head of IR is inside the room when the decisions are made.

An effective IR strategy also includes empowerment: Jack did something to bolster my ability to get access to the entire senior management team. He said to senior management: The second most important call you will get is from Mark Begor—you have to help him communicate our message to the Street and be responsive to their issues. That was a huge asset. Thanks to Jack, I was never denied information or any other resource I needed.

What's the Message?

An engaged CEO, an empowered head of IR with access to the top—those are vital tools. The next question is: What do you do with them?

In my view, the most important thing to do with those tools is to use them to carve out a consistent and clear message. In that respect, IR is a form of finance marketing and communications. The goal of investor relations cannot be simply to distribute pieces of information. The challenge is to tie all of those pieces together to shape a message, one that gives a bird's-eye view of the entire company—and a vantage point to see its future. That may be especially important to GE, because it is so large and so diverse. But increasingly, all companies have some degree of diversity, so GE's experience is not all that different from other companies trying to sell their stock to the Street.

Of course, we never ignored the details. Our approach was always to have plenty of news and detail about each of our different businesses. We would thoroughly and carefully walk analysts through NBC, Plastics, Aircraft Engines, and all of the other businesses.

But even as we talked about the pieces, we always brought it back to the whole of GE. We tried to answer the big questions—stated or unstated—that we knew were on the analysts' minds: What are the broad, far-reaching initiatives that GE has? What differentiates GE from other large-cap industrials? We tried to boil all of the information down to the key initiatives the company was focused on. We always stressed the big themes that told the company's overall story.

Take the theme of the company's globalization. In the mid-'90s, globalizing GE was a major, across-the-board company initiative. In all of our IR initiatives, we spent a lot of time talking about that, bringing the story back to the globalization of GE . . . by globalizing each business. For example, if we brought our Power Systems head to an analysts' meeting, he would talk about power systems and turbine orders—you can't ignore the specifics. But we would also tie it back to the big GE message—in this case, the globalization of power systems.

We would take the same approach to our service strategy. GE had found that servicing some of our products yielded a higher margin than manufacturing them. We built that into our investor communications strategy. In all of our analyst meetings, we devoted time to demonstrating our increased focus on service activities. If the focus of the meeting was Aircraft Engines, we would provide data that demonstrated how we were moving beyond just building and delivering aircraft engines to servicing them.

We would take the same thematic approach in focusing our message on Six Sigma—GE's disciplined statistical approach, aimed at constantly improving the company's products and services—and our digitization strategy, aimed at bolstering access to information across the company. Since Jeff Immelt has taken over as CEO, he has added two new themes to stress with investors: customer-centricity—GE's ability to embed itself in the customer's business and understand and respond to the customer's needs and technical leadership—and GE's continued investment in new products and features. Jeff held an investor meeting at our research center in upstate New York to introduce the new technology initiative.

In most large companies, there are so many moving parts that it is difficult to boil down what the business is all about and where you are trying to take it. That is one of the biggest challenges of investor relations, and it is one that no company can shrink from. It is crucial to give portfolio managers and investors something to think about beyond that aircraft-engine order, that power-systems shipment, or how appliance sales are going with Sears. It gives them something broader to think about—and that is one of the primary goals of IR strategy: to get the investment community thinking about the company's big picture.

Who's the Audience?

Shaping the message is half the job. The other half is delivering it. IR has to deliver the company's investor message continually—and with immediacy. There is little point in trying to provide a perspective on old news. If you are not talking to the analysts about whatever it was the company did yesterday, somebody else is in there getting their message out.

I strongly believe that one of the key elements of success in investor relations is to treat as customers the investors and analysts with whom you are communicating. IR's job is to service the people who have influence over the company's share price, just as the sales and marketing divisions service the people who have influence over the company's revenue.

I saw my work as dealing with two groups of customers: sell-side analysts and buy-side analysts.

We have seen a significant change in the role and nature of sell-side analysts, who depend on the company for information, which they publish to the Street. Sell-side analysts traditionally have acted as reporters. But for reporters to be credible, their objectivity must be unquestioned, even taken for granted. Unfortunately, sell-side analysts recently have found themselves in conflicts within their firm and clients. The companies being analyzed were potential investment-banking clients, and no firm wanted to antagonize them. As a result, there was a tendency for the firm's analysts to cultivate relations with the management of the companies they were following.

Given the considerable controversy that has surrounded the relationship between analysts and companies, sell-side analysts today are more sensitive about covering bad news. Now they want to be the first and the loudest to cover it—even pounding on companies over small issues—in order to demonstrate their independence. That makes it important to keep in close touch with the analysts, in order to get a sense of any tough questions that may be coming down the road. The key is continual contact. About thirty sell-side analysts followed GE; I would have a conversation with close to half of them on a daily basis.

But sell-side analysts have seen a slide in their influence. So while we continue to spend time with them, our focus is on spending our time with the buy-side—portfolio managers or analysts for mutual funds who make the decisions about buying stock. In fact, when it came to the buy-side analysts, I didn't just invest my own time—we invested Jack Welch's. For example, we would go to Boston two to three times a year to visit the large mutual funds like Putnam, Wellington, and Fidelity. In fact, if we believed it was important enough, on a minute's notice he would do a one-on-one meeting with a buy-side manager or analyst.

But no company is all about one person, no matter how dynamic he or she may be. I would take CEOs of other GE businesses to mutual funds, such as Bob Wright of NBC to T. Rowe Price in Baltimore. When you have great leaders on your team, you want to get them out to meet with the investment community. We believed it was important to make sure that investors saw not just the CEO who was batting cleanup but also the depth of the GE bench. That demonstrates to the Street that the company is more than one person. It puts a face to a broader group of people.

It's a battle for "share of mind" among the analysts and investors. If you are not in front of Fidelity or Putnam or Janus, someone else is. IR at GE is a marketing-communications job—the link between GE and Wall Street. In order to communicate with investors, you have to spend time with them—on the road, face to face.

And you have to marshal the numbers that allow you to target investors and back up your case as to why they should be investing in your company. Before I would go to see a customer—such as a mutual fund or a large portfolio—I would analyze what other big-cap stocks they had in their portfolio. I would compare their growth rate to GE's growth rate. In understanding how to deal with the buy-side analysts, we employed plenty of analytics about GE stock—who was buying it and who was selling it. We would look at who didn't own stock and who should. Jack used to say, "Everyone should own GE stock, and everyone should own more of it!" So we would examine the funds, profile them, and make an assessment as to whether the profile of their investments met the profile of GE. Based on that, we would determine if their portfolio was underweighted in the stock and then target the fund for owning more GE.

Take Fidelity. When I came into the job, Fidelity was underweighted in GE stock. So I made that a priority, spending enormous amounts of time helping fund managers to understand the company, our strategy, our growth potential, and our future. That involved a great many face-to-face meetings.

Of course, big investors are inundated with information and visits. How to make your company stand out? My view of that is somewhat counterintuitive. Rather than hold back because analysts are flooded with information, I believe it's important to keep up a constant drumbeat of communications and information to the investment community. If your customers hear from you on a continual basis, they will be comfortable with you. That comfort level allows information about your company to stand out.

For that reason, GE constantly provides analysts and large investors with information about what the company is doing. Working closely with the corporate-communications department, IR would send out information any time there was any news that would make a difference to investors, such as when GE got a big customer order, or there was news concerning NBC or GE Capital or a development in Plastics. We had a fax/e-mail list of more than two thousand analysts and investors and used the Internet to communicate information on our website; I would follow up with phone calls to key investors.

The IR Mantra: Proactive, Proactive, Proactive

I've always believed that one of the keys to an effective investor-communication program was being proactive. The role of IR is getting in front of issues, not just responding to them. At GE, we always had a rolling twelve-month communication plan for IR, one that included details such as when we were going to meet with an investor group, or even when the next investor group was going to be invited to NBC or another GE business. Today, that is more important than ever. Investors are demanding transparency. That is why CEOs and CFOs and heads of businesses are meeting so frequently with the investment community, far more frequently than ever before.

Let me give you an example of the increasingly proactive nature of IR. At GE, as I explained, we always made it a point of keeping in touch with analysts and large investors. But we never did quarterly-earnings conference calls until recently. We would release earnings, and we would have one-on-one meetings with the analysts. But quarterly calls were seen as a lot of work offering little reward, especially when a call became dominated by an analyst who wanted to talk about one small aspect of GE that would have little to do with the big picture, or someone who would want us to comment on our competitive positioning vis-à-vis another company. The big picture would tend to be obscured. But today, quarterly calls are absolutely necessary. It is the best way to provide the transparency that the market demands.

Being proactive also includes focusing on potential problems, such as an analyst who is skeptical about the company. On Wall

Street, there is a practice known as "icing"—that's when you freeze an analyst who is critical of the company, cut him or her off from information. I believe that is a big mistake. Rather than freeze them out, the best way to deal with doubters is to draw them in. Spend more time with analysts who have concerns—otherwise, their view of the company grows darker and darker, and they will never see your perspective. It is necessary to spend time with them, to put forward the company's strategy, its strengths, and how the strategy and the strengths build on each other.

If you are the head of IR and haven't heard from an analyst in a while, then the mountain has to go to Mohammed. It's important to get on the phone and, perhaps, invite the analyst in to see some of the businesses.

One of the most crucial tools of the IR trade is the airplane—almost as valuable as the telephone and e-mail. Information is what the IR business is all about, and the best way for anyone to really digest information is in person. If a picture is worth a thousand words, an on-site visit is worth a million. We would take analysts on tours of our European operations and our Asian operations. Or we would take some lucky analysts to Erie, Pennsylvania, to show them what was happening in our locomotive business or to Milwaukee, Wisconsin, to review GE's new medical-imaging equipment.

It comes down to telling a story. If you have a story to tell that you believe in, a story that you are proud of—a story that the investment community will find compelling—there is no excuse for not constantly getting it out. The important thing is to have the active support of the CEO and use that to marshal the resources of the company—including the heads of businesses, the internal experts, the data, and the leverage that comes from being a dynamic company's voice on the Street. Clearly, the world has changed since I was in the investor-communications game, but the success drivers are the same: access, communication, communication, and communication.

CHAPTER NINETEEN

Controlling the Message

Christoph J. Walther, founding partner and CEO of (Communications & Network Consulting) AG and former senior vice president and head of Global Communications at DaimlerChrysler

As the head of communications for Daimler-Benz and then, following the historic merger, DaimlerChrysler, Christoph Walther during the late 1990s had a front-row seat at one of the most important transatlantic mergers of the decade. Jürgen Schrempp, Daimler's CEO, was already widely known in Europe, and the merger with Chrysler made him among the most prominent global chief executives.

Walther soon found himself shuttling across the Atlantic to keep the DaimlerChrysler story straight in both Auburn Hills, Michigan, and Stuttgart, Germany. His work for the company won broad recognition, including the *Financial Times* award for the best reputation of a German company in 1999 and the Best Automative Company award from the *Wall Street Journal*'s Image Study in 2000.

The lessons that Walther drew from his experience would not necessarily please the reporters who always wanted access to Jürgen Schrempp and other senior executives from the company. Walther counsels other CEOs to focus their message clearly, limit the number of people with access to the press, and repeat the same message continuously—something many executives must do if they are going to penetrate the press.

In 2001, Walther left DaimlerChrysler to found his own communications firm.

WHEN THE EUROPEAN EDITION of the *Wall Street Journal* hit the streets on May 6, 1998—just hours before Daimler-Benz and Chrysler announced that we were engaged in merger talks—it was the first time that word of these discussions had leaked beyond a small circle of senior executives of the two companies. In any major corporate action, there is a reason for including in the loop only those who absolutely need to know. Controlling the information is crucial to controlling the message.

Any time a company takes its case to the public—proactively in announcing a major move such as a merger, reactively in response to a crisis—it must decide on a message and shape a strategy to support it. The press sometimes compares a major announcement to an earthquake, referring to it as "earth-shattering news." That is an apt comparison. Like an earthquake, a major announcement has aftershocks. An important story will last more than a couple of news cycles.

The first blast has to come from the company. Its message has to be the one that makes the noise. But one big bang isn't sufficient for a strategy to be successful. A successful strategy must take into account the aftershocks; the company's message must resonate through each of them. If a company cannot control the news—if word leaks out before it is prepared to make the announcement *and* follow up on it—then it will be unable to back up its messaging through each successive round of news coverage.

Nail Down the Message

The substance of the message is central to the success of the strategy. If your message is indistinct, you lose focus. Some seem to think that in order to make a message compelling, it is necessary to educate the broad public on all of the factors that contributed to making a corporate decision necessary. But there is a huge difference between conducting a symposium and conducting a communications strategy. In conducting a symposium, there might be dozens of aspects of an issue you would need to discuss, starting with the economic factors that caused it. In conducting a communications strategy, there should be no more than three or four factors to emphasize. Each of them should be of relevance to the people with whom you are trying to communicate, and all of them should lead clearly to and directly back up the corporate action you are trying to promote.

Consider the DaimlerChrysler merger. No doubt it stemmed from a number of factors that reflected the state of the international auto industry in the mid-1990s, including increased industry consolidation and the need to economize. There was an internal debate about whether to explain this environment, emphasizing the impact of globalization on the auto industry and the various alternative ways of dealing with it as a prelude to setting up our message. But that would have diluted the impact of the initial announcement. We would have been providing the media and the public with an interesting analysis, not a persuasive message.

Our starting point had to be why the merger was the right thing to do, most importantly for the companies' shareholders and other stakeholders.

We started with a four-part message: This was a merger to promote growth, a merger of complementary brands and products, a merger to ensure global reach, and a merger to bolster technological leadership. What we were saying to Daimler and Chrysler shareholders, employees, suppliers, and interested communities was "Here are the ways this merger will benefit you." That is what investors and stakeholders want to know. It is important that they hear a clear answer and that the first answer they hear to their questions is the one that underpins the decision you are building support for.

To ensure that a message will be understandable and persuasive to the broad spectrum of people at whom it is aimed, I like to make sure it passes what might be called the "man-on-the-street test." If someone who isn't involved in planning the strategy—someone I know who has about as much information as the average man or woman on the street—is able to understand the message and relate to it, then I am confident that I have a solid message. Otherwise, it is time to go back to the drawing board.

Nailing down the right message is not optional. If you don't focus attention on the elements of the story you want to convey, you can be assured that someone else will draw attention to the elements of the story that you *don't* want to convey. Having started my communications career in Europe, I am intimately familiar with the tabloid newspapers. But they are not the only ones in the media capable of sensationalizing a story and headlining its most negative aspects. Either you tell the story, or someone will tell it for you.

Conveying the Message

How do you ensure that your message gets across? The following elements are crucial.

Limit the Messengers:

Any choir leader knows that the bigger the choir, the harder it is to make sure that all the members carry the tune. The same is true of corporate communications. The more people who are empowered to speak on behalf of the company, the greater the risk is of the message breaking down, with everyone running off in all directions with his or her own favorite argument. In the first weeks of the DaimlerChrysler merger, only four people—the two CEOs, Jürgen Schrempp of Daimler and Robert Eaton of Chrysler; the head of communications, Steve Harris of Chrysler; and myself—were allowed to talk about it once it was announced. While it is difficult to manage that kind of tight control for an extended period of time, experience has shown that the more control you have over the process, the better the outcome is. In any major announcement, I would advise limiting the authorized spokespeople to the chairman, CEO, COO, CFO, head of communications, and maybe the head of the business unit, as long as they are properly prepared and have undergone extensive periodic media training.

Plan for Follow-Up:

As I mentioned, no major news story lasts only one news cycle. Major news stories break in waves. The first wave is the announcement itself. That one is the easiest to control, as long as you have successfully kept the announcement under wraps and used your time to prepare for the kick-off. It is important to have a second and third wave of news planned well in advance. That is not as difficult as it sounds, because one can anticipate the various news angles the media will pursue.

Inevitably, for example, the media will follow an important corporate announcement with stories about the reaction of "respected third parties," experts in the field such as academics and industry and financial analysts. It is important to anticipate who will be asked for comment and, beforehand, provide them with the background information that underlines and supports your message. It is important to have hard data in visual form—maps, charts, models—that paint pictures in people's minds.

"Second-party" reaction comes from a smaller group—such as employees and union representatives—who can be reached with greater ease. Since they are more likely to have a direct stake in the issue, it is important to identify those who are likely to be supportive of the announcement and ensure that they understand its benefits and that they have the information they need. When people talk about communication, the emphasis is usually on external communication. But in-house communication has an equally important role to play. How often do you see employees being interviewed on television or quoted in the newspapers regarding their reaction to a major corporate announcement? If it is an important story, you will see it quite often. While very few can be in the loop before an announcement is made, it is important to open up as soon as the story breaks.

Repeat, Repeat, Repeat:

A CEO or any other corporate spokesperson has to be prepared to sound like a broken record. The message should become the spokesperson's mantra and be repeated over and over again. That quickly becomes boring to the person doing all of the repeating. CEOs don't usually like that. They are intelligent, creative people, and they are used to showing leadership. Constantly repeating the same points can become boring quite quickly. I know many CEOs who absolutely dislike it. But they do it, because they understand its importance. What CEOs have to keep in mind is that it may be boring for them to repeat the message, but the people listening to them are probably hearing it for the first time or, at least, focusing on it for the first time. Look at it this way: Even *Hamlet* could become boring if you have performed the part thousands of times. But that doesn't mean the audience isn't paying attention.

Never Answer a Hypothetical Question:

That first *what if* question may seem like a no-brainer. But it sets up the next one. Pretty soon you find yourself trapped in a maze of hypotheticals. Even that might not seem so bad when you are sitting there with a reporter engaged in a theoretical discussion. But when your answer becomes a television clip or a newspaper quote, it creates the impression that the hypothetical scenario is a real possibility. The only way to avoid this problem is to cut it off at the pass, by using five of the most valuable words in communications: *"I don't answer hypothetical questions."*

Turning Negatives into Positives

Unfortunately, corporate communications is not just about proactively making announcements and following up on them. Life would be a lot easier if it were. But there is also the matter of news that a company does not want to make. Very often it is therefore even more necessary to be able to deal with the bad-news story.

When I signed on with Daimler-Benz, I knew that my expertise in crisis management would be put to the test. I had been working for the tobacco industry, which meant that I was more than familiar with high-profile public-relations challenges. The chairman was planning to turn Daimler from a technology conglomerate into one of the world's leading automotive manufacturers, so I knew that there would be a number of communications challenges.

In many respects, the principles of crisis management are the same as the principles of making a major "good news" announcement. It is important to shape a message, as soon as possible, and repeat it as often as possible. It is important to identify a limited group of authorized spokespeople, and it is crucial to avoid responding to hypothetical questions. But there are some important differences. When responding to a crisis, you are under pressure and under the glare of the media spotlight, rather than presenting the story in a time and manner of your own choosing. It is crucial that a company not fall into the trap of saying something it will regret.

In these situations, I recommend what many would regard as a contrarian approach. In a crisis, most communications consultants advise a client always to be proactive. I believe that depends on the nature of the crisis. There are some crises that demand an immediate, proactive response in which the CEO takes center stage. A plane crash, a natural disaster—an event in which lives are lost or endangered—demands a visible company presence at the highest level, one that demonstrates empathy and involvement. Those are characteristics that by definition cannot be delegated or postponed.

On the other hand, there are crises that do not present such a black-and-white issue. There are crises, such as an environmental or product-safety problem, in which the causes and effects are not clear and no clear solution has been identified. In my view, the CEO should not immediately be center stage in those situations, because he or she will face pressure to make a snap decision or at least hint at some kind of solution. The CEO (and therefore the entire company) will have to end up having to flip-flop and, therefore, sacrifice corporate credibility. The CEO should not be visible until the appropriate policy decision is clear; at that point, and that point only, it is time for the CEO to move to the center of the stage. Until then, statements should go out in the name of the senior person directly responsible for the specific business that is involved.

At Daimler, we faced such a challenge in October 1997. It landed at our doorstep when a car failed something called an "Elk Test." The Elk Test originated in Sweden, where it is not all that unusual for a moose or elk to jump out onto the road and become a dangerous obstacle. Under the test, to be considered safe a car needs to be able to approach an elk at a minimum of thirty-seven miles per hour and be able to swerve and return to the proper lane. Daimler faced a potential crisis when a Swedish journalist wrote that the soon-to-be launched Mercedes A-class model would flip over if an elk ran out of the woods and a driver had to avoid hitting the animal. Within two weeks, it seemed like everybody in Europe was talking about the A class and the dreaded elk.

At that point, we did not have a clear understanding of the degree of the problem, much less a solution. Until we had that nailed down, Daimler's CEO kept a low public profile. The head of the division—Mercedes-Benz Passenger Cars—was the spokesman. We didn't have a solid answer for the press, so it was his job to convince the public that we take the problem seriously and that we were working on a solution.

Once the facts were in, the engineers were able to address the problem. At that point, Jürgen Schrempp came out to talk to the media, announcing that within three months we would—among other modifications—introduce an electronic stability system in every Class A car. By doing so, he demonstrated the full commitment of the company and its board.

Schrempp's announcement was the "first wave" of our media strategy to regain our credibility. As with any announcement, we also had to deal with the second and third wave of media coverage. We obtained a third-party testimonial from Formula One driver and world champion Niki Lauda, who proclaimed the Mercedes A the safest car he had ever driven. Obviously, we wanted to reach the widest possible audience for Lauda's endorsement, but we did not want to do it in the form of an advertisement. That would have diminished the credibility of his judgment. Instead, we produced a documentary focused on the elk test with the "new" A class driven by Lauda.

Before we launched production of the modified A-class model, we prepared for the next wave—the investigative-journalism phase—by conducting workshops for journalists, explaining the physical dynamics so they could understand the effectiveness of the modifications we were making.

Managing the Elk Test crisis was not just a matter of communications strategy. Daimler had to solve the engineering problem before we could shape any kind of message. Even then, it was not a one-dimensional communications strategy. It required use of several media (including the documentary). It required a testimonial from a respected third party. It demanded an intense educational effort among journalists. But with all of that, it might well not have succeeded if the CEO had been out front from the beginning. Under the circumstances, a CEO might feel pressure to say something off-message (an especially risky proposition when a message has yet to be developed). He might have been put in the situation of defending a class of car that we would subsequently have to modify. If that had been the case, the ultimate story would not have been "Daimler makes major investment to make Mercedes Class A safe." The story would have been "Daimler forced to re-work model that CEO claimed was safe."

More than anything, this incident reinforced for me the importance of using a CEO strategically. As in chess, the best way to protect the king is to keep him out of danger. That is why I have a slightly different approach from many communications consultants. Many PR professionals emphasize the importance of a "visible" CEO. I agree with that wholeheartedly. But there is a difference between being visible and being accessible. CEOs should speak only when they have something to say. If they go out without a clear message, the media will keep pressing until they are able to come up with their own angle. CEOs should grant interviews, but they should be carefully targeted, in-depth interviews. The CEO should be trying to build relationships with top journalists, and you can't build a relationship in ten minutes. It makes more sense to grant three one-hour interviews rather than twenty ten-minute quickies. The emphasis should be on quality time.

If I were to sum up these strategic concepts—strict messaging, constant repetition, discerning use of the CEO, carefully planned and prepared phases for all announcements—they are characterized by one word: *discipline*. Without it, a company cannot make its case, no matter how many arguments it has on its side. With it, a company can get its story across in a way that people can relate to. Ultimately, that is the purpose of corporate communications.

CHAPTER TWENTY

Getting Fair News Coverage

Matthew Bishop, business editor of *The Economist*

At some point in their tenure, all CEOs must deal with the media. When pressed, most concede that it is a part of their job they would rather do without. Although many executives have been the subject of fawning and flattering press coverage—and, indeed, some have actively courted it—most business leaders tread carefully around reporters. A single "negative" story can not only embarrass the CEO who cooperated with the reporter, it can also do substantial damage to the company's reputation and stock price. For this reason, CEOs often regard the business press as a kind of adversary, sometimes relying on a public relations staff to keep the most persistent reporters at bay.

Yet relationships with the press remain a critical part of a CEO's responsibility—and, some would argue, even more critical in the new era of public skepticism toward corporations. For this reason, the CEO Academy has always invited a leading member of the business press to provide his or her perspective on covering executives and their companies.

In his presentation to the Academy and in this chapter, Matthew Bishop argues that CEOs ought to strike a less defensive posture toward journalists and invest more time in developing a cordial and professional relationship with them. The contemporary business journalist is an educated professional trying to capture the most interesting and accurate information about a company and its leaders. When CEOs are able to establish a trusting dialogue with good reporters, the result is better quality business coverage.

Bishop has worked at *The Economist* for 12 years, where he has served as American finance editor, New York bureau chief, and now business editor. Prior to that he was on the faculty of the London Business School.

GETTING FAIR NEWS COVERAGE

AS STORY-HUNGRY journalists, there is nothing we like more than to talk to business executives. But why, I ask with tongue slightly in cheek, would a business executive ever want to talk to a reporter?

One of the most refreshing interviews I ever took part in was with the CEO of a Wall Street trading firm who had spent a long time avoiding the interview. We eventually arranged to get together, and the first question put to him was why he had been so elusive. His answer cut right to the chase. As he put it, "I hate talking to you bastards in the press and I'm only talking to you now because my PR person has told me I've got to." I thought that was a nice refreshing breath of honesty, and we went on from there to complete a very productive interview.

The reality is that there are all sorts of ways of avoiding talking to the press or managing your press relations. If they are determined and have decent luck, CEOs can get away without ever speaking to the media. So why do it?

At bottom, the main argument for talking to a reporter is that if an executive doesn't tell us his or her story, somebody else will. The difference is that "somebody else" might not be shy at all about talking—particularly since they probably won't have a PR person sitting there censoring what they say and may well be talking off the record. For that matter, "somebody else" might even have an ax to grind, deliberately trying to put the worst possible spin on a story. In short, executives and their corporate communication staff should understand that business stories that interest the public often can't be suppressed simply because an executive refuses to talk to a reporter. Any executive who is weighing a decision about whether to talk to the press should assume that a good (i.e., often bad for the company) story will find its way into the media regardless.

Getting a Fair Hearing

CEOs and executives who spend time with the press have many different motivations. Some do so out of a vague sense of civic duty, a belief that the corporate world must communicate on an ongoing basis with the broad public. This is something that I as a journalist thoroughly applaud—however much I suspect it is often a bad strategy for the bosses concerned! Some do so in hopes of getting flattering profiles. Of course, many do it thinking, often wishfully, that it will help raise their company's share price. However, I actually believe that if there is one overriding reason to talk to the media—particularly the high-end media whom people trust, such as the *Wall Street Journal, The Economist*, the *New York Times, Financial Times*, and *Business Week*—it is to get a fair hearing when things get tough. A CEO needs to have a relationship with people in publications such as these in order to obtain the benefit of the doubt when a potentially bad story breaks—at least in the early rounds. Good ongoing media relations do not buy good media coverage, but they often do buy a chance to put your side of the story to someone who knows more about you than that you are in trouble. They give a CEO or a company the credibility that can counteract any tendency in the media to present a story from only one side, often the most negative one.

The media coverage that Jacques Nasser received as a result of the recall of Bridgestone/Firestone tires may not have seemed all that friendly, but the truth is that the media tended initially to assign most of the blame to the tiremakers, rather than the automaker. Nasser's constant mantra—"It's a tire problem, not a vehicle problem"—seemed to be assigned more credibility by the media, even as Ford became the target of millions of dollars in lawsuits. How did Nasser initially manage to deflect so much of the blame to the tire company? He had an opening advantage: good and established relations with the media—good enough to get the benefit of the doubt. The Japan-based leaders of Bridgestone/Firestone, by contrast, were barely known to American business reporters. Good relations with reporters can't buy good press when a company is in the wrong. But at the outset of a crisis, they may buy time and ensure a fair hearing when a company is besieged by critics.

Consider another example from the opposite side of the media-sympathy spectrum: John Meriwether, one of the leaders of Long-Term Capital Management. One of his deepest regrets was that he just didn't have people in the press to whom he talked on a regular basis. The mistake had been failing to cultivate that kind of relationship. As a result, alternative interpretations of Long-Term's financial implosion (e.g., Wall Street investment banks were using Long-Term's troubles to their own advantage and thereby making its problems worse), which might have put the hedge fund in a better light, did not get reported much. Without Mr. Meriwether to put such stories to them, the press were content to feast on the failed genius angle.

Pitfalls to Avoid

Whatever one's reasons for talking to the news media, there are good ways and bad ways of going about it. Too often, executives believe they need an array of maneuvers to "deal" with the press—steps that often backfire.

Pressure

The first tactic I would avoid is trying to intimidate a journalist or a publication in the wake of a negative article. No one likes criticism or what they believe is unfair reporting. However, it amazes me how prickly some CEOs can get at profiles that are largely positive except for the odd line of criticism, sometimes thrown in to add both balance and levity to a business article. Yet that single line of criticism sometimes becomes a preoccupation of the business executive and his organization. Rather than accepting the fact the company has received a positive piece, the executive and his senior staff complain to the reporter and his editors, invariably poisoning the relationship for the future.

In some cases, though, companies unhappy with their press coverage express their anger over it in far worse ways. One favorite is to threaten to cancel—or even to actually cancel—advertising, to punish the newspaper or magazine. But however unfairly an executive feels that he or his company has been treated, the confrontational mode—including the decision to pull advertising—is one of the least effective ways to make your case to the press, or at least the serious press. Indeed, in some cases it might even make more sense to run an advertisement in the offending publication, spelling out the company's position and "correcting" the perceived mistakes in the article. Alternatively, firms can make their case in a letter to the editor, or in future meetings with the journalists concerned. But threats that create an atmosphere of tension between a company and a journalist almost never help the company in the long run. If anything, they may embolden the journalist, making him or her feel like a hero, standing up against a powerful corporate leader. It may inspire the editors, who feel proud of standing by a report they believe is accurate. And the decision of a business publication to ignore the pressure from a large company, especially an advertiser, reminds the whole organization of the "Chinese wall" that separates a publication's commercial and editorial interests.

The Press Conference

A press conference should only be held after careful thought. Especially during a corporate crisis, it can be a godsend to desperate journalists—for which reason, being a journalist myself, I think you should hold many more of them. However, I should point out in fairness that although press conferences can create a sense of occasion, they do not provide a vehicle for putting out a complex story that requires some degree of detail. They are often superficial events, generating few intelligent questions. A press conference, if as well attended as it often is during a crisis, will include a large number of reporters with whom you do not really have a close relationship. More to the point, it is likely to be controlled by journalists with their own agendas, and the questioning is likely to be especially aggressive, as each reporter tries to outdo the other in demonstrating how tough they can be. One-on-one interviews may make far more sense, providing an opportunity to focus on a more thoughtful message with reporters whom you perceive to be more likely to understand it and be open to it, though such interviews are unlikely to allow you to escape tough but fair questioning.

Selective Leaks

A favorite but often ineffectual maneuver that companies often try is the strategic leak, typically given to the *Wall Street Journal* or *Financial Times,* with the hope of winning favorable coverage when the story first breaks. During the height of the corporate merger frenzy, it seemed almost a required maneuver, and many times it seems to work. With little reporting time and a scoop to protect (which discourages normal thorough reporting, such as talking to critics and others outside the firms involved), the newspaper reporter may end up writing a story with little initial criticism. The day the story appears, corporate communications teams think they have won over the press, but the victory is often short-lived. Competing reporters who did not get the scoop hand-delivered to them now have an incentive to write a more critical piece, focusing on precisely the negative aspects of the deal that the carefully leaked piece neglected. Good initial press can quickly sour into second-guessing and contrarian press treatment. Releasing major announcements to all press outlets at the same time may result in a better overall range of coverage.

Misleading Statements

No corporate executive is required to answer every question asked, but every response needs to be truthful. Making an evasive statement or telling a half-truth (or worst of all an outright lie) is the most damaging thing an executive or company spokesperson can do to corporate credibility. It is always better just to say nothing. Similarly, people unaccustomed to talking to business reporters should be very clear about what the phrase "off the record" means. The precise definition varies among different journalists, different publications, and even different countries—but the best strategy is to assume that it means that you will not be quoted or attributed directly, but that what you say may well be used anonymously in a story. Most journalists, mindful of the need to keep valuable relationships with their sources, will make an effort to ensure that the information they use cannot be traced back—but they will also assume, reasonably enough, that they would not have been told an interesting piece of information if a particular source had not wanted it to be made public. Misunderstanding of this is often the source of embarrassment for a company official who thinks—wrongly—that he has been betrayed. The basic rule is the simplest rule: If you don't want something to appear in a publication, don't say it.

The Ongoing Relationship

CEOs who want to see fair and smart coverage of their company are well advised to get to know journalists who are willing to get to know them and their business. That often means that a CEO should have face-to-face meetings with a journalist without the corporate public relations staff policing every word being said. Indeed, many public relations people hinder a true relationship between a journalist and an executive. PR staff often see themselves as controllers of the information flow, sometimes even as stars of the show, but it makes far more sense for them to accept their roles as messengers and go-betweens. They cannot control information or suppress stories any more than a CEO can. The companies that are most confident in dealing with the press are those who recognize that the CEO should be the primary source and spokesperson. CEOs are never really going to earn trust if someone is guarding them all of the time.

The best way to build a positive relationship with a reporter is to get together occasionally, perhaps even in a social setting that is not set up as a formal interview. This is usually attractive to the journalist, and the executive is put at ease. It is a comfortable environment for both sides, but it needs to be handled carefully. The journalist must never feel that an outing with a CEO is intended as a "bribe." No doubt some executives quietly hope that such a meeting will have the effect of a bribe, however, and sometimes they may succeed—though nowadays probably not with the top business journalists and papers. One of New York's oldest companies was known for having good seats for the top sporting events, some of which went to journalists. It has been said that the company managed to get all the way to Chapter 11 bankruptcy without having a single bad article written about it.

Relationship-building is a critical responsibility in thinking about how a business executive wants to interact with the journalists who cover his company or industry. Executives who want to tell their stories to leading journalists need to devote a significant amount of time to the project. A twenty-minute phone interview provides information but doesn't cultivate a deeper connection. That requires formal and informal meetings and contacts that are kept up over time. A long lunch to present the general state of the business at least once a year is a good investment of time. Even when there is no particular news, executives should keep up with the journalists who follow their company, setting up time to talk with them at industry conferences, or at the World Economic Forum in Davos, Switzerland, or other CEO gatherings.

And one shouldn't simply target the beat reporters. It also makes sense to forge a relationship with business editors and others who have influence on what is actually published.

Nor is it sufficient to get to know just the one or two regulars who cover your company. A savvy press strategy means reaching out to meet or know the more senior journalists who cover an industry or write the larger business trend stories. These are writers who are assigned the very biggest stories, and the benefits of knowing them become clear when a bad story starts to break about a company. At that moment, editors frequently do not leave the story exclusively in the hands of the reporter who had been covering the company in question. It is the top reporters—usually the toughest reporters—who are able to say, "This is my story," regardless of who the beat journalist happens to be. An executive is in a much stronger and much more confident position if he or she already knows these top reporters, can reach out to them, and can feel comfortable offering them the corporate perspective on a scandal, bad news, or a misunderstood event.

The idea that a CEO or other executive has to invest time to know a wide range of the best reporters runs counter to the prevailing wisdom in corporate PR, which has been trying to categorize members of the media and determine which ones are the most likely to write a favorable article, which reporters aren't so bright, which ones are most likely to be flattered by being brought in to see the CEO, and so on. True, there are some easy reporters who gladly write the occasional puff piece—though not at *The Economist,* of course—but when a potentially troublesome story breaks, the reporter who handles it is often going to be the old bruiser who likes to tackle the hard stories. If you haven't built a relationship with that bruiser, then all the trust in the world from the lightweight novice who doesn't get the story will do you no good whatsoever.

A New Era?

Journalists have been writing about business and business executives for centuries, but we now do seem to be in an era when the rules that govern the relationship between the media and corporations are changing. In the aftermath of corporate scandals, journalists feel they have an even greater obligation to scrutinize the corporate world, and more authority to do so. CEOs recognize that they are more exposed to the media, even to its whims. At this stage, the business world hasn't yet figured out what the right media relations model is, but clearly the trend is toward a greater show of openness. The secretive public company will be an increasingly rare animal.

Company executives and their public relations staffs worry about whether the press has sufficient understanding of their business, but the best way of appreciating what drives the media is to understand that it is *their* business. In many ways, the best contemporary journalists have more in common with today's business executives than the reporters of yesteryear. The best publications are staffed these days by extremely professional, talented people, often with M.B.A.s or specialist training. Many have worked on Wall Street or in the City of London and understand the details of balance sheets and financial transactions. They rarely drink at lunch (much to the regret of their older colleagues), they are extremely ambitious, and they really want to get noticed and get ahead. They work for multibillion-dollar companies that are extremely competitive and put a great value on getting stories first and being right—and are very embarrassed when they get things wrong. (Consider the upheaval in May 2003 at the *New York Times* when a journalist was found to be plagiarizing and occasionally inventing stories.) What they want is professional but very open relationships with the subjects they cover so their audience can get the best, most interesting, and most accurate information.

Too many in-house press strategies ignore these genuine motivations of journalism. Too often they assume that favorable press coverage is a product of spin, massive PR campaigns, and careful manipulation of public information. That is an old model that no longer serves the interests of the company, if it ever did, and rarely leads to quality press coverage. Business journalists don't usually have an agenda—other than to uncover interesting, important stories. What they want, ideally, is access, trust, and the ability to build a relationship. While there is clearly going to be confrontation and disagreement from time to time, and journalists will sometimes be the last people on earth that an executive wants to talk to, those goals of the contemporary reporter ought to be the same goals of any executive's press strategy.

CHAPTER TWENTY-ONE

Right Versus Right: Dealing with Ethical Dilemmas in Business

Joseph L. Badaracco Jr., John Shad Professor of Business Ethics at Harvard Business School

Ethical decision-making has been a part of business-school curricula for a number of years, but in the wake of much-publicized incidents of corporate malfeasance, these courses are likely to take on a new prominence.

Business ethics must, of course, go beyond the obvious prohibitions against fraud, deception, or criminal wrongdoing. Corporate leaders need a broader framework in which tough decisions with ethical implications can be easily made.

Joseph L. Badaracco approaches the topic in this way. He has become well known for his course at the Harvard Business School, "The Moral Leader," in which students read classic and contemporary works of literature, as well as the required Strategy course.

He is a widely published author, having examined the relationships between business and government, leadership, and the role of ethical decision-making in business. He has taught and lectured on these subjects before a wide variety of audiences in the United States and Japan, including the World Bank, UBS Warburg, the Boston Police Department, and Hewlett-Packard. In addition to his teaching duties at Harvard, he is the faculty chair of the Nomura School of Advanced Management in Tokyo.

Badaracco's most recent books are *Business Ethics: Roles and Responsibilities*, *Defining Moments: When Managers Must Choose Between Right and Right*, and *Leading Quietly: An Unorthodox Guide to Doing the Right Thing.*

IN 1982 THE United States was beset by a new form of terrorism aimed at consumers. Bottles of Tylenol had been tampered with and cyanide had been found in the medication. The manufacturer, Johnson & Johnson, had already decided to pull Tylenol off the shelves, but the CEO, Jim Burke, felt that before announcing the decision he should go to Washington, D.C., to talk to the heads of the FBI and the Food and Drug Administration. When he told them what he planned to do, he was stunned by their response. They told Burke that they wanted him to keep Tylenol on the shelves for a while. When Burke asked why, the head of the FBI, William Webster, said that the Tylenol killings might be a terrorist act, and the government didn't want to accede to terrorism. The head of the FDA said that Halloween was coming up, and the last thing they wanted to do was take the risk of encouraging copycats.

At that moment, Burke faced the most difficult decision of his life. As a human being, a fiduciary for the owners, and somebody trying to defend his company's brand, he wanted Tylenol off the shelves. But as an American citizen, he was being asked to do otherwise. Right in front of him were the chief law-enforcement officer of the United States and the regulatory guardian of the food and drug system, asking him to leave the product out there.

This was a moral question but not a matter of black and white—not a question of right versus wrong. It was an issue colored by various shades of gray—an issue of right versus right. Burke says that to this day he does not know what he would have done if forced to make a decision. Fortunately, he got lucky. There was a knock on the door, and Webster was handed a note. He read it, talked with his FDA counterpart, and said to Burke: Go ahead and pull the product. The note had conveyed the information that there had been another poisoning, this time in California. It was strychnine rather than cyanide. Apparently, FBI analysts had concluded that it wasn't terrorism, and since copycatting was already under way, it made sense to get the product off the shelf lest it be a target for somebody else. But for a moment, Burke had been faced with a high-stakes moral dilemma—an issue of right versus right.

Moral Dilemmas in Everyday Business Life

While few of us are called upon to deal with issues of life-or-death, we are all confronted from time to time with issues of right versus right. There are the everyday examples: You have an enormous backlog of work, but you have a family to spend time with, a kid to take to a soccer game, a friend to visit in the hospital. These are not choices between right and wrong. These are choices between two commitments, both of which you *ought* to make good on.

How do you deal with such questions in business? Consider a specific example, one that could be faced by a number of managers. Over the past few years, I've heard the same basic story several times. A boss—usually a mid-level manager—is informed that the company is about to downsize and told who is on the list of employees to go. But he is also told to keep it confidential for a while. Soon afterward, a longtime employee comes in and says that he and his wife are thinking of buying the house of their dreams. The boss knows that the employee would have a hard time making the mortgage payments—he is on the list of people to be let go. Let's even suppose that the employee has heard through the grapevine that there might be some staff reductions coming and asks his manager if buying the house is a good idea. If you are the manager, what do you say? You want to do the right thing—but what is the right thing? Is it being loyal to your friend, and telling him the truth? Or is it being loyal to your company, and respecting your duty of confidentiality?

I think almost everybody, if they look back on the decisions that leave them even now with a wrenching feeling in their stomach, recognizes that the toughest choices are those in which they can make a moral case for each side. The moral compass is hardest to follow when different sets of responsibilities point in different directions.

No one can tell you what decision to make in such a situation. But what I will try to do is suggest a framework for making such decisions. It is a framework that has stood the test of time—literally centuries. Some of the brightest people in history have engaged in a long conversation about the fundamental questions of how to use power and responsibility, and how to sort through conflicts that have challenged human beings since the dawn of reason. This historical conversation is the source of the framework I am presenting. Essentially, it revolves around four questions.

The Greatest Good for the Greatest Number

Question number one: Faced with a moral dilemma, which of the alternaives will do the greatest good and cause the least harm for everybody affected? In effect, this is a form of cost-risk, cost-benefit analysis. Put in the most mechanical fashion, it is a matter of getting out a piece of paper, drawing a line down the middle, and for every one of your alternatives, sorting out who would benefit and who would suffer. Then it is a matter of calculating the alternative that does the most good and causes the least harm. The intellectual pedigree of this is the eighteenth-century British philosopher and social reformer John Stuart Mill, who argued that the essence of responsible behavior is acting in a way that promotes the greatest happiness for the greatest number of people. By happiness, he meant everything that gives life value and dignity and worth.

This is only the first question, but in my experience most smart, practical people initially think it is the only one you need. It seems to really get to the heart of the matter. Some may wonder: Why are there four questions to consider, rather than just this one? Let me assure you—the other three questions are more than just spare tires.

The shortfall of the "greatest good for the greatest number" is that it leaves out an important consideration. To get a clear sense of it, consider a hypothetical circumstance. It starts with some good news: You have just had a medical exam, and based on it and on an actuarial program, it is apparent that you are going to live a long time—say, another fifty years. But the bad news is that at a major hospital in your city there are seven people who are on life support, in need of organ transplants. Your body contains healthy organs that would keep each of these people alive; combined, they would be able to live at least another three hundred years. In addition, one of the people in need of a vital organ is working on a scientific breakthrough that could wipe out a serious infectious disease. Based on the first question—what would promote the greatest happiness for the greatest number?—the right thing to do would be to use your vital organs to let these people live. But is that the right thing to do? Few would think so. Why? Because forcing you to die so that others may live in these circumstances is a violation of your basic rights.

A Matter of Basic Rights

That sets up the second of the four questions. In sorting through moral issues, a question that has to be asked is: Which individuals or groups affected by the decision have basic rights that must be respected?

At this point, you might imagine a potential formula for allowing one to objectively balance the considerations raised by these two questions. If you're analytically minded, you can picture a formula that says maximize "net, net, net" consequences for everybody affected, subject to the constraint of not violating anybody's rights. Okay? But in a lot of right-versus-right dilemmas, what you find is that looking at it in that way only tightens the dilemma.

Take President Harry Truman's momentous decision to launch the first nuclear strike in the history of the world to end the Second World War. In terms of consequences—net, net, net—he saved the lives of American and Allied soldiers. Arguably, he even saved the lives—net, net—of Japanese soldiers and civilians. Many more might have been killed in the invasion of the Japanese islands. But he was also responsible for the deaths of many small children. Truman suffered headaches for several years afterward. A few days after the attacks, he complained to one of his cabinet members, who asked him whether he meant literal or figurative headaches. Truman said both—he hated the thought of killing all those kids—and then gave the order that no more bombs would be dropped in the Pacific theater without his permission. Fortunately, the Japanese surrendered, ending the war. But it was not an issue that Truman could resolve morally in his own mind regardless of how confident he was that he had made the right decision.

What Would a Person of Good Character Do?

The third question has probably the oldest roots of any I am putting forward. In the Western tradition, it goes back to Aristotle—in the East, to Confucius. For them, doing the right thing in a tough situation with the pressure on is not a matter of calculating consequences or looking up rights. It is a matter of character—the character of individuals, and the character of the communities that produced them and hopefully supported them in doing the right thing. As to the right thing to do, Aristotle punted on the question. In effect, he said that the right thing to do in a tough situation is whatever a person with good judgment and good character who has thoroughly immersed himself in the particulars of the situation would do. Typically, there are lines almost everybody has that he or she will not cross. Faced with one of these right-versus-right decisions, what lines are there that I am unwilling to cross or that we as an institution should be unwilling to cross? When you make these decisions, people are watching. You're writing your permanent biography. But unlike a word processor, you cannot delete words or move blocks of copy. It's done, and word will go around that you had certain priorities and not others. I suspect that we all can think of a number of defining moments that determined our attitude toward people, for good or ill. In many cases, we can trace our attitude about others to a situation in which they made a tough decision—they drew a line they could have drawn elsewhere—and then it was pretty clear what they stood for. It is in moments such as these that you answer Aristotle's question.

What Works in the World as It Is?

The fourth question was developed by someone whom many may regard as a surprising source of moral guidance: Niccolò Machiavelli. A great many people think of Machiavelli as someone best described as the high priest of unscrupulousness. That is a common interpretation of his seminal work *The Prince*. But would Machiavelli be remembered if his advice came down to the notion that you can get ahead in life by being unscrupulous? After all, unscrupulousness was not a product of the sixteenth century. Simply repeating millennia-old attitudes devoid of moral content would not have made Machiavelli one of the commanding intellectual figures of the Western tradition.

One of the most important points that Machiavelli makes is that if you are responsible for an organization, you may be faced with decisions in which the moral choice you would make in personal life—such as telling a friend not to take out the mortgage on that new house because unemployment beckons—is not something that one is able to reconcile with institutional responsibilities. Machiavelli teaches that one has to find a course of action that will work in the world as it is, not as one might like it to be. Machiavelli does not recommend taking the easy way out, or searching for the lowest common denominator. In fact, he says, fortune favors the bold. He admired the entrepreneurs of his era, people who were changing the entire Western way of thinking about the role of religion, government, business, and the individual. But at the end of the day, he concluded, if a supposedly ethical course of action does not work, it is of no substantive value. Looked at this way, if a business leader gives speeches that consist of inspiring words not matched by effective action, he or she is making a serious mistake. Unless people in the organization know that the CEO is following through, it just contributes to cynicism and, ultimately, demoralization.

So the fourth question is: What works in the world as it is?

Three Tests to Help Answer the Questions

These four questions are deeply etched in the human psyche. When we ponder right and wrong—and when we ponder right and right—we think naturally in these terms. Consider how often the answers to these four questions are the underlying basis for important decisions:

- We've thought hard, and we're going to take a certain action because for everybody affected it's the best decision we can come up with.
- We've thought hard, and we're going to do this because it respects the rights of people involved.
- We're going to do this because it makes good on the commitments we've made and the kind of organization we are.
- We're going to do it this way because it is the best we can do in the world as it is.

I cannot offer a formula for answering the four questions. But I can suggest three tests—tests that point you in a direction in which you can sort out the conflicting elements when faced with a right-versus-right kind of problem.

First is the so-called newspaper test or Internet test. What plan of action would look best to you if it were going to be published on a Web page or on the front page of your local newspaper tomorrow? H. L. Mencken once described our conscience as "the inner voice that warns us that someone may be looking." That is a typically cynical way of putting it, but imagining that large numbers of people will learn of your actions is a good way of assessing their net consequences, or what is the greatest good for the greatest number. It is also a way of looking at Machiavelli's question of what will work in the world as it is.

The second test takes different forms—the golden rule of "do unto others," or the Native American advice to walk a mile in the other person's moccasins. Sometimes people find that the most illuminating way to put the test is in terms of their children: If a child of yours was going to be the one affected by the decision, how would you want him or her to be treated? This is a way of dealing with the question: What are people's basic rights in this situation? It allows you to consider issues that are often elusive to someone in a powerful position who can become insulated from the human impact of their decisions.

The final test—allowing you to focus on Aristotle's question about what a person of character would do—comes in two forms. The somber form is called the obituary test. Which way of resolving this problem would you want to look back on, and would you want people whose respect you seek to look back on it? It is a way of thinking of an issue not in the swirl of events of the moment but from the standpoint of the totality of your life. The less somber version of this question is: How would you want to resolve this in a way that is part of a good life for yourself, for the people you work with, and for the people who depend on you? This is a way of looking at the issue in broader terms, but with a sense of immediacy.

Leadership Moments: Balancing Right Versus Right

Using these questions as a basis for choosing between right and right is not just a matter of picking your favorite and running with it. Each of these questions balances and corrects the flaws in the other. If you think only about consequences, you can run roughshod over people's rights. If you think just about people's rights, you can be paralyzed into inaction, especially in a litigious society such as ours. If you think exclusively about what you can live with, you have to ask what makes your conscience so true that it trumps consequences for other people and their rights. If you think only about what will work in the world as it is, your choice can end up devoid of moral content.

A leader looks at an issue from a number of perspectives. Leaders face defining moments, moments that rip off their masks. Almost everybody, no matter how hard an effort they make to be honest and candid, wears masks in varying degrees. But when you have to choose, and indicate your priority among important considerations, you're revealing a little bit about yourself. People are watching, they are assessing, and the resulting buzz ripples through an organization's grapevine. These are not just matters of personal reflection and choice—they are leadership moments. It is important for leaders to recognize them, and act accordingly.

acknowledgments

ORGANIZING AND EDITING a book with twenty different contributors cannot, by definition, be the work of just one person. In putting together this volume, we relied on a large cast of people who have organized a succession of CEO Academy and G100 meetings—meetings that made the content of this book possible.

Pamela Preisendoerfer and Heike Straub, the staff of G100, which hosts the regular meetings of the CEO Academy, have played an indispensable role in creating lively, professional gatherings where our contributors felt comfortable first sharing their thoughts with a tough audience of CEOs. Donna Gregor and Kelly Gallagher have provided unvaluable help in working with our authors and helping us plan our meetings. Gocki von Kageneck has always offered the best creative input to create supporting materials for our CEO Academy participants. The peerless photographer, Richard Avedon, put together a tremendous visual record of our Academy participants. His presence has made every gathering memorable. Our meetings have been held at the Harold Pratt House in Manhattan, home to the Council on Foreign Relations. We are indebted to the Council and its staff for their help and forbearance.

Daniel Casse of the White House Writers Group first proposed a book based on the proceedings of the CEO Academy. Since then, he has worked closely with every one of our authors to shape the final manuscript. Without his relentless persistence and his professionalism this book would not have come together.

Larry Bossidy, Ray Gilmartin, and Jack Welch have each served as program leaders of our CEO Academy. They are the best "faculty members" a business group can have and we are grateful to them for steering the conversation toward essential questions.

During the process of putting together the book, we turned to Professor Michael Useem of the Wharton School of Business (who is also a speaker at the CEO Academy) to help us focus on the key issues that readers might want to learn about from CEOs. His judgment and advice were tremendously helpful.

James Levine, our literary agent, saw the potential for the book and helped us with its organization. John Mahaney, our editor at Crown Books, provided superb advice and showed endless patience. His assistant Shana Wingert Drehs made sure everything went according to plan—and adjusted when it didn't. Tara Gilbride began thinking about how to market the book early on and we benefited from her ideas.

The G100 owes much of its success to its board of advisors: Ray Gilmartin, Hans-Joachim Körber, A.G. Lafley, Bob Lane, and Bob Nardelli. The CEO Academy advisors—Steve Kaufman, Mackey McDonald, Ira Millstein, Marilyn Carlson Nelson, and Bill Stavropoulos—have been just as indispensable. Neither of these projects would have taken off without the support of our partners, Blue Capital, David Fuente, Six Sigma, Spencer Stuart, and Jack Welch.

Finally, we are most grateful to the contributors themselves (along with their very patient and able assistants), who not only participated in the CEO Academy but also set aside time to work with us, sometimes under tight deadlines. Their enthusiasm for the project and their keen attention to the content of their chapters has made this project both possible and rewarding.

On a personal note, Marie-Caroline von Weichs would like to thank Dayton Ogden and David Daniel of Spencer Stuart for their continuous support.

Dennis Carey would like to acknowledge his children, Maggie and Matt, who gave up time with their dad while he got involved in founding the CEO Academy and G100.

index

INDEX

INDEX

INDEX

about the authors

DENNIS C. CAREY is vice chairman of Spencer Stuart, U.S., and has recruited CEOs and directors for some of the largest global companies. He is the founder of G100, an exclusive forum for leading CEOs, and the CEO Academy. In addition to numerous articles on corporate governance, succession planning, and business strategy, he is the coauthor (with Dayton Ogden) of *CEO Succession* and *The Human Side of M&A*. Dennis holds a Ph.D. in finance and administration from the University of Maryland and was a post-doctoral fellow at Harvard University in 1982–1983.

MARIE-CAROLINE VON WEICHS is CEO of G100 and dean of the CEO Academy. For more than six years she has worked as a recruiter of senior management talent for Spencer Stuart's Global Life Sciences Practice, and currently serves as a director of the Jackson Laboratory. Prior to joining Spencer Stuart, Marie-Caroline was a consultant in the health-care industry with a leading European strategy-consulting firm. She has also been a research scientist at the Rockefeller University and Oxford University. Marie-Caroline holds a Ph.D. in biochemistry/molecular biology from Oxford University.